CW00820953

The History of the Common law of England. Divided Into Twelve Chapters. Written by a Learned Hand

BOOKS printed for, and are to be fold by
J. Walthoe in the *Middle-Temple* Cloyfters,
and at his Shop in *Stafford*.

1 A General Abridgment of the Common Law, Alphabetically digefted under proper Titles, with Notes and References to the whole By *Knightley D'Aivers*, of the *Inner-Temple*, Efq; Dedicated to the Lord Chief Juftice *Holt*, with the Allowance of the Lord Keeper, and all the reft of the Judges

2 The Law of Laft Wills and Teftaments, containing Rules for the Conftruction of Laft Wills

3. The Compleat Sheriff, to which is added, the Office of a Coroner The 2d Edition

4. The Modern Conveyancer, or Conveyancing improved ; being a choice Collection of Prefidents on moft Occafions, drawn after the manner of Conveyancing, now in Ufe by the greateft Hands of the Age, in 3 Vol. The Third Edition, with large Additions.

5 The Clergyman's Law, or Compleat Incumbent, collected from the Common and Statute Laws relating to the Church and Clergy of *England* By *W. Watfon*, Dr. of Laws. The 2d Edition with Additions, in 2 Vol.

6. The Juftice of Peace his Companion , or a Summary of all the Acts of Parliament to 1712 whereby one, two, or more Juftices of the Peace are authorized to act, not only in, but out of the Seffions of the Peace · With an exact Alphabetical Table. By *Samuel Blackerby*, of *Grays-Inn*, Efq;

7. Crown Law ; or the Common and Statute Law of *England*, concerning Trials of High Treafon, Mifprifion of Treafon, and in all other Crimes and Offences relating to the Crown ; Alphabetically digefted under proper Heads, and brought down to the Year 1710, with an exact Table. By *W. J* Barrifter at Law

8. Legal Provifions for the Poor ; or a Treatife of the Common and Statute Laws concerning the Poor, either as to Relief, Settlement, or Punifhment. Being a Methodical Guide for Juftices of the Peace, Church wardens, and Overfeers. Wherein are explained all the Statutes relating to that Subject ; with the Ancient and Modern Law-Cafes and Refolutions of the Judges: And alfo many Precedents proper for fuch a Treatife. By *S C*. of the *Inner-Temple*, Efq;

THE
HISTORY
OF THE
Common Law
OF
ENGLAND.

Divided into Twelve Chapters.

Written by a Learned Hand.

Ἱερὸν ὁ ΝΟΜΟΣ ἐςὶ ἄρχοντα.

In the SAVOY:

Printed by J. Nutt, Assignee of *Edw. Sayer* Esq;
for J. Walthoe, in the *Middle-Temple* Cloy-
sters; and at his Shop in *Stafford*, 1713.

THE
CONTENTS.

CHAP. I.

Concerning the Diſtribution of the Laws of England into Common Law, and Statute Law. And Firſt, concerning the Statute Law, or Acts of Parliament. Page 1.

CHAP. II.

Concerning the Lex non Scripta, i. e. The Common or Municipal Laws of this Kingdom. Page 23.

CHAP. III.

Concerning the Common Law of England, its Uſe and Excellence, and the Reaſon of its Denomination. Page 45.

A 3   C H A P.

The CONTENTS.

The CONTENTS.

THE

THE
HISTORY
OF THE
Common Law
OF
ENGLAND.

CHAP. I.

*Concerning the Distribution of the Laws of
England into Common Law, and Statute
Law. And First, concerning the Statute
Law, or Acts of Parliament.*

THE Laws of *England* may aptly The Kinds of Laws.
enough be divided into Two
Kinds, *viz.* *Lex Scripta,* the written Law; and *Lex non Scripta,* the
unwritten Law: For although (as shall be
shewn hereafter) all the Laws of this Kingdom have some Monuments or Memorials
there-

thereof in Writing, yet all of them have not their Original in Writing, for some of those Laws have obtain'd their Force by immemorial Usage or Custom, and such Laws are properly called *Leges non Scriptæ*, or unwritten Laws or Customs.

1. Leges nonScriptæ

2 Leges Scriptæ

Those Laws therefore that I call *Leges Scriptæ*, or written Laws, are such as are usually called *Statute Laws*, or Acts of Parliament, which are originally reduced into Writing before they are enacted, or receive any binding Power, every such Law being in the first Instance formally drawn up in Writing, and made, as it were, a *Tripartite Indenture*, between the King, the Lords and the Commons, for without the concurrent Consent of all those Three Parts of the Legislature, no such Law is, or can be made. But the Kings of this Realm, with the Advice and Consent of both Houses of Parliament, have Power to make New Laws, or to alter, repeal, or enforce the Old And this has been done in all Succession of Ages.

Statute Laws of Two Kinds.

Now *Statute Laws*, or Acts of Parliament, are of Two Kinds, *viz* First, Those Statutes which were made *before Time of Memory*, and, Secondly, Those Statutes which were made *within* or *since Time of Memory*, wherein observe, That according to a juridical Account and legal Signification, *Time within Memory* is the Time of Limitation in a Writ of Right; which by the Statute of *Westminster* 1. *cap* 38 was settled, and reduced to the Beginning of the Reign of King Richard I. or *Ex prima Coronatione Regis Richardi Primi,*

Time of M-mory

Primi, who began his Reign the 6th of *July* 1189, and was crown'd the 3d of *September* following: So that whatsoever was before that Time, is *before* Time of Memory; and what is since that Time, is, in a legal Sense, said to be *within* or since the Time of Memory.

And therefore it is, that those Statutes or Acts of Parliament that were made before the beginning of the Reign of King *Richard* I. and have not since been repealed or altered, either by contrary Usage, or by subsequent Acts of Parliament, are now accounted Part of the *Lex non Scripta*, being as it were incorporated thereinto, and become a Part of the Common Law; and in Truth, such Statutes are not now pleadable as Acts of Parliament, (because what is *before* Time of Memory is supposed without a Beginning, or at least such a Beginning as the Law takes Notice of) but they obtain their Strength by meer immemorial Usage or Custom

And doubtless, many of those Things that now obtain as Common Law, had their Original by Parliamentary Acts or Constitutions, made in Writing by the King, Lords and Commons, though those Acts are now either not extant, or if extant, were made before Time of Memory; and the Evidence of the Truth hereof will easily appear, for that in many of those old Acts of Parliament that were made before Time of Memory, and are yet extant, we may find many of those Laws enacted which

Ancient Statutes.

B 2   now

now obtain meerly as Common Law, or the General Custom of the Realm : And were the rest of those Laws extant, probably the Footsteps of the Original Institution of many more Laws that now obtain meerly as Common Law, or Customary Laws, by immemorial Usage, would appear to have been at first Statute Laws, or Acts of Parliament.

Of Two Periods. Those ancient Acts of Parliament which are ranged under the Head of *Leges non Scriptæ*, or Customary Laws, as being made before Time of Memory, are to be considered under Two Periods. *Viz.* First, Such as were made before the coming in of King *William* I. commonly called, *The Conqueror*; or, Secondly, Such as intervened between his coming in, and the beginning of the Reign of *Richard* I which is the legal Limitation of Time of Memory.

1 Before W 1 The former Sort of these Laws are mentioned by our ancient Historians, especially by *Brompton*, and are now collected into one Volume, by *William Lambard* Esq; in his *Tractatus de priscis Anglorum Legibus*, being a Collection of the Laws of the Kings, *Ina, Alfred, Edward, Athelstane, Edmond, Edgar, Ethelred, Canutus*, and of *Edward the Confessor*; which last Body of Laws, compiled by *Edward the Confessor*, as they were more full and perfect than the rest, and better accommodated to the then State of Things, so they were such whereof the *English* were always very zealous, as being the great Rule and Standard of their

Rights

Rights and Liberties. Whereof more hereafter.

The fecond Sort are thofe Edicts, Acts of
Parliament, or Laws, that were made after
the coming in of King *William*, commonly
named, *The Conqueror*, and before the beginning of the Reign of King *Richard* I. and
more efpecially are thofe which follow;
whereof I fhall make but a brief Remembrance here, becaufe it will be neceffary
in the Sequel of this Difcourfe (it may be
more than once) to refume the Mention of
them; and befides, Mr. *Selden*, in his Book
called, *Janus Anglorum*, has given a full Account of thofe Laws, fo that at prefent it
will be fufficient for me, briefly to collect
the Heads or Divifions of them, under the
Reigns of thofe feveral Kings wherein they
were made, *viz.*

Firft, The Laws of King *William* I. Thefe
confifted in a great Meafure of the Repeti-
tion of the Laws of King *Edward the Confeffor*, and of the enforcing them by his own
Authority, and the Affent of Parliament, at
the Requeft of the *Englifh*; and fome new
Laws were added by himfelf with the like
Affent of Parliament, relating to Military Tenures, and the Prefervation of the
publick Peace of the Kingdom; all which
are mention'd by Mr. *Lambart*, in the Tractate before-mentioned, but more fully by
Mr. *Selden*, in his Collections and Obfervations upon *Eadmerus*

Secondly, We find little of new Laws after
this, till the Time of King *Henry* I. who

2 From W 1 to R. 1.

K W. 1.

K H. 1

B 3 be-

besides the Confirmation of the Laws of the
Confessor, and of King *William* I brought
in a new Volume of Laws, which to this
Day are extant, and called the *Laws* of
King *Henry* I. The entire Collection of
these is entered in the Red Book of the *Exchequer*, and from thence are transcribed and
published by the Care of Sir *Roger Twisden*,
in the latter End of Mr. *Lambart's* Book
before mention'd, what the Success of those
Laws were in the Time of King *Steven*,
and King *Henry* II. we shall see hereafter: But
they did not much obtain in *England*, and
are now for the most Part become wholly
obsolete, and in Effect quite antiquated

K. H 2.   *Thirdly*, The next considerable Body of
Acts of Parliament, were those made under
the Reign of King *Henry* II. commonly
called, *The Constitutions of* Clarendon; what
they were, appears best in *Hoveden* and *Mat
Paris*, under the Years of that King We
have little Memory else of any considerable
Laws enacted in this King's Time, except
his Assizes, and such Laws as related to the
Forests; which were afterwards improv'd
under the Reign of King *Richard* I. But
of this hereafter, more at large

And this shall serve for a short Instance
of those Statutes, or Acts of Parliament,
that were made *before Time of Memory*;
whereof, as we have no Authentical Records, but only Transcripts either in our
ancient Historians, or other Books and Ma-
nuscripts; so they being Things done before Time of Memory, obtain at this Day
no further than as by Usage and Custom they
are,

are, as it were, engrafted into the Body of the Common Law, and made a Part thereof

And now I come to thofe *Leges Scriptæ*, or Acts of Parliament, which were made fince or within the Time of Memory, *viz* Since the beginning of the Reign of *Richard* I and thofe I fhall divide into Two General Heads, *viz.* Thofe we ufually call the *Old* Statutes, and thofe we ufually call the *New* or later Statutes : And becaufe I would prefix fome certain Term or Boundary between them, I fhall call thofe the *Old* Statutes which end with the Reign of King *Edward* II. and thofe I fhall call the *New* or later Statutes which begin with the Reign of King *Edward* III. and fo are derived through a Succeffion of Kings and Queens down to this Day, by a continued and orderly Series

Leges Scriptæ. Two Kinds

Old Statutes

Touching thefe later Sort I fhall fay nothing, for they all keep an orderly and regular Series of Time, and are extant upon Record, either in the Parliament Rolls, or in the Statute Rolls of King *Edward* III. and thofe Kings that follow. For excepting fome few Years in the beginning of K *Edward* III. *i. e* 2, 3, 7, 8 & 9 *Edw* 3. all the Parliament Rolls that ever were fince that Time have been preferved, and are extant, and, for the moft Part, the Petitions upon which the Acts were drawn up, or the very Acts themfelves

Later Statutes.

Now therefore touching the elder Acts of Parliament, *viz* Thofe that were made between the Firft Year of the Reign of K. *Richard* I. and the laft Year of K. *Edward* II

Old Statutes in the Time of K R

we

we have little extant in any authentical
History; and nothing in any authentical
Record touching Acts made in the Time

K. *Rich.* I. of K. *Rich* I. unless we take in those Constitutions and Assizes mentioned by *Hoveden*
as aforesaid.

Neither is there any great Evidence,
what Acts of Parliament pass'd in the Time

K. *John.* of King *John,* tho' doubtless many there
were both in his Time, and in the Time of
K. *R.ch.* I. But there is no Record extant of
them, and the *English* Histories of those
Times give us but little Account of those
Laws; only *Matthew Paris* gives us an Historical Account of the *Magna Charta,* and

His two *Charta de Foresta,* granted by King *John* at
Charters. *Running Mead* the 15th of *June,* in the Seventeenth Year of his Reign

And it seems, that the Concession of these

Granted Charters was in a Parliamentary Way, you
in a Parli- may see the Transcripts of both Charters
amentary *verbatim* in *Mat Paris,* and in the Red Book
Way of the *Exchequer* There were seven Pair of
these Charters sent to some of the Great
Monasteries under the Seal of King *John,* one
Part whereof sent to the *Abby* of *Tewkesbu-*
ry I have seen under the Seal of that King;
the Substance thereof differs something from
the *Magna Charta,* and *Charta de Foresta,* granted by King *Hen* III. but not very much, as
may appear by comparing them.

But tho' these Charters of King *John* seem
to have been passed in a kind of Parliament,
yet it was in a Time of great Confusion between that King and his Nobles; and therefore

fore they obtained not a full Settlement till the Time of King *Hen* III. when the Subſtance of them was enacted by a full and ſolemn Parliament

· I therefore come down to the Times of thoſe ſucceeding Kings, *Hen* III. *Edw* I. and *Edw* II. and the Statutes made in the Times of thoſe Kings, I call the *Old Statutes*; partly becauſe many of them were made but in Affirmance of the Common Law; and partly becauſe the reſt of them, that made a Change in the Common Law, are yet ſo ancient, that they now ſeem to have been as it were a Part of the Common Law, eſpecially conſidering the many Expoſitions that have been made of them in the ſeveral Succeſſions of Times, whereby as they became the great Subject of Judicial Reſolutions and Deciſions; ſo thoſe Expoſitions and Deciſions, together alſo with thoſe old Statutes themſelves, are as it were incorporated into the very Common Law, and become a Part of it

In the Times of thoſe three Kings laſt mentioned, as likewiſe in the Times of their Predeceſſors, there were doubtleſs many more Acts of Parliament made than are now extant of Record, or otherwiſe, which might be a Means of the Change of the Common Law in the Times of thoſe Kings from what it was before, tho' all the Records or Memorials of thoſe Acts of Parliament introducing ſuch a Change, are not at this Day extant: But of thoſe that are extant, I ſhall give you a brief Account,

not

not intending a large or accurate Treatiſe touching that Matter.

K. H 3. The Reign of *Hen* III was a trouble-ſome Time, in reſpect of the Differences be-tween him and his Barons, which were not compoſed till his 51ſt Year, after the Battle of *Eveſham*. In his Time there were many Parliaments, but we have only one Sum-mons of Parliament extant of Record in his Reign, *viz.* 49 *Hen* III. and we have but few of thoſe many Acts of Parliament that paſſed in his Time, *viz.* The great Char-ter, and *Charta de Foreſta*, in the Ninth Year of his Reign, which were doubtleſs paſs'd in Parliament; the Statute of *Merton*, in the 20th Year of his Reign; the Statute of *Marlbridge*, in the 52d Year; and the *Dictum ſive Edictum de Kenelworth*, about the ſame Time; and ſome few other old Acts.

K E 1. In the Time of K *Edw* I there are many more Acts of Parliament extant than in the Time of K *Hen*. III. Yet doubtleſs, in this King's Time, there were many more Sta-tutes made than are now extant: Thoſe that are now extant, are commonly bound to-gether in the old Book of *Magna Charta*. By *thoſe Statutes*, great Alterations and Amendments were made in the Common Law; and by thoſe that are now extant, we may reaſonably gueſs, that there were conſiderable Alterations and Amendments made by thoſe that are not extant, which poſſibly may be the real, tho' ſudden Means of the great Advance and Alteration of the Laws of *England* in the King's Reign, over what

what they were in the Time of his Predeceſſors

The firſt Summons of Parliament that I
remember extant of Record in this King's
Time, is 23 *Edw*. 1. tho' doubtleſs there were
many more before this, the Records whereof are either loſt or miſlaid. For many Parliaments were held by this King before that
Time, and many of the Acts paſs'd in thoſe
Parliaments are ſtill extant ; as, the Statutes
of *Weſtminſter* 1. in the 3d of *Edw*. 1. The
Statutes of *Glouceſter*, 6 *Edw* 1. The Statutes
of *Weſtminſter* 2. and of *Winton*, 13 *Edw*. 1.
The Statutes of *Weſtminſter* 3. and of *Quo
Warranto*, 18 *Edw*. 1. And divers others in
other Years, which I ſhall have Occaſion to
mention hereafter

In the Time of K. *Edw*. II many Parlia- K E 2.
ments were held, and many Laws were enacted, but we have few Acts of Parliament
of his Reign extant, eſpecially of Record.
" The Statutes of this King's Reign which
" are in Print, are theſe, *viz* The Statutes
" *De Militibus, & de Frangentibus Priſonas*,
" 1 *Edw* 2. *Articuli Cleri*, 9 *Edw*. 2. De
" *Gaveletto* in *London*, 10 *Edw* 2. The Sta-
" tutes of *York*, of Eſſoins and View of Land,
" 12 *Edw* 2, *Weſtminſter* 4 13 *Edw* 2. Of
" Eſtreats, 15 *Edw*. 2. *Prerogativa Regis*,
" 17 *Edw* 2 tho' ſome think this Statute
" to be made *Temp Edw* 1. The Statute
" of Homage, and the Statute *De Terris
" Templarior'*, alſo 17 *Edw*. 2. View of
" Frankpledge, 18 *Edw* 2 And divers other
" Sta-

" Statutes in this King's Reign, but of un-
" certain Time.

And now, because I intend to give some
short Account of some general Observations touching Parliaments, and of Acts of
Parliament pass'd in the Times of those
three Princes, *viz. Hen* III *Edw* I. and
Edw. II. because they are of greatest Antiquity, and therefore the Circumstances
that attended them most liable to be worn
out by Process of Time, I will here mention some Particulars relating to them to
preserve their Memory, and which may also be useful to be known in relation to other
Things

Parlia-   We are therefore to know, That there are
mentary these several Kinds of Records of Things
Records. done in Parliament, or especially relating
thereto, *viz.* 1 The Summons to Parliament. 2. The Rolls of Parliament 3. Bundles of Petitions in Parliament. 4. The
Statutes, or Acts of Parliament themselves.
And, 5. The *Brevia de Parliamento*, which for
the most Part were such as issued for the
Wages of Knights and Burgesses; but with
these I shall not meddle.

Summons   *First*, As to the Summons to Parliament.
to Parlia- These Summons to Parliament are not all
ment. entred of Record in the Times of *Hen* III.
and *Edw* I none being extant of Record
in the Time of *Hen* III but that of 49 *Hen.* 3.
and none in the Time of *Edw.* I. till the
23 *Edw.* 1. But after that Year, they are
for the most part extant of Record, *viz. In*
Dorso

Dorſo Claus' Rotulorum, in the Backſide of the Cloſe Rolls.

Secondly, As to the Rolls of Parliament, Rolls of *viz* The Entry of the ſeveral Petitions, Parliament. Anſwers and Tranſactions in Parliament. Thoſe are generally and ſucceſſively extant of Record in the *Tower*, from 4 *Edw*. 3. downward till the End of the Reign of *Edw*. IV. Excepting only thoſe Parliaments that intervened between the 1ſt and the 4th, and between the 6th and the 11th, of *Edw*. III.

But of thoſe Rolls in the Times of *Hen*. III. Many and *Edw*. I. and *Edw*. II many are loſt, and loſt, *&c* few extant; alſo, of the Time of *Hen*. III. I have not ſeen any Parliament Roll; and all that I ever ſaw of the Time of *Edw*. I. was one Roll of Parliament in the Receipt of the *Exchequer* of 18 *Edw*. 1. and thoſe Proceedings and Remembrances which are in the *Liber placitor' Parliamenti* in the *Tower*, begiming as I remember with the 20th Year of *Edw*. I. and ending with the Parliament of *Carliſle*, 35 *Edw* 1. And not continued between thoſe Years with any conſtant Series ; but including ſome Remembrances of ſome Parliaments in the Time of *Edw*. I and others in the Time of *Edw* II.

In the Time of *Edw* II beſides the *Rotulus Ordinationum*, of the Lords Ordoners, about 7 *Edw*. 2 we have little more than the Parliament Rolls of 7 & 8 *Edw* 2. and what others are interſperſed in the Parliament Book of *Edw* I above-mention'd, and, as I remember, ſome ſhort Remembrances.

ces of Things done in Parliament in the
19 *Edw.* 3

Bundles of Petitions

Thirdly, As to the Bundles of Petitions in
Parliament They were for the moſt part
Petitions of private Perſons, and are commonly endorſed with Remiſſions to the ſeveral Courts where they were properly determinable   There are many of thoſe Bundles
of Petitions, ſome in the Times of *Edw* I.
and *Edw* II. and more in the Times of
Edw. III. and the Kings that ſucceeded him.

Acts, or Statutes

Fourthly, The Statutes, or Acts of Parliament themſelves   Theſe ſeem, as if in the
Time of *Edw.* I they were drawn up into
the Form of a Law in the firſt Inſtance, and
ſo aſſented to by both Houſes, and the
King, as may appear by the very Obſervation of the Contexture and Fabrick of the

Manner of Paſſing anciently

Statutes of thoſe Times   But from near the
beginning of the Reign of *Edw* III till
very near the end of *Hen.* VI. they were
not in the firſt Inſtance drawn up in the
Form of Acts of Parliament, but the Petition and the Anſwer were entred in the
Parliament Rolls, and out of both, by Advice of the Judges and others of the King's
Council, the Act was drawn up conformable to the Petition and Anſwer, and the
Act it ſelf for the moſt part entred in a
Roll, called, *The Statute Roll,* and the Tenor
thereof affixed to Proclamation Writs, directed to the ſeveral Sheriffs to proclaim it
as a Law in their reſpective Counties

End of later Times

But becauſe ſometimes Difficulties and
Troubles aroſe, by this extracting of the Statute

tute out of the Petition and Anfwer ; about
the latter end of *Hen.* VI. and beginning of
Edw. IV. they took a Courfe to reduce
'em, even in the firft Inftance, into the
full and compleat Form of Acts of Parliament, which was profecuted (or Entred)
commonly in this Form : *Item quædam Petitio
exhibita fuit in hoc Parliamento formàm actus in
fe continens, &c.* and abating that Stile, the
Method ftill continues much the fame,
namely; That the entire Act is drawn up
in Form, and fo comes to the King for his
Affent.

The ancient Method of paffing Acts of
Parliament being thus declared, I fhall now
give an Account touching thofe Acts of Par- Statutes
liament that are at this Day extant of the extant.
Times of *Hen.* III *Edw* I and *Edw* II. and
they are of two Sorts, *viz.* Some of them Two
are extant of Record ; others are extant in Sorts.
ancient Books and Memorials, but not of
Record. And thofe which are extant of Re- 1. Of Record, are either Recorded in the proper and cord
natural Roll, *viz. the Statute Roll* ; or they
are entred in fome other Roll, efpecially in
the *Clofe Rolls* and *Patent Rolls*, or in both.
Thofe that are extant, but not of Record,
are fuch as tho' they have no Record extant of them, but poffibly the fame is loft;
yet they are preferved in ancient Books
and Monuments, and in all Times have had
the Reputation and Authority of Acts of
Parliament.

For an Act of Parliament made within
Time of Memory, lofes not its being fo,
be-

becaufe not extant of Record, efpecially
if it be a general Act of Parliament. For
of general Acts of Parliament, the Courts
of Common Law are to take Notice without pleading of them; and fuch Acts fhall
never be put to be tried by the Record, upon an Iffue of *Nul tiel Record*, but it fhall be
tried by the Court, who, if there be any
Difficulty or Uncertainty touching it or the
right Pleading of it, are to ufe for their
Information ancient Copies, Tranfcripts,
Books, Pleadings and Memorials to inform
themfelves, but not to admit the fame to
be put in Iffue by a Plea of *Nul tiel Record*.

For, as fhall be fhewn hereafter, there are
very many old Statutes which are admitted
and obtain as fuch, tho' there be no Record at this Day extant thereof, nor yet any
other written Evidence of the fame, but
what is in a manner only Traditional, as
namely, Ancient and Modern Books of
Pleadings, and the common received Opinion and Reputation, and the Approbation
of the Judges Learned in the Laws: For the
Judges and Courts of Juftice are, *ex Officio,*
(bound) to take Notice of publick Acts of
Parliament, and whether they are truly
pleaded or not, and therefore they are the
Triers of them. But it is otherwife of private Acts of Parliament, for they may be
put in Iffue, and tried by the Record upon
Nul tiel Record pleaded, unlefs they are pro
duced Exemplified, as was done in the
Prince's Cafe in my Lord *Cook's* 8th *Rep.* and
therefore

therefore the Averment of *Nul tiel Record* was refused in that Case

The old Statutes or Acts of Parliament that are of Record, as is before said, are entred either upon the proper Statute Roll, or some other Roll in *Chancery*

The first Statute Roll which we have, is in the *Tower*, and begins with *Magna Charta*, and ends with *Edw* III and is called *Magnus Rotulus Statutor'*. There are five other Statute Rolls in that Office, of the Times of *Rich.* II *Hen* IV *Hen.* V *Hen.* VI. and *Edw* IV. ***The first Statute Roll***

I shall now give a Scheme of those ancient Statutes of the Times of *Hen* III *Edw.* I. and *Edw* II that are recorded in the first of those Rolls or elsewhere, to the best of my Remembrance, and according to those Memorials I have long had by me, *viz.* ***Ancient Statutes of Record***

Magna Charta Magno Rot. Stat. membr 49 *& Rot Cartar* 28 E. 1 *membr* 16.

Charta de Foresta Mag Rot. Stat membr 19 *& Rot Cartar* 28 E 1 *membr* 26

Sat de Gloucestre. Mag Rot Stat membr 47 *Westm.* 2. *Rot Mag Stat membr* 47

Westm 3. *Rot. Clauso,* 18 E. 1. *membr* 6 *Dorso.*

Winton. Rot Mag. Stat membr 41 *Rot Clauso,* 8 E 3 *membr* 6 *Dorso Pars* 2 *Rot Clauso,* 5 R 2. *membr* 13 *Rot Paten* 25 E 1. *membr* 13.

De Mercatoribus Mag Rot. Stat membr 47 *In Dorso.*

C De

De Religiosis. Mag. Rot Stat. membr. 47

Articuli Cleri. Mag. Rot. Stat membr 34.
Dorso 2 Pars Pat. E. 1 2. membr. 34 2 Pars.
Pat 2 E. 3. membr 15

De his qui ponendi sunt in Assisis. Mag Rot.
Stat. membr 41.

De Finibus levatis. Mag Rot Stat memb 37
De defensione Juris liberi Parliam. Lib Parl.
E. 1. fo. 32

Stat Eborum Mag Rot. Stat membr 32.

De conjunctis infeofatis. Mag Rot Stat.
membr 34

De Escaetoribus Mag Rot Stat. membr. 35.
Dorso, & Rot Clauf 29 E 1 membr 14.
Dorso

Stat de Lincolne Mag Rot Stat memb. 32.

Stat de Juses Rot Mag Stat membr. 33.
In Schedula de libertatibus perquirendis, vel Rot.
Clauf. 27 E 1 membr 24

Stat de Acton Burnel. Rot. Mag Stat.
membr 46. Dorso, & Rot. Clauf. 11 E 1
membr. 2

Juramentum Vicecomit. Rot Mag Stat.
membr 34. Dorso, & Rot. Clauf 5 E. 2
membr 23

Articuli Stat. Gloucestriæ Rot Clauf 2 E. 2
Pars 2. membr 8

De Pistoribus & Braciatoribus 2 Pars Clauf.
vel Pat 2 R 2 membr 29

De asportatis Religiosi Mag Rot Stat
membr 33

Westm. 4. De Vicecomitibus & Viridi cæra.
Rot Mag Stat memb. 33 In Dorso

Confirmationes Chartarum Mag. Rot. Stat.
membr. 28

De

*De Terris Templariorum. Mag Rot. Stat.
memb.* 31 *in Dorfo, & Clauf* 17 E. 2. *membr.* 4.

*Litera patens fuper prifis bonorum Cleri. Rot.
Mag. Stat membr.* 33 *In Dorfo*

*De Forma mittendi extractas ad Scaccar. Rot
Mag. Stat. membr* 36. & *membr* 30 *In Dorfo.*

Statutum de Scaccai   Mag Rot Stat

Statutum de Rutland   Rot Clauf. 12 E 1.

Ordinatio Foreftæ   Mag Rot. Stat memb. 30.
& *Rot. Clauf.* 17 E 2 *Pars* 2. *membr.* 3.

According to a ftrict Inquiry made about
30 Years fince, thefe were all the old Statutes of the Times of *Hen.* III. *Edw* I. and
Edw II that were then to be found of Record; what other Statutes have been found
fince, I know not.

The Ordinance called *Butlers,* for the Heir to punifh Waft in the Life of the Anceftor, tho' it be of Record in the Parlia-
ment Book of *Edw* I yet it never was a
Statute, nor never fo received, but only
fome Conftitution of the King's Council or
Lords in Parliament, and which never obtain'd the Strength or Force of an Act of
Parliament

Butler's Ordinance

Now thofe Statues that enfue, tho' moft
of 'em are unqueftionable Acts of Parliament, yet are not of Record that I know of,
but only their Memorials preferved in
ancient Printed and Manufcript Books of
Statutes, yet they are at this Day for the
moft part generally accepted and taken as
Acts of Parliament tho' fome of 'em are
now antiquated, and of little Ufe, *viz*

Ancient Statutes not of Record.

C 2   The

The Statutes of *Merton, Marlbridge, Westm* 1. *Explanatio Statuti Glouceſtriæ, De Champertio, De viſu Frankplegii, De pane & Cerviſia, Articuli Inquiſitionis ſuper Stat de Winton, Circumſpecte agatis, De diſtrictione Scaccarii, De Conſpirationibus, De vocatis ad Warrant Statut de Carliol, De Prerogativa Regis, De modo faciendi Homag De Wardis & Relev, Dies Communes in Banco. Stat de Bigamis, Dies communes in Banco in caſu conſimili Stat Hiberniæ, De quo Warranto, De Eſſoin calumpniand. Judicium colliſtrigii, De Frangentibus Priſonar' De malefactoribus in Parcis, De Conſultationibus, De Officio Coronatoris, De Protectionibus, Sententia lata ſuper Chartas, Modus levandi Fines Statut de Gavelet, De Militibus, De Vaſto, De anno Biſſextili, De appellatis, De Extenta Manerii, Compoſitio Menſearum vel* Computatio Menſarum *Stat de Quo Warranto, Ordinatio de Inquiſitionibus, Ordinatio de Foreſta, De admenſura Terre, De dimiſſione Denarioi. Statut. de Quo Warranto novum, Ne Rector proſternat arbores in Cæmeterio, Conſuetudines & Aſſiſa de Foreſta,* Compoſitio de Ponderibus, De Tallagio, De viſu Terræ & ſervitio Regis, Compeſitio ulnarum & particarum, De Terris amortizandis, Dictum de Kenelworth, *&c*

From whence we may collect theſe Two Obſervations, *viz*

Firſt, That altho' the Record it ſelf be not extant, yet general Statutes made within Time of Memory, namely, ſince 1° *Richardi Primi*, do not loſe their Strength, if any authentical

thentical Memorials thereof are in Books, and seconded with a general received Tradition attesting and approving the same.

Secondly, That many Records, even of Acts of Parliament, have in long Process of Time been lost, and possibly the Things themselves forgotten at this Day, which yet in or near the Times wherein they were made, might cause many of those authoritative Alterations in some Things touching the Proceedings and Decisions in Law: The original Cause of which Change being otherwise at this Day hid and unknown to us, and indeed, Histories (and Annals) give us an Account of the Suffrages of many Parliaments, whereof we at this Time have none, or few Footsteps extant in Records or Acts of Parliament. The Instance of the great Parliament at *Oxford*, about 40th of *Hen* III. may, among many others of like Nature, be a concurrent Evidence of this: For tho' we have Mention made in our Histories of many Constitutions made in the said Parliament at *Oxford*, and which occasioned much Trouble in the Kingdom, yet we have no Monuments of Record concerning that Parliament, or what those Constitutions were.

Many Acts of Parliament lost.

And thus much shall serve touching those Old Statutes or *Leges Scriptæ*, or Acts of Parliament made in the Times of those three Kings,

Kings, *Hen* III. *Edw.* I and *Edw* II. Those that follow in the Times of *Edw.* III. and the succeeding Kings, are drawn down in a continued Series of Time, and are extant of Record in the Parliament Rolls, and in the Statute Rolls, without any remarkable Omission, and therefore I shall say nothing of them.

CHAP.

CHAP. II.

Concerning the Lex non Scripta, i. e.
*The Common or Municipal Laws of
this Kingdom.*

IN the former Chapter, I have given you
a short Account of that Part of the
Laws of *England* which is called *Lex Scripta*,
namely, Statutes or Acts of Parliament,
which in their original Formation are reduced into Writing, and are so preserv'd in
their Original Form, and in the same Stile
and Words wherein they were first made :
I now come to that Part of our Laws called, *Lex non Scripta*, under which I include
not only General Customs, or the Common
Law properly so called, but even those
more particular Laws and Customs applicable to certain Courts and Persons, whereof
more hereafter

And when I call those Parts of our Laws
Leges non Scriptæ, I do not mean as if all
those Laws were only Oral, or communicated from the former Ages to the later,
merely by Word   For all those Laws have
their several Monuments in Writing, whereby they are transferr'd from one Age to another, and without which they would soon
lose all kind of Certainty · For as the Civil
and Canon Laws have their *Responsa Pru-*
dentum,

The Com-
mon Law
consists
of

General
Customs,

And par=
ticular

Written
in Books,
&c

C 4

dentum, Confilia & Decifiones, i e. their Canons, Decrees, and Decretal Determinations extant in Writing, fo thofe Laws of *England* which are not comprized under the Title of Acts of Parliament, are for the moft part extant in Records of Pleas, Proceedings and Judgments, in Books of Reports, and Judicial Decifions, in Tractates of Learned Men's Arguments and Opinions, preferv'd from ancient Times, and ftill extant in Writing.

Hath its
Force by
Ufage

But I therefore ftile thofe Parts of the Law, *Leges non Scriptæ*, becaufe their Authoritative and Original Inftitutions are not fet down in Writing in that Manner, or with that Authority that Acts of Parliament are; but they are grown into Ufe, and have acquired their binding Power and the Force of Laws by a long and immemorial Ufage, and by the Strength of Cuftom and Reception in this Kingdom   The Matters indeed, and the Subftance of thofe Laws, are in Writing, but the formal and obliging Force and Power of them grows by long Cuftom and Ufe, as will fully appear in the enfuing Difcourfe.

Now the Municipal Laws of this Kingdom, which I thus call *Leges non Scriptæ*, are of a vaft Extent, and indeed include in their Generalty all thofe feveral Laws which are allowed, as the Rule and Direction of Juftice and Judicial Proceedings, and which are applicable to all thofe various Subjects, about which Juftice is converfant. I fhall, for more Order, and the better to guide

my

my Reader, diftinguifh them into Two Kinds, *viz*

Firft, The Common Law, as it is taken in its proper and ufual Acceptation

Secondly, Thofe particular Laws applicable to particular Subjects, Matters or Courts.

1 Touching the former, *viz* The Common Law in its ufual and proper Acceptation This is that Law by which Proceedings and Determinations in the King's Ordinary *Courts* of Juftice are directed and guided This directs the Courfe of Difcents of Lands, and the Kinds; the Natures, and the Extents and Qualifications of Eftates; therein alfo the Manner, Forms, Ceremonies and Solemnities of transferring Eftates from one to another · The Rules of Settling, Acquiring, and Transferring of Properties; The Forms, Solemnities and Obligation of Contracts; The Rules and Directions for the Expofition of Wills, Deeds and Acts of Parliament. The Procefs, Proceedings, Judgments and Executions of the King's Ordinary *Courts* of Juftice; The Limits, Bounds and Extents of Courts, and their Jurifdictions The feveral Kinds of *Temporal* Offences, and Punifhments at Common Law; and the Manner of the Application of the feveral Kinds of Punifhments, and infinite more Particulars which extend themfelves as large as the many Exigencies in the Diftri-

Diftribution of the King's *Ordinary* Juftice requires.

And befides thefe more common and ordinary Matters to which the Common Law extends, it likewife includes the Laws applicable to divers Matters of very great Moment; and tho' by reafon of that Application, the faid Common Law affumes divers Denominations, yet they are but **Its Denominations.** Branches and Parts of it; like as the fame Ocean, tho' it many times receives a different Name from the Province, Shire, Ifland or Country to which it is contiguous, yet thefe are but Parts of the fame Ocean.

Thus the Common Law includes, *Lex Prerogativa*, as 'tis applied with certain Rules to that great Bufinefs of the King's Prerogative; fo 'tis called *Lex Foreftæ*, as it is applied under its fpecial and proper Rules to the Bufinefs of Forefts, fo it is called *Lex Mercatoria*, as it is applied under its proper Rules to the Bufinefs of Trade and Comerce; and many more Inftances of like Nature may be given. Nay, the various and particular Cuftoms of Cities, Towns and Manors, are thus far Parts of the Common Law as they are applicable to thofe particular Places, which will appear from thefe Obfervations, *viz*

Its Effects on particular Cuftoms *Firft*, The Common Law does determine what of thofe Cuftoms are good and reafonable, and what are unreafonable and void. *Secondly*, The Common Law gives to thofe Cuftoms that it adjudges reafonable, the Force and Efficacy of their Obligation.

gation *Thirdly*, The Common Law determines what is that Continuance of Time that is sufficient to make such a Custom. *Fourthly*, The Common Law does interpose and authoritatively decide the Exposition, Limits and Extension of such Customs

This Common Law, though the Usage, Practice and Decisions of the King's Courts of Justice may expound and evidence it, and be of great Use to illustrate and explain it; yet it cannot be authoritatively altered or changed but by Act of Parliament But of this Common Law, and the Reason of its Denomination, more at large hereafter. *Not alterable but by Statute*

Now, *Secondly*, As to those particular Laws I before mentioned, which are applicable to particular Matters, Subjects or Courts: These make up the second Branch of the Laws of *England*, which I include under the general Term of *Leges non Scriptæ*, and by those particular Laws, I mean the Laws Ecclesiastical, and the Civil Law, so far forth as they are admitted in certain Courts, and certain Matters allow'd to the Decision of those Courts, whereof hereafter *2dly, Particular Laws, viz.*

It is true, That those Civil and Ecclesiastical Laws are indeed Written Laws; The Civil Law being contain'd in their Pandects, and the Institutions of *Justinian*, &c (their Imperial Constitutions or Codes answering to our *Leges Scriptæ*, or Statutes) And the Canon or Ecclesiastical Laws contained for the most part in the Canons and Constitutions of Councils and Popes, collected in their *1. Civil. 2 Ecclesiastical.*

their *Decretum Gratiani*, and the Drecretal
Epistles of Popes, which make up the Body
of their *Corpus Juris Canonici*, together with
huge Volumes of Councils, and Expositions,
Decisions, and Tractates of learned Civilians and Canonists, relating to both Laws,
so that it may seem at first View very im-
proper to rank these under the Branch of
Leges non Scriptæ, or Unwritten Laws

*Why ac-
counted
Leges non
Scriptæ*
But I have for the following Reason rang'd
these Laws among the Unwritten Laws of
England, v.z. because it is most plain, That
neither the Canon Law nor the Civil Law
have any Obligation as Laws within this
Kingdom, upon any Account that the Popes
or Emperors made those Laws, Canons, Re-
scripts or Determinations, or because *Justinian* compiled their *Corpus Juris Civilis*,
and by his Edicts confirm'd and publish'd
the same as authentical, or because this or
that Council or Pope made those or these
Canons or Decrees, or because *Gratian*, or
Gregory, or *Boniface*, or *Clement*, did as much
as in them lie authenticate this or that
Body of Canons or Constitutions; for the
King of *England* does not recognize any
Foreign Authority, as superior or equal to
him in this Kingdom, neither do any Laws
of the Pope or Emperor, as they are such,
bind here : But all the Strength that either
the Papal or Imperial Laws have obtained
in this Kingdom, is only because they have
been received and admitted either by the
Consent of Parliament, and so are part of
the Statute Laws of the Kingdom, or else
by

by immemorial Ufage and Cuftom in fome particular Cafes and Courts, and no otherwife, and therefore fo far as fuch Laws are received and allowed here, fo far they obtain, and no further; and the Authority and Force they have here is not founded on, or derived from themfelves, for fo they bind no more with us than our Laws bind in *Rome* or *Italy*. But their Authority is founded merely on their being admitted and received by us, which alone gives 'em their Authoritative Effence, and qualifies their Obligation

Allowed by Ufage only

And hence it is, That even in thofe Courts where the Ufe of thofe Laws is indulged according to that Reception which has been allowed 'em : If they exceed the Bounds of that Reception, by extending themfelves to other Matters than has been allowed 'em; or if thofe Courts proceed according to that Law, when it is controuled by the Common Law of the Kingdom: The Common Law does and may prohibit and punifh them, and it will not be a fufficient Anfwer, for them to tell the King's Courts, that *Juftinian* or Pope *Gregory* have decreed otherwife. For we are not bound by their Decrees further, or otherwife than as the Kingdom here has, as it were, tranfpofed the fame into the Common and Municipal Laws of the Realm, either by Admiffion of, or by Enacting the fame, which is that alone which can make 'em of any Force in *England*. I need not give Particular Inftances herein, the Truth thereof is

And controul'd by the Common Law

plain

plain and evident, and we need go no further than the Statutes of 24 *H* 8 *cap.* 12.
25 *H* 8. *c* 19, 20, 21 and the learned Notes
of *Selden* upon *Fleta*, and the Records there
cited, nor shall I spend much Time touching the Use of those Laws in the several
Courts of this Kingdom. But will only
briefly mention some few Things concerning them

3 Courts using the Civil and Comon Law.   There are Three Courts of Note, wherein
the Civil, and in one of them the Canon or
Ecclesiastical Law, has been with certain
Restrictions allowed in this Kingdom, *viz.*
1*st* The Courts Ecclesiastical, of the Bishops
and their derivative Officers 2*dly* The Admiralty Court 3*dly* The *Curia Militaris*, or
Court of the Constable and Marshal, or
Persons commissioned to exercise that Jurisdiction I shall touch a little upon each
of these.

.. Eccle- fiastical Courts 2 Kinds   *First*, The Ecclesiastical Courts, they are
of two Kinds, *viz.* 1*st* Such as are derived
immediately by the Kings Commission;
such was formerly the Court of High Commission, which tho', without the help of an
Act of Parliament, it could not in Matters
of Ecclesiastical Cognizance use any Temporal Punishment or Censure, as Fine, Imprisonment, *&c* Yet even by the Common
Law, the Kings of *England*, being delivered
from *Papal Usurpation*, might grant a Commission to hear and determine Ecclesiastical
Causes and Offences, according to the
King's Ecclesiastical Laws, as *Cawdry's*
Case, *Cook's* 5th Report. 2*dly*. Such as are

not derived by any immediate Commiſſion
from the King; but the Laws of *England*
have annexed to certain Offices, Eccleſiaſtical Juriſdiction, as incident to ſuch Offices:
Thus every Biſhop by his Election and Confirmation, even before Conſecration, had
Eccleſiaſtical Juriſdiction annex'd to his Office, as *Judex Ordinarius* within his Dioceſe;
and divers Abbots anciently, and moſt
Archdeacons at this Day, by Uſage, have
had the like Juriſdiction within certain
Limits and Precincts.

Qr.

But altho' theſe are *Judices Ordinarii*, and
have Eccleſiaſtical Juriſdiction annex'd to
their Eccleſiaſtical Offices, yet this Juriſdiction Eccleſiaſtical *in Foro Exteriori* is derived from the Crown of *England*: For
there is no External Juriſdiction, whether
Eccleſiaſtical or Civil, within this Realm,
but what is derived from the Crown: It is
true, both anciently, and at this Day, the
Proceſs of Eccleſiaſtical Courts runs in the
Name, and Iſſues under the Seal of the
Biſhop; and that Practice ſtands ſo at this
Day, by Vertue of ſeveral Acts of Parliament, too long here to recount But that
is no Impediment of their deriving their
Juriſdiction from the Crown, for till 27 *H* 8.
cap. 24. the Proceſs in Counties Palatine
ran in the Name of the Counts Palatine, yet no Man ever doubted, but that
the Palatine Juriſdictions were deriv'd from
the Crown

Their Ju-
riſdiction
derived
from the
Crown

Touching the Severance of the Biſhops
Conſiſtory from the Sheriff's Court: See
the

the Charter of King *Will.* I and Mr *Selden's*
Notes on *Eadmerus*

*Ecclefia-
ftical Ju-
rifdiction
of Two
Kinds.*
Now the Matters of Ecclefiaftical Jurifdiction are of Two Kinds, Criminal and
Civil

*1ft Cri-
minal*
The Criminal Proceedings extend to fuch
Crimes, as by the Laws of this Kingdom are
of Ecclefiaftical Cognizance, as Herefie, For-
nication, Adultery, and fome others, wherein their Proceedings are, *Pro Reformatione
Morum & pro Salute Animæ*, and the Reafon
why they have Conuzance of thofe and the
like Offences, and not of others, as Mur-
ther, Theft, Burglary, &c is not fo much
from the Nature of the Offence (for furely
the one is as much a Sin as the other, and
therefore if their Cognizance were of Offences *quatenus peccata contra Deum*, it fhould
extend to all Sins whatfoever, it being
againft God's Law) But the true Reafon
is, becaufe the Law of the Land has indulged unto that Jurifdiction the Conuzance of fome Crimes, and not of others.

2d Civil.
The Civil Caufes committed to their Cognizance, wherein the Proceedings are *ad Inftantiam Partis*, ordinarily are Matters of
Tythes, Rights of Inftitution and Inducti-
on to Ecclefiaftical Benefices, Cafes of Ma-
trimony and Divorces, and Teftamentary
Caufes, and the Incidents thereunto, as In-
finuation or Probation of Teftaments, Con-
troverfies touching the fame, and of Legacies of Goods and Monies, &c.

Altho' *de Jure Communi* the Cognizance
of Wills and Teftaments does not belong

to the Ecclesiastical Court, but to the Temporal or Civil Jurisdiction; yet *de Confuetudine Angliæ pertinet ad Judices Ecclefiafticos*, as *Linwood* himself agrees, *exercit de Teftamentis, cap 4 in Gloffa.* So that it is the Custom or Law of *England* that gives the Extent and Limits of their external Jurisdiction in *Foro Cortentiofo*

The Rule by which they proceed, is the Canon Law, but not in its full Latitude, and only so far as it stands uncorrected, either by contrary Acts of Parliament, or the Common Law and Custom of *England*, for there are divers Canons made in ancient Times, and Decretals of the Popes that never were admitted here in *England*, and particularly in relation to Tytles, many Things being by our Laws Priviledg'd from Tythes, which by the Canon Law are chargable, (as Timber, Oat, Coals, *&c*) without a Special Custom subjecting them thereunto.

They Use the Canon Law,

Where the Canon Law, or the *Stylus Curiæ*, is silent, the Civil Law is taken in as a Director, especially in Points of Exposition and Determination, touching Wills and Legacies

And Civil.

But Things that are of Temporal Cognizance only, cannot by Charter be delivered over to Ecclefiaftical Jurisdiction, nor be judged according to the Rules of the Canon or Civil Law, which is *aliud Examen*, and not competent to the Nature of Things of Common Law Cognizance And therefore, *Mic. 8 H. 4. Rot. 72. coram Rege,* when the

Not to judge of Temporal Matters.

D Chan-

Chancellor of *Oxford* proceeded according to the Rule of the Civil Law in a Case of Debt, the Judgment was reversed in *B. R.* wherein the Principal Error assigned was, because they proceeded *per Legem Civilem ubi quilibet ligens Domini Regis Regni sui Angliæ in oribuscunque placitis & querelis infra hoc Regnum factis & emergentibus de Jure tractari debet per Communem Legem Angliæ*; and altho' King *H* 8 14 *Anno Regni sui*, granted to the University a liberal Charter to proceed according to the Use of the University, *viz.* By a Course much conform'd to the Civil Law, yet that Charter had not been sufficient to have warranted such Proceedings without the Help of an Act of Parliament. And therefore in 1<u>3</u> *Eliz* an Act passed, whereby that Charter was in effect enacted; and 'tis thereby that at this Day they have a kind of Civil Law Proceedure, even in Matters that are of themselves of Common Law Cognizance, where either of the Parties to the Suit are priviledg'd

Priviledge of the University

Sentence enforced The Coertion or Execution of the Sentence in Ecclesiastical Courts, is only by Excommunication of the Person contumatious, and upon Signification thereof into *Chancery*, a Writ *de Excommunicato capiendo* issues, whereby the Party is imprisoned till Obedience yielded to the Sentence But besides this Coertion, the Sentences of the Ecclesiastical Courts touching some Matters do introduce a real Effect, without any other Execution; as a Divorce, a *Vinculo Matrimonii* for the Causes of Consanguinity,

Pre-

Precontract, or Frigidity, do induce a legal
Diſſolution of the Marriage; ſo a Sentence
of Deprivation from an Eccleſiaſtical Bene-
fice, does by Vertue of the very Sentence,
without any other Coertion or Execution,
introduce a full Determination of the Intereſt of the Perſon deprived

And thus much concerning the Eccleſiaſtical Courts, and the Uſe of the Canon
and Civil Law in them, as they are the
Rule and Direction of Proceedings therein.

Secondly, The Second Special Juriſdiction
wherein the Civil Law is allow'd, at leaſt
as a Director or Rule in ſome Caſes, is the
Admiral Court or Juriſdiction This Juriſdiction is derived alſo from the Crown of
England, either immediately by Commiſſion
from the King, or mediately, which is ſeveral Ways, either by Commiſſion from the
Lord High Admiral, whoſe Power and
Conſtitution is by the King, or by the
Charters granted to particular Corporations
bordering upon the Sea, and by Commiſſion from them, or by Preſcription, which
nevertheleſs in Preſumption of Law is derived at firſt from the Crown by Charter
not now extant

The Admiral Juriſdiction is of Two Kinds,
viz. Juriſdictio Voluntaria, which is no other
but the Power of the Lord High Admiral,
as the King's General at Sea over his Fleets;
or *Juriſdictio Contentioſa,* which is that Power
of Juriſdiction which the Judge of the Admiralty has in *Foro Contentioſo;* and what I
have to ſay is of this later Juriſdiction

D 2

The

The Jurisdiction of the Admiral Court,
How Re- as to the Matter of it, is confined by the
strained. Laws of this Realm to Things done upon
the High Sea only ; as Depredations and
Piracies upon the High Sea, Offences of
Masters and Mariners upon the High Sea ;
Maritime Contracts made and to be executed upon the High Sea; Matters of Prize
and Reprizal upon the High Sea But
touching Contracts or Things made within
the Bodies of *English* Counties, or upon the
Land beyond the Sea, tho' the Execution
thereof be in some Measure upon the High
Sea, as Charter Parties, or Contracts made
even upon the High Sea, touching Things
that are not in their own Nature Maritime,
as a Bond or Contract for the Payment of
Money; so also of Damages in Navigable
Rivers, within the Bodies of Counties,
Things done upon the Shore at Low-Water,
Wreck of the Sea, *&c.* These Things belong not to the Admiral's Jurisdiction . And
thus the Common Law, and the Statutes of
13 *Rich* 2. *cap* **15** **15** *Rich.* 2. *cap* **3.** confine
and limit their Jurisdiction to Matters Mari-
time, and such only as are done upon the
High Sea

The   This Court is not bottom'd or founded
Ground upon the Authority of the Civil Law, but
of its has both its Power and Jurisdiction by the
Autho- Law and Custom of the Realm, in such
rity. Matters as are proper for its Cognizance;
and this appears by their Process, *viz* The
Arrest of the Persons of the Defendants as
well as by Attachment of their Goods ; and
like-

likewife by thofe Cuftoms and Laws Maritime, whereby many of their Proceedings are directed, and which are not in many Things conformable to the Rules of the Civil Law, fuch are thofe ancient Laws of *Oleron*, and other Cuftoms introduced by the Practice of the Sea, and Stile of the Court.

Alfo, The Civil Law is allowed to be the Rule of their Proceedings, only fo far as the fame is not contradicted by the Statute of this Kingdom, or by thofe Maritime Laws and Cuftoms, which in fome Points have obtain'd in Derogation of the Civil Law: But by the Statute 28 *Hen* 8 *cap* 15. all Treafons, Murders, Felonies, done on the High Sea, or in any Haven, River, Creek, Port or Place, where the Admirals have, or pretend to have Jurifdiction, are to be determined by the King's Commiffion, as if the Offences were done at Land, according to the Courfe of the Common Law

And thus much fhall ferve touching the Court of *Admiralty*, and the Ufe of the Civil Law therein

Thirdly, The Third Court, wherein the Civil Law has its Ufe in this Kingdom, is the Military Court, held before the Conftable and Marfhal anciently, as the *Judicis Ordinarii* in this Cafe, or otherwife before the King's Commiffioners of that Jurifdiction, as *Judices Delegati*.

3 The Military Court.

D 3   The

The Matter of their Jurisdiction is declared and limited by the Statutes of 8 *R.* 2. *cap* 5 & 13 *R* 2 *cap* 2 And not only by those Statutes, but more by the very Common Law is their Jurisdiction declared and limited as follows, *viz*

Negatively

First, Negatively They are not to meddle with any Thing determinable by the Common Law. And therefore, in as much as Matter of Damages, and the Quantity and Determination thereof, is of that Conuzance, the Court of Constable and Marshal cannot, even in such Suits as are proper for their Conuzance, give Damages against the Party convicted before them, and at most can only order Reparation in Point of Honour, as *Mendacium sibi ipsi imponere*. Neither can they, as to the Point of Reparation, in Honour, hold Plea of any such Words or Things, wherein the Party is relievable by the Courts of the Common Law.

Affirmatively

Secondly, Affirmatively. Their Jurisdiction extends to Matters of Arms and Matters of War, *viz*.

First, As to Matters of Arms (or Heraldry), the Constable and Marshal had Conuzance thereof, *viz* Touching the Rights of Coat-Armour, Bearings, Crests, Supporters, Pennons, &c. And also touching the Rights of Place and Precedence, in Cases where either Acts of Parliament or the King's Patent (he being the Fountain of

of Honour) have not already determined it,
for in such Cases they have no Power to alter it. Those Things were anciently allowed to the Conuzance of the Conſtable Office of
and Marſhal, as having ſome Relation to Conſtable
Military Affairs, but ſo reſtrain'd, that and Mar-
they were only to determine the Right, ſhal
and give Reparation to the Party injured
in Point of Honour, but not to repair him
in Damages

But, *Secondly*, As to Matters of War. The
Conſtable and Marſhal had a double Power,
viz

1. A Miniſterial Power, as they were
Two great ordinary Officers, anciently, in
the King's Army, the Conſtable being in
Effect the King's General, and the Marſhal
was imployed in marſhalling the King's
Army, and keeping the Liſt of the Officers
and Soldiers therein, and his Certificate
was the Trial of thoſe whoſe Attendance
was requiſite, *Vide Littleton*, § 102

Again, 2 The Conſtable and Marſhal
had alſo a Judicial Power, or a Court
wherein ſeveral Matters were determinable: As 1*ſt*, Appeals of Death or Murder
committed beyond the Sea, according to
the Courſe of the Civil Law 2*dly*, The
Rights of Priſoners taken in War 3*dly*, The
Offences and Miſcarriages of Soldiers,
contrary to the Laws and Rules of the Army For always preparatory to an actual
War, the Kings of this Realm, by Advice
of the Conſtable (and Marſhal), were uſed
to compoſe a Book or *Rules* and *Orders* for
the

C 4

the due Order and Discipline of their Officers and Soldiers, together with certain Penalties on the Offenders, and this was called, *Martial Law* We have extant in the Black Book of the Admiralty, and elsewhere, several Exemplars of such Military Laws, and especially that of the 9th of *Rich* 2. composed by the King, with the Advice of the Duke of *Lancaster*, and others

Of Law Martial

But touching the Business of Martial Law, these Things are to be observed, *viz.*

First, That in Truth and Reality it is not a Law, but something indulged rather than allowed as a Law; the Necessity of Government, Order and Discipline in an Army, is that only which can give those Laws a Countenance, *Quod enim Necessitas cogit defendit*

Secondly, This indulged Law was only to extend to Members of the Army, or to those of the opposite Army, and never was so much indulged as intended to be (executed or) exercised upon others; for others who were not listed under the Army had no Colour of Reason to be bound by Military Constitutions, applicable only to the Army; whereof they were not Parts, but they were to be order'd and govern'd according to the Laws to which they were subject. though it were a Time of War.

Thirdly, That the Exercise of Martial Law, whereby any Person should lose his Life or Member, or Liberty, may not be
per-

permitted in Time of Peace, when the Kings Courts are open for all Persons to receive Justice, according to the Laws of the Land. This is in Substance declared by the Petition of Right, 3 *Car* 1. whereby such Commissions and Martial Law were repealed and declared to be contrary to' Law: And accordingly was that famous Case of *Edmond* Earl of *Kent*, who being taken at *Pomfret*, 15 *Ed* 2 the King and divers Lords proceeded to give Sentence of Death against him, as in a kind of Military Court by a Summary Proceeding; which Judgment was afterwards in 1 *Ed* 3 revers'd in Parliament And the Reason of that Reversal serving to the Purpose in Hand, I shall here insert it as entered in the Record, *viz.*

Quod cum quicunq; homo ligeus Domini Regis pro Seditionibus, &c tempore pacis captus & in quacunq, Curia Domini Regis ductus fuerit de ejusmodi Seditionibus & aliis Feloniis sibi impositis per Legem & Consu tudine Regni arrestari debet & ad Responsionem adduci, Et inde per Communem Legem, antequam fuerit Mort' adjudicand' (triari) &c Unde cum notorium sit & manifestum quod totum tempus quo impositum fuit eidem Comiti propter Mili & Facinora fecisse, ad tempus in quo captus fuit & in quo Morti adjudicatus fuit, fuit tempus Pacis maximæ, Cum per totum tempus predictum & Cancellaria & aliæ plac Curiæ Domini Regis apertæ fuer' in quibus cuilibet Lex fiebatur sicut fieri consuevit, Nec idem Dominus Rex unquam tempore illo cum vexillis explicatis

explicatis Equitabat, &c And accordingly
the Judgment was revers'd ; for Martial
Law, which is rather indulg'd than allowed,
and that only in Cafes of Neceffity, in
Time of open War, is not permitted in
Time of Peace, when the ordinary Courts
of Juftice are open.

In this Military Court, Court of Honour, or Court Martial, the Civil Law has
been ufed and allowed in fuch Things as
belong to their Jurifdiction ; as the Rule or
Direction of their Proceedings and Decifions, fo far forth as the fame is not controuled by the Laws of this Kingdom, and
thofe Cuftoms and Ufages which have obtain'd in *England*, which even in Matters of
Honour are in fome Points derogatory to
the Civil Law But this Court has been
long difufed upon great Reafons.

And thus I have given a brief Profpect of
thefe Courts and Matters, wherein the
Canon and Civil Law has been in fome
Meafure allowed, as the Rule or Direction
of Proceedings or Decifions But although
in thefe Courts and Matters the Laws of
England, upon the Reafons and Account before expreffed, have admitted the Ufe and
Rule of the Canon and Civil Law ; yet even
herein alfo, the Common Law of *England*
Prehemi-
nence of
the Com-
mon Law. has retain'd thofe *Signa Superioritatis*, and the
Preference and Superintendence in relation
to thofe Courts . Namely,

1   1ft As the Laws and Statutes of the
Realm have prefcribed to thofe Courts their
Bounds

Bounds and Limits, fo the Courts of Common Law has the Superintendency over thofe Courts to keep them within the Limits and Bounds of their feveral Jurifdictions, and to judge and determine whether they have exceeded thofe Bounds, or not; and in cafe they do exceed their Bounds, the Courts at Common Law iffue their Prohibitions to reftrain them, directed either to the Judge or Party, or both : And alfo, in cafe they exceed their Jurifdiction, the Officer that executes the Sentence, and in fome Cafes the Judge that gives it, are punifhable in the Courts at Common Law ; fometimes at the Suit of the King, fometimes at the Suit of the Party, and fometimes at the Suit of both, according to the Variety and Circumftances of the Cafe.

2dly. The Common Law, and the Judges of the Courts of Common Law, have the Expofition of fuch Statutes or Acts of Parliament as concern either the Extent of the Jurifdiction of thofe Courts (whether Ecclefiaftical, Maritime or Military) or the Matters depending before them; and therefore, if thofe Courts either refufe to allow thefe Acts of Parliament, or expound them in any other Senfe than is truly and properly the Expofition of them, the King's Great Courts of the Common Law (who next under the King and his Parliament have the Expofition of thofe Laws) may prohibit and controul them

And thus much touching thofe Courts wherein the Civil and Canon Laws are allowed

2.

lowed as Rules and Directions under the Reftrictions above-mentioned: Touching which, the Sum of the Whole is this:

1. *First*, That the Jurifdiction exercifed in thofe Courts is derived from the Crown of *England*, and that the laft Devolution is to the King, by Way of Appeal

2. *Secondly*, That although the Canon or Civil Law be refpectively allowed as the Direction or Rule of their Proceedings, yet that is not as if either of thofe Laws had any original Obligation in *England*, either as they are the Laws of Emperors, Popes, or General Councils, but only by Vertue of their Admiffion here, which is evident; for that thofe Canons or Imperial Conftitutions which have not been received here do not bind, and alfo, for that by feveral contrary Cuftoms and Stiles ufed here, many of thofe Civil and Canon Laws are comptrouled and derogated.

3. *Thirdly*, That although thofe Laws are admitted in fome Cafes in thofe Courts, yet they are but *Leges fub graviori Lege*, and the Common Laws of this Kingdom have ever obtain'd and retain'd the Superintendency over them, and thofe *Signa Superioritatis* before-mentioned, for the Honour of the King and the Common Laws of *England*.

CHAP.

C H A P. III.

Concerning the Common Law of England, *its Use and Excellence, and the Reason of its Denomination.*

I Come now to that other Branch of our Laws, the common Municipal Law of this Kingdom, which has the Superintendency of all those other particular Laws used in the before-mentioned Courts, and is the common Rule for the Administration of common Justice in this great Kingdom; of which it has been always tender, and there is great Reason for it; for it is not only a very just and excellent Law in it self, but it is singularly accommodated to the Frame of the *English* Government, and to the Disposition of the *English* Nation, and such as by a long Experience and Use is as it were incorporated into their very Temperament, and, in a manner, become the Complexion and Constitution of the *English* Commonwealth.

Insomuch, that even as in the natural Body the due Temperament and Constitution does by Degrees work out those accidental Diseases which sometimes happen, and do reduce the Body to its just State and Constitution, so when at any Time through the Errors, Distempers or Iniquities of Men or Times,

Times, the Peace of the Kingdom, and right Order of Government, have received Interruption, the Common Law has wasted and wrought out those Distempers, and reduced the Kingdom to its just State and Temperament, as our present (and former) Times can easily witness

This Law is that which asserts, maintains, and, with all imaginable Care, provides for the Safety of the King's Royal Person, his Crown and Dignity, and all his just Rights, Revenues, Powers, Prerogatives and Government, as the great Foundation (under God) of the Peace, Happiness, Honour and Justice, of this Kingdom; and the Law is also, that which declares and asserts the Rights and Liberties, and the Properties of the Subject, and is the just, known, and common Rule of Justice and Right, between Man and Man, within this Kingdom

And from hence it is, that the Wisdom of the Kings of *England*, and their great Council, the Honourable Houses of Parliament, have always been jealous and vigilant for the Reformation of what has been at any Time found defective in it, and so to remove all such Obstacles as might obstruct the free Course of it, and to support, countenance and encourage the Use of it, as the best, safest and truest Rule of Justice in all Matters, as well Criminal as Civil

I should be too Voluminous to give those several Instances that occur frequently in the Statutes, the Parliament Rolls, and
Par-

Parliamentary Petitions, touching this Matter; and shall therefore only instance in some few Particulars in both Kinds, *viz.* Criminal and Civil: And First, in Matters Civil

In the Parliament 18 *Ed* 1. In a Petition 1. Civil in the Lords House, touching Land between Cases *Hugh Lowther* and *Adam Edingthorp*. The Defendant alledges, That if the Title should in this Manner be proceeded in, he should lose the Benefit of his Warranty, and also, that the Plaintiff, if he hath any Right, hath his Remedy at Common Law by Assize of *Mortdancestor*, and therefore demands Judgment, *Si de Libero Tenemento debeat hic sine brevi Respondere*; and the Judgment of the Lords in Parliament thereupon is entered in these Words, *viz. Et quia actio de predicto Tenemento petendo & etiam suum recuperare, si quid habere debeat vel possit eidem Adæ per Assisam mortis Antecessoris competere debet nec est juri consonum vel hactenus in Curia ista usitat' quod aliquis sine Lege Communi, & Brevi de Cancellaria de libero Tenemento suo respondeat & maxime in Casu ubi Breve de Cancellaria Locum habere potest, dictum est præfato Adæ quod sibi perquirat per Breve de Cancellaria, si sibi viderit Expedire*

Rot. Parl. 13 *R* 2 N° 10 *Adam Chaucer* preferred his Petition to the King and Lords in Parliament, against Sir *Robert Knolles*, to be relieved touching a Mortgage, which he supposed was satisfied, and to have Restitution of his Lands The Defendant appeared, and upon the several Allegations on both Sides,

Sides, the Judgment is thus entered, *viz. Et apres les Raisons & les Allegeances de l'un party & de l'autre, y sembles a Seigneurs du Parlement que le dit Petition ne estoit Petition du Parlement, deins que le mattier en icel comprize* doutt *estre* discuss *per le Commune Ley   Et pur ceo agard fuit que le dit* Robert *troit eut sans jour & que le dit* Adam *ne p endroit rien per sa suit icy, eins que il suerott p.r le Commune Ley si il luy sembloit ceo faire*   Where we may note, the Words are *Doutt estre,* and not *Poet estre discusse per le, &c.*

Rot. Parl. 50 *Ed* 3. Nº 43. A Judgment being given against the Bishop of *Norwich,* for the Archdeaconry of *Norwich,* in the Common Bench, the Bishop petitioned the Lords in Parliament, that the Record might be brought into that House, and to be reversed for Error. *Et quoy a luy estoit finalement Respondu per common Assent des ils les Justices que si Error y fust si ascun a fine force per le Ley de* Angleterre *tiel Error fuit voire en Parlement immediatement per voy de Error ains en Bank le Roy, & en nul part ailhors, Mais si le Case avenoit que Error fust fait en Bank le Roy adonque ceo serra amendes en Parlement*

And let any Man but look over the Rolls of Parliament, and the Bundles of Petitions in Parliament, of the Times of *Ed* I *Ed* II. *Ed* III *Hen* IV. *H* V. *& H* VI. he will find Hundreds of Answers of Petitions in Parliament concerning Matters determinable at Common Law, endorsed with Answers to this, or the like Effect, *viz. Suez vous a le*

Commune Ley ; sequatur ad Communem Legem ;
Perquirat Breve in Cancellaria si sibi viderit ex-
pedire ; ne est Petition du Parlement ; Mandetur
ista Petitio in Cancellarium, vel Cancellario, vel
Justiciarus de Banco, vel Thesaurario & Baroni-
bus de Scaccario, and the like.

And these were not barely upon the *Bene
placita* of the Lords, but were *De jure,* as
appears by those former Judgments given in
the Lords House in Parliament, and the
Reason is evident : *First,* Because if such a
Course of Extraordinary Proceeding should
be had before the Lords in the first Instance,
the Party should lose the Benefit of his
Appeal by Writ of Error, according as the
Law allows, and that is the Reason, why
even in a Writ of Error, or Petition of Error upon a Judgment in any inferior Court,
it cannot go *per Saltum* into Parliament, till
it has passed the Court of *King's-Bench* ; for
that the First Appeal is thither. *Secondly,*
Because the Subject would by that Means
lose his Trial *per Pares,* and consequently
his Attaint, in case of a Mistake in Point
of Issue or Damages : To both which he is
entitled by Law.

And although some Petitions of this Nature have been determined in that Manner,
yet it has been (generally) when the Exception has not been started, or at least not in-
sisted upon : And One Judgment in Parliament, that Cases of that Nature ought to
be determined according to the Course of the
Common Law, is of greater Weight than
many Cases to the contrary, wherein the

E   Question

Queſtion was not ſtirred Yea, even tho'
it ſhould be ſtirred, and the contrary affirm'd
upon a Debate of the Queſtion, becauſe
greater Weight is to be laid upon the Judgment of any Court when it is excluſive of
its Juriſdiction, than upon a Judgment of
the ſame Court in Affirmance of it

2 Crim-
nal Caſes. Now as to Matters Criminal, whether
Capital or not, they are determinable by the
Common Law, and not otherwiſe, and in
Affirmance of that Law, where the Statutes
of *Magna Charta*, cap 29. 5 *Ed* 3 *cap* 9
25 *Ed*. 3. *cap*. 4. 29 *Ed*. 3 *cap* 3. 27 *Ed* 3
cap. 17. 38 *Ed*. 3 *cap* 9 & 40 *Ed* 3 *cap*. 3.
The Effect of which is, That no Man ſhall
be put out of his Lands or Tenements, or
be impriſoned upon any Suggeſtion, unleſs
it be by Indictment or Preſentment of lawful Men, or by Proceſs at Common Law.

And by the Statute of 1 *Hen*. 4. *cap* 14.
it is enacted, That no Appeals be ſued in
Parliament at any Time to come · This
extends to all Accuſations by particular
Perſons, and that not only of Treaſon or
Felony, but of other Crimes and Miſdemeanors It is true, the Petition upon
which that Act was drawn up, begins with
Appeals of Felony and Treaſon, but the
Cloſe thereof, as alſo the King's Anſwer,
refers as well to Miſdemeanors as Matters
Capital, and becauſe this Record will give
a great Light to this whole Buſineſs, I will
here ſet down the Petition and the Anſwer
verbatim. *Vide Rot Parl*. 1 *Hen* 4. N° 144.

Item,

Item, *Supplyont les Commens que defore en* Petition.
avant nul appele de Traifon ne de autre Felony 1 Hen 4.
quelconq; foit accept ou receive en le Parlement Nº. 144.
ains en vous autres Courts de dans voftre Realm
dementiers que en vous dits Courts purra eftre
Terminer come ad ote fait & ufe ancienement
en temps de vous noble Progeniteurs, Et que
chefcun Perfon qui en temps a venir ferra accufe ou
impeach en voftre Parlement ou en afcuns des vos
dits Courts per les Seigniors & Commens di voftre
Realm ou per afcun Perfon & defence ou Refponfe a
fon Accufement ou Empeachment & fur fon Refponfe
reafonable Record Jugement & Tryal come de an-
cienement temps ad eftre fait & ufe per les bones
Leges de voftre Realm, nient obftant que les dits
Empeachements ou Accufements foient faits per les
Seigneurs ou Commens de voftre Relme come que
de novel en temps de Ric. nadgarius Roy ad eftre
fait & ufe a contrar, a tres grand Mifchief &
tres grand Maleveys Exemple de voftre Realm.

Le Roy voet que de cy en avant toutes les Ap- Anfwer.
peles de chofes faits deins le Relme foient tryez
& terminez per les bones Leys faits en temps de
tres noble Progeniteurs de noftre dit Seigneur le
Roy, Et que touts les Appeles de chofes faits hors
du Realm, foient triez & terminez devant le
Conftable & Marfhal de Angleterre, *& que*
nul Appele foit fait en Parlement defore en afcun
temps a venir.

This is the Petition and Anfwer. The Stat 1 H 4
Statute as drawn up hereupon, is *general,* cap 14
and runs thus: Item, *Pur plufieurs grands In-*
convemencies & Mifcheifs que plufieurs fait ont

advenus

advenus per colour des plusieurs Appeles faits deins
le Realm avant ces heurs ordain est & establuz, Que
desore en avant touts Appeles de choses faits deins
le Realm soient tries & termines per les bones Leys
de le Realm faits & uses en temps de tres noble
Progeniteurs de dit nostre Seigneur le Roy, Et
que ils les Appeles de choses faits hors du Realm
soient tries & termines devant le Constable &
Marshel pur les temps esteant ; Et ouster accordes
est & assentus que nulls Appeles soient desore faits
ou pursues en Parlement en nul temps avenir.

Where we may obferve, That though
the Petition expreffes (only) Treafon and
Felony, yet the Act is general againft all
Appeals in Parliament ; and many Times
the Purview of an Act is larger than the
Preamble, or the Petition, and fo 'tis here: For
the Body of the Act prohibits all Appeals
in Parliament, and there was Reafon for it :
For the Mifchief, *viz.* Appeals in Parliament in the Time of King *Richard* II. (as
in the Petition is fet forth) were not only
of Treafon and Felony, but of Mifdemea-
nors alfo, as appears by that great Proceeding, 11 R 2. againft divers, by the Lords
Appellants, and confequently it was neceffary to have the Remedy as large as the
Mifchief. And I do not remember that
after this Statute there were any Appeals
in Parliament, either for Matters Capital
or Criminal, at the Suit of any Particular
Perfon or Perfons.

It is true, Impeachments by the Houſe of
Commons, ſent up to the Houſe of Lords,
were fiequent as well after as before this
Statute, and that juſtly, and with good
Reaſon; for that neither the Act nor the
Petition ever intended to reſtrain them, but
only to regulate them, *viz.* That the Parties might be admitted to their Defence to
them, and as neither the Words of the Act
nor the Practice of After-times extended to
reſtrain ſuch Impeachments as were made
by the Houſe of Commons, ſo neither do
thoſe Impeachments and Appeals agree in
their Nature or Reaſon, for Appeals were
nothing elſe but Accuſations, either of Capital or Criminal Miſdemeanors, made in
the Lords Houſe by particular Perſons; but
an Impeachment is made by the Body of
the Houſe of Commons, which is equivalent
to an Indictment *pro Corpore Regni*, and
therefore is of another Nature than an Ac-
cuſation or Appeal, only herein they a-
gree, *viz.* Impeachments in Caſes Capital
againſt Peers of the Realm, have been ever
tried and determined in the Lords Houſe;
but Impeachments againſt a Commoner
have not been uſual in the Houſe of Lords,
unleſs preparatory to a Bill, or to direct an
Indictment in the Courts below. But Impeachments at the Proſecution of the Houſe
of Commons, for Miſdemeanors as well
againſt a Commoner as any other, have
uſually received their Determinations and
final Judgments in the Houſe of Lords,
whereof there have been numerous Prece-

E 3   dents

dents in all Times, both before and since the said Act

And thus much in general touching the great Regard that Parliaments and the Kingdom have had, and that most justly to the Common Law, and the great Care they have had to preserve and maintain it, as the Common Interest and Birthright of the King and Kingdom.

Appellation of the Common Law

I shall now add some few Words touching the Stiles and Appellations of the Common Law, and the Reasons of it · 'Tis called sometimes by Way of Eminence, *Lex Terræ*, as in the Statute of *Magna Charta, cap* 29. where certainly the Common Law is at least principally intended by those Words, *aut per Legem Terræ*, as appears by the Exposition thereof in several subsequent Statutes, and particularly in the Statute 28 *Ed* 3. *cap* 3. which is but an Exposition and Declaration of that Statute . Sometimes 'tis called, *Lex Angliæ*, as in the Statute of *Merton, cap*... *Nolumus Leges Angliæ mutare, &c* Sometimes 'tis called, *Lex & Consuetudo Regni*, as in all Commissions of *Oyer* and *Terminer*, and in the Statutes of 18 *Ed* 1. *cap* . and *De Quo Warranto,* and divers others; but most commonly 'tis call'd, *The Common Law,* or, *The Common Law of* England, as in the Statute of *Articuli super Chartas, cap* 15 in the Statute 25 *Ed.* 3. *cap* 5. and infinite more Records and Statutes

Now the Reason why 'tis call'd, *The Common Law,* or what was the Occasion that first

firſt gave that Determination to it, is va- *The Rea-* riouſly aſſigned, *viz* *fonsthere-* *of*

Firſt, Some have thought it to be ſo called by Way of Contradiſtinction to thoſe other Laws that have obtain'd within this King- dom; as, 1*ſt* By Way of Contradiſtinction to the Statute Law, thus a Writ of Entry *ad Com- munem Legem*, is ſo call'd in Contradiſtinction to Writs of Entry in *Caſu conſimili*, and in *Caſu proviſo*, which are given by Act of Par- liament. 2*dly*, By Way of Contradiſtinction to particular Cuſtomary Laws: Thus Diſ- cents at Common Law, Dower at Com- mon Law, are in Contradiſtinction to ſuch Dowers and Diſcents as are directed by par- ticular Cuſtoms And 3*dly*, In Contradi- ſtinction to the Civil, Canon, Martial and Military Laws, which are in ſome particu- lar Caſes and Courts admitted, as the Rule of their Proceedings

Secondly, Some have conceived, that the Reaſon of this Appellation was this, *viz* In the beginning of the Reign of *Edward* III. before the Conqueſt, commonly called, *Edward the Confeſſor*, there were ſeveral Laws, and of ſeveral Natures, which obtain'd in ſeveral Parts of this Kingdom, *viz* The *Mercian Laws*, in the Counties of *Glouceſter*, *Worceſter*, *Hereford*, *Warwick*, *Oxon*, *Cheſter*, *Salop* and *Stafford* The *Daniſh* Laws, in the Counties of *York*, *Derby*, *Nottingham*, *Lei- ceſter*, *Lincoln*, *Northampton*, *Bedford*, *Bucks*, *Hartford*, *Eſſex*, *Middleſex*, *Norfolk*, *Suffolk*, *Cam- bridge* and *Huntington*. The *Weſt-Saxon* Laws, in the Counties of *Kent*, *Suſſex*, *Surrey*, *Berks*,

E 4 *Southamp-*

Southampton, Wilts, Somerset, Dorset, and *Devon.*

This King, to reduce the Kingdom as well under one Law, as it then was under one Monarchical Government, extracted out of all those Provincial Laws, one Law to be observed through the whole Kingdom : Thus *Ranulphus Cestrensis,* cited by Sir *Henry Spelman* in his *Glossary,* under the Title, *Lex,* says, *Ex tribus his Legibus Sanctus Edvardus unam Legem &c* And the same in *totidem verbis,* is affirm'd in his History of the last Year of the same King *Edward (Vide ibid plura de hoc)* But *Hoveden* carries up the *Common Laws,* or those stiled the *Confessor's Laws,* much further, for he in his History of *Henry* II. tells us, *Quod istæ Leges prius inventæ & constitutæ erant Tempore* Edgari, *Avi sui, &c (Vide Hoveden)* And possibly the Grandfather might be the first Collector of them into a Body, and afterwards *Edward* might add to the Composition, and give it the Denomination of the Common Law; but the Original of it cannot in Truth be referred to either, but is much more ancient, and is as undiscoverable as the Head of *Nile* Of which more at large in the following Chapter.

Thirdly, Others say, and that most truly, That it is called the Common Law, because it is the common Municipal Law or Rule of Justice in this Kingdom : So that *Lex Communis,* or *Jus Communus,* is all one and the same with *Lex Patriæ,* or *Jus Patrium;* for although there are divers particular Laws,

some

(margin note) The Confessor's Laws

some by Custom applied to particular Places, and some to particular Causes; yet that Law which is common to the generality of all Persons, Things and Causes, and has a Superintendency over those particular Laws that are admitted in relation to particular Places or Matters, is *Lex Communis Angliæ*, as the Municipal Laws of other Countries may be, and are sometimes call'd, *The Common Law of that Country*, as, *Lex Communis Norrica, Lex Communis Burgundica, Lex Communis Lombardica, &c.* So that although all the former Reasons have their Share in this Appellation, yet the principal Cause thereof seems to be the later: And hence some of Ancients call'd it *Lex Communis*, others *Lex Patriæ*, and so they were called in their Confirmation by King *William* I. Whereof hereafter.

C HAP.

CHAP. IV.

Touching the Original of the Common Law of England.

THE Kingdom of *England* being a very ancient Kingdom, has had many Vicissitudes and Changes (especially before the coming in of King *William* I) under several either Conquests or Accessions of Foreign Nations. For tho' the *Britains* were, as is supposed, the most ancient Inhabitants, yet there were mingled with them, or brought in upon them, the *Romans*, the *Picts*, the *Saxons*, the *Danes*, and lastly, the *Normans*; and many of those Foreigners were as it were incorporated together, and made one Common People and Nation, and hence arises the Difficulty, and indeed Moral Impossibility, of giving any satisfactory or so much as probable Conjecture, touching the Original of our Laws, for the following Reasons, *viz*

The Difficulty of discovering their Original

First, From the Nature of Laws themselves in general, which being to be accommodated to the Conditions, Exigencies and Conveniencies of the People, for or by whom they are appointed, as those Exigencies and Conveniencies do insensibly grow upon the People, so many times there grows insensibly a Variation of Laws, especially in a long tract of Time, and hence it is, that tho' for the Purpose in some particular Part

of

of the Common Law of *England*, we may
eafily fay, That the Common Law, as it is
now taken, is otherwife than it was in that
particular Part or Point in the Time of
Hen II when *Glanville* wrote, or than it was
in the Time of *Hen* III. when *Bracton* wrote,
yet it is not poffible to affign the certain
Time when the Change began ; nor have we
all the Monuments or Memorials, either of
Acts of Parliament, or of Judicial Refolutions, which might induce or occafion fuch
Alterations ; for we have no authentick
Records of any Acts of Parliament before
9 H 3 and thofe we have of that King's
Time, are but few Nor have we any Reports of Judicial Decifions in any conftant
Series of Time before the Reign of *Edw* I
tho' we have the Plea Rolls of the Times of
Hen. III and King *John,* in fome remarkable
Order. So that Ufe and Cuftom, and Judicial Decifions and Refolutions, and Acts
of Parliament, tho' not now extant, might
introduce fome *New* Laws, and alter fome
Old, which we now take to be the very
Common Law it felf, tho' the Times and
precife Periods of fuch Alterations are not
explicitely or clearly known But tho' thofe
particular Variations and Acceffions have
happened in the Laws, yet they being only
partial and fucceffive, we may with juft
Reafon fay, They are the fame *Englifh* Laws
now, that they were 600 Years fince in the
general. As the *Argonauts* Ship was the
fame when it returned home, as it was when
it went out, tho' in that long Voyage it had
fuc-

successive Amendments, and scarce came back with any of its former Materials, and as *Titius* is the same Man he was 40 Years since, tho' Physitians tell us, that in a Tract of 7 Years, the Body has scarce any of the same Material Substance it had before.

Secondly, The 2d Difficulty in the Search of the Antiquity of Laws and their Original, is in relation to that People unto whom the Laws are applied, which in the Case of *England*, will render many Observables, to to shew it hard to be traced. For,

1*st*. It is an ancient Kingdom, and in such Cases, tho' the People and Government had continued the same *ab Origine*, (as they say the *Chinefes* did, till the late Incursion of the *Tartars*) without the Mixture of other People, or Laws, yet it were an impossible Thing to give any certain Account of the Original of the Laws of such a People, unless we had as certain Monuments thereof as the *Jews* had of theirs, by the Hand of *Moses*, and that upon the following Accounts, *viz.*

First, We have not any clear and certain Monuments of the Original Foundation of the *English* Kingdom or State, when, and by whom, and how it came to be planted. That which we have concerning it, is uncertain and traditional; and since we cannot know the Original of the planting of this Kingdom, we cannot certainly know the Original of the Laws thereof, which may be well presum'd to be very near as ancient as the Kingdom it self. Again, 2*dly*, Tho'

Tra

Tradition might be a competent Difcoverer of the Original of a Kingdom or State, I mean Oral Tradition, yet fuch a Tradition were incompetent without written Monuments to derive to us, at fo long a Diftance, the Original Laws and Conftitutions of the Kingdom, becaufe they are of a complex Nature, and therefore not orally traducible to fo great a Diftance of Ages, unlefs we had the Original or Authentick Tranfcript of thofe Laws, as the People the *Jews* had of their Law, or as the *Romans* had of their Laws of the Twelve Tables engraven in Brafs. But yet further, 3*dly*, It is very evident to every Day's Experience, that Laws, the further they go from their original Inftitution, grow the larger, and the more numerous: In the firft Coalition of a People, their Profpect is not great, they provide Laws for their prefent Exigence and Convenience. But in Procefs of Time, poffibly their firft Laws are changed, altered or antiquated, as fome of the Laws of the Twelve Tables among the *Romans* were. But whatfoever be done touching their *Old* Laws, there muft of Neceffity be a Provifion of *New*, and other Laws fuccefively, anfwering to the Multitude of fucceffive Exigencies and Emergencies, that in long Tract of Time will offer themfelves; fo that if a Man could at this Day have the Profpects of all the Laws of the *Britains* before any Invafion upon them, it would yet be impoffible to fay, which of them were *New*, and which were *Old*, and the feveral Seafons and Periods

riods of Time wherein every Law took its
Rise and Original, especially since it ap-
pears, that in those elder Times, the *Bri-
tains* were not reduc'd to that civiliz'd
Estate, as to keep the Annals and Memo-
rials of their Laws and Government, as the
Romans and other civiliz'd Parts of the
World have done

It is true, when the Conquest of a Country appears, we can tell when the Laws of
conquering People came to be given to
the Conquered. Thus we can tell, that in
the Time of *Hen.* II when the Conquest of
Ireland had obtain'd a good Progress, and in
the Time of K *John*, when it was compleated, the *English* Laws were settled in *Ireland*
But if we were upon this Inquiry, what
were the Original of those *English* Laws that
were thus settled there; we are still under
the same Quest and Difficulty that we
are now, *viz* What is the Original of the
English Laws For they that begin New Colonies, Plantations and Conquests; if they
settle *New* Laws, and which the Places had
not before, yet for the most part (I don't
say altogether) they are the *Old* Laws which
obtain'd in those Countries from whence
the Conquerors or Planters came

Secondly, The 2d Difficulty of the Discovery of the Original of the *English* Laws is
this, That this Kingdom has had many and
great Vicissitudes of People that inhabited
it, and that in their several Times prevail'd
and obtain'd a great Hand in the Government of this Kingdom, whereby it came to

pass, that there arose a great Mixture and Variety of Laws: In some Places the Laws of the *Saxons*, in some Places the Laws of the *Danes*, in some Places the Laws of the ancient *Britons*, in some Places the Laws of the *Mercians*, and in some Places, or among some People (perhaps) the Laws of the *Normans*: For altho', as I shall shew hereafter, the *Normans* never obtain'd this Kingdom by such a Right of Conquest, as did or might alter the Established Laws of the Kingdom, yet considering that K. *William* I. brought with him a great Multitude of that Nation, and many Persons of great Power and Eminence, which were planted generally over this Kingdom, especially in the Possessions of such as had oppos'd his coming in, it must needs be suppos'd, that those Occurrences might easily have a great Influence upon the Laws of this Kingdom, and secretly and insensibly introduce *New* Laws, Customs and Usages; so that altho' the Body and Gross of the Law might continue the same, and so continue the ancient Denomination that it first had, yet it must needs receive divers Accessions from the Laws of those People that were thus intermingled with the ancient *Britains* or *Saxons*, as the Rivers of *Severn, Thames, Trent, &c.* tho' they continue the same Denomination which their first Stream had, yet have the Accession of divers other Streams added to them in the Tracts of their Passage which enlarge and augment them. And hence grew those several Denominations of the *Saxon, Mercian,* and *Danish* Laws,

out

out of which (as before is shewn) the Confeſſor extracted his Body of the Common
Law, and therefore among all thoſe various
Ingredients and Mixtures of Laws, it is almoſt an impoſſible Piece of Chymiſtry to
reduce every *Caput Legis* to its true Original,
as to ſay, This is a piece of the *Daniſh,* this
of the *Norman,* or this of the *Saxon* or *Britiſh*
Law . Neither was it, or indeed is it much
Material, which of theſe is their Original ;
for 'tis very plain, the Strength and Obligation, and the formal Nature of a Law,
is not upon Account that the *Danes,* or the
Saxons, or the *Normans,* brought it in with
them, but they became Laws, and binding
in this Kingom, by Vertue only of their
being received and approved here

Thirdly, A Third Difficulty ariſes from
thoſe accidental Emergencies that happened,
either in the Alteration of Laws, or communicating or conveying of them to this
Kingdom : For firſt, the Subdiviſion of the
Kingdom into ſmall Kingdoms under the
Heptarchy, did moſt neceſſarily introduce
a Variation of Laws, becauſe the ſeveral
Parts of the Kingdom were not under one
common Standard, and ſo it will ſoon be
in any Kingdoms that are cantonized, and
not under one common Method of Diſpenſation of Laws, tho' under one and the
ſame King. *Again,* The Intercourſe and
Traffick with other Nations, as it grew
more or greater, did gradually make a
Communication and Tranſmigration of
Laws from us to them, and from them to us.

Again,

Again, The growth of Chriſtianity in this Kingdom, and the Reception of Learned Men from other Parts, eſpecially from *Rome*, and the Credit that they obtained here, might reaſonably introduce ſome *New* Laws, and antiquate or abrogate ſome *Old* ones that ſeem'd leſs conſiſtent with the Chriſtian Doctrines, and by this Means, not only ſome of the Judicial Laws of the *Jews*, but alſo ſome Points relating to, or bordering upon, or derived from the Canon or Civil Laws, as may be ſeen in thoſe Laws of the ancient Kings, *Ini, Alphred, Canutus, &c.* collected by Mr *Lambard*.

Having thus far premiſed, it ſeems, upon the whole Matter, an endleſs and inſuperable Buſineſs to carry up the *Engliſh* Laws to their ſeveral Springs and Heads, and to find out their firſt Original, neither would it be of any Moment or Uſe if it were done: For whenever the Laws of *England*, or the ſeveral *Capita* thereof began, or from whence or whomſoever derived, or what Laws of other Countries contributed to the Matter of our Laws, yet moſt certainly their Obligation ariſes not from their Matter, but from their Admiſſion and Reception, and Authorization in this Kingdom, and thoſe Laws, if convenient and uſeful for the Kingdom, were never the worſe, tho' they were deſumed and taken from the Laws of other Countries, ſo as they had their Stamp of Obligation and Authority from the Reception and Approbation of this Kingdom by Vertue of the Common Law, of which

F   this

this Kingdom has been always jealous, especially in relation to the Canon, Civil, and *Norman* Law, for the Reasons hereafter shewn

Three Constituents of the Common Law   Passing therefore from this unsearchable Inquiry, I shall descend to that which gives the Authority, *viz* The formal Constituents, as I may call them, of the Common Law, and they seem to be principally, if not only, those three, *viz* 1*st*, The Common Usage, or Custom, and Practice of this Kingdom, in such Parts thereof as lie in Usage or Custom 2*dly*, The Authority of Parliament, introducing such Laws; and, 3*dly*, The Judicial Decisions of Courts of Justice, consonant to one another in the Series and Successions of Time.

1. Customs   1 As to the first of these, Usage and Custom generally received, do *Obtinere vim Legis*, and is that which gives Power sometimes to the Canon Law, as in the Ecclesiastical Courts, sometimes to the Civil Law, as in the Admiralty Courts, and again, controules both, when they cross other Customs that are generally received in the Kingdom This is that which directs Discents, has settled some ancient Ceremonies and Solemnities in Conveyances, Wills and Deeds, and in many more Particulars And if it be inquired, What is the Evidence of this Custom, or wherein it consists, or is to be found? I answer, It is not simply an unwritten Custom, nor barely *Orally* derived down from one Age to another, but it is a Custom that is derived down

down in Writing, and tranfmitted from Age
to Age, efpecially fince the beginning of
Edw I to whofe Wifdom the Laws of *England* owe almoft as much as the Laws of
Rome to *Juftinian*

2. Acts of Parliament. And here it muft ²ly Sta-
not be wonder'd at, that I make Acts of tutes.
Parliament one of the Authoritative Con-
ftituents of the Common Law, tho' I had
before contradiftinguifhed the one from the
other ; for we are to know, that altho' the
Original or Authentick Tranfcripts of
Acts of Parliament are not before the Time
of *Hen* III and many that were in his
Time are perifh'd and loft, yet certainly
fuch there were, and many of thofe Things
that we now take for Common Law, were
undoubtedly Acts of Parliament, tho' now
not to be found of Record And if in the
next Age, the Statutes made in the Time
of *Hen.* III. and *Edw* I were loft, yet even
thofe would pafs for Parts of the Common
Law, and indeed, by long Ufage, and the
many Refolutions grounded upon them, and
by their great Antiquity, they feem even
already to be incorporated with the very
Common Law; and that this is fo, may appear, tho' not by Records, for we have none
fo ancient, yet by an authentical and unqueftionable Hiftory, wherein a Man may,
without much Difficulty, find, That many
of thofe *Capitula Legum* that are now ufed
and taken for Common Law, were Things
enacted in Parliaments or Great Councils
under *William* I and his Predeceffors, King's

of *Ergland*, as may be made appear hereafter. But yet, thofe Conftitutions and Laws being made before Time of Memory, do now obtain, and are taken as part of the Common Law, and Immemorial Cuftoms of the Kingdom : And fo they ought now to be efteem'd, tho' in their firft Original they were Acts of Parliament.

3 dly Judicial Decifions

3 Judicial Decifions. It is true, the Decifions of Courts of Juftice, tho' by Vertue of the Law of this Realm they do bind, as a Law between the Parties thereto, as to the particular Cafe in Queftion, till revers'd by Error or Attaint, yet they do not make a Law properly fo called, (for that only the King and Parliament can do), yet they have a great Weight and Authority in in Expounding, Declaring, and Publifhing what the Law of this Kindom is, efpecially when fuch Decifions hold a Confonancy and Congruity with Refolutions and Decifions of former Times; and tho' fuch Decifions are lefs than a Law, yet they are a greater Evidence thereof, than the Opinion of any private Perfons, as fuch, whatfoever

1ft, Becaufe the Perfons who pronounce thofe Decifions, are Men chofen by the King for that Employment, as being of greater Learning, Knowledge, and Experience in the Laws than others. 2dly, Becaufe they are upon their Oaths to judge according to the Laws of the Kingdom 3dly, Becaufe they have the beft Helps to inform their Judgments. 4thly, Becaufe they

they do *Sedere pro Tribunali*, and their Judgments are strengthen'd and upheld by the Laws of this Kingdom, till they are by the same Law revers'd or avoided.

Now Judicial Decisions, as far as they refer to the Laws of this Kindom, are for the Matter of them of Three Kinds: Of Three Kinds.

First, They are either such as have their Reasons singly in the Laws and Customs of this Kingdom, as, Who shall succeed as Heir to the Ancestor, what is the Ceremony requisite for passing a Freehold, what Estate, and how much shall the Wife have for her Dower? And many such Matters, wherein the ancient and express Laws of the Kindom give an express Decision, and the Judge seems only the Instrument to pronounce it. And in these Things, the Law or Custom of the Realm is the only Rule and Measure to judge by, and in reference to those Matters, the Decisions of Courts are the Conservatories and Evidences of those Laws.

Secondly, Or they are such Decisions, as by way of Deduction and Illation upon those Laws are framed or deduced, as for the Purpose, Whether of an Estate thus or thus limited, the Wife shall be endowed? Whether if thus or thus limited, the Heir may be bair'd? And infinite more of the like complicated Questions. And herein the Rule of Decision is, First, the Common Law and Custom of the Realm, which is

F 3   the

the great *Substratum* that is to be maintain'd;
and then Authorities or Decisions of former
Times in the same or the like Cases, and
then the Reason of the Thing it self.

Thirdly, Or they are such as seem to have
no other Guide but the common Reason of
the Thing, unless the same Point has been
formerly decided, as in the Exposition of
the Intention of Clauses in Deeds, Wills,
Covenants, *&c.* where the very Sense of the
Words, and their Positions and Relations,
give a rational Account of the Meaning of
the Parties, and in such Cases the Judge
does much better herein, than what a bare
grave Grammarian or Logician, or other
prudent Man could do; for in many Cases
there have been former Resolutions, either
in Point, or agreeing in Reason or Analogy with the Case in Question; or perhaps also, the Clause to be expounded is
mingled with some Terms or Clauses that
require the Knowledge of the Law to help
out with the Construction or Exposition:
Both which do often happen in the same
Case, and therefore it requires the Knowledge of the Law to render and expound
such Clauses and Sentences, and doubtless a
good Common Lawyer is the best Expositor
of such Clauses, *&c. Vide Plowden*, 122, to
130. 140, *&c*

CHAP.

CHAP. V.

How the Common Law of England *stood at and for some Time after the coming in of King* William I.

IT is the Honour and Safety, and therefore the just Desire of Kingdoms that recognize no Superior but God, that their Laws have those two Qualifications, *viz.* 1*st.* That they be not dependent upon any Foreign Power; for a Dependency in Laws derogates from the Honour and Integrity of the Kingdom, and from the Power and Sovereignty of the Prince thereof. *Secondly,* That they taste not of Bondage or Servitude; for that derogates from the Dignity of the Kingdom, and from the Liberties of the People thereof

In relation to the former Consideration, the Kings of this Realm, and their great Councils, have always been jealous and careful, that they admitted not any Foreign Power, (especially such as pretended Authority to impose Laws upon other free Kingdoms or States) nor to countenance the Admission of such Laws here as were derived from such a Power

Rome, as well Ancient as Modern, pretended a kind of Universal Power and Interest, the former by their Victories,

Two Qualifications of the Laws of England

F 4   which

which were large, and extended even to
B: · · it ſelf, and the later upon the Pretence of being Univerſal Biſhop or Vicar-
General in all Matters Eccleſiaſtical, ſo
that upon Pretence of the former, the Civil
Law, and upon Pretence of the later, the
Canon Law was introduc'd, or pretended
to ſome kind of Right in the Territories of
ſome abſolute Princes, and among others
here in Eng. d. But this Kingdom has been
always very jealous of giving too much
Countenance to either of thoſe Laws, and
has always ſhewn a juſt Indignation and Re-
ſentment againſt any Encroachments of this
Kind, either by the one Law or the other.
It it true, as before is ſhewn, that in the
Admiralty and Military Courts, the Civil
Law has been admitted, and in the Eccleſiaſtical Courts, the Canon Law has been in

Neither
Canon
nor Civil
Law the
Rule of
Juſtice
here

ſome Particulars admitted But ſtill they
carry ſuch Marks and Evidences about
them, whereby it may be known that they
bind not, nor have the Authority of Laws
from themſelves, but from the authoritative
Admiſſion of this Kingdom

And, as thus the Kingdom, for the Reaſons before given, never admitted the Civil
or the Canon Law to be the Rule of the
Adminiſtration of Common Juſtice in this
Kingdom, ſo neither has it endured any
Laws to be impoſed upon the People by
any Right of Conqueſt, as being unſuita-
ble to the Honour or Liberty of the *Engliſh*
Kingdom, to recognize their Laws as given
them at the Will and Pleaſure of a Conqueror.

queror. And hence it was, that altho' the
People unjuftly affifted King *Hen.* IV. in
his Ufurpation of the Crown, yet he was
not admitted thereunto, until he had Declared, that he claimed not as a Conqueror,
but as a Succeffor, only he referved to himfelf the Liberty of extending a Pretence
of Conqueft againft the *Scroops* that were
Slain in Battle againft him; which yet he
durft not reft upon without a Confirmation
in Parliament *Vide Rot Parl.* 1 H 4 Nº 56.
& *Pars* 2 *Ib* Nº 17.

*Our Laws
not Im-
pos'd by
Conqueft.*

And upon the like Reafon it was, That
King *William* I. tho' he be called the Conqueror, and his attaining the Crown here,
is often in Hiftory, and in fome Records,
called, *Conqueftus Angliæ;* yet in Truth it
was not fuch a Conqueft as did, or could,
alter the Laws of this Kingdom, or impofe
Laws upon the People, *per Modum Conqueftus,* or *Jure Belli* And therefore, to wipe off
that falfe Imputation upon our Laws, as if
they were the Fruit or Effect of a Conqueft,
or carried in them the Badge of Servitude
to the Will of the Conqueror, which Notion
fome ignorant and prejudiced Perfons have
entertain'd; I fhall rip up, and lay open
this whole Bufinefs from the Bottom, and
to that End enquire into the following Particulars, *viz.*

 1 Of the Thing called Conqueft, what
it is, when attained, and the Rights thereof

        2 Of

2. Of the feveral Kinds of Conqueſt, and their Effects, as to the Alteration of Laws by the Victor.

3. How the *Engliſh* Laws ſtood at the Entry of King *William* the Firſt.

4. By what Title he entred, and whether by ſuch a Right of Conqueſt as did, or could, alter the *Engliſh* Laws

5 Whether *De Facto* there was any Alteration of the ſaid Laws, and by what Means after his coming in

Conqueſt,   *Firſt*, Touching the firſt of theſe, *viz.* what it is. Conqueſt, what it is, when attain'd, and the Rights thereof. It is true, That it ſeems to be admitted as a kind of Law among all Nations, That in caſe of a Solemn War between Supream Princes, the Conqueror acquires a Right of Dominion, as well as a Property over the Things and Perſons that are fully conquered, and the Reaſons aſſigned are Principally theſe, *viz.*

1ſt. Becauſe both Parties have appealed to the higheſt Tribunal that can be, *viz.* The Trial by War, wherein the great Judge and Sovereign of the World, *The Lord of Hoſts*, ſeems in a more eſpecial manner than in other Caſes to decide the Controverſy. 2dly, Becauſe unleſs this ſhould be a final Deciſion, Mankind would be deſtroy'd by endleſs Broils, Wars and Contentions, therefore, for the Preſervation of Mankind, this great Deciſion ought to be final, and the Conquer'd ought to acquieſce in it 3dly, Becauſe if this ſhould not be admitted, and

be

be by, as it were, the tacite Consent of Mankind accounted a lawful Acquisition, there
would not be any Security or Peace under
any Government: For by the various Re-
volutions of Dominion acquired by this
Means, have been, and are to this Day the
Successions of Kingdoms and States preserved. What was once the *Romans*, was before that the *Græcians*, and before them
the *Persians*, and before the *Persians* the
Assyrians, and if this just Victory were not
allowed to be a firm Acquest of Dominion,
the present Possessors would be still obnoxi-
ous to the Claim of the former Proprietors,
and so they would be in a restless State of
Doubts, Difficulties and Changes upon the
Pretension of former Claims. Therefore, to
cut off this Instability and Unsettledness in
Dominion and Property, it would seem
that the common Consent of all Nations
has tacitely submitted, that Acquisition by
Right of Conquest, in a Solemn War between Persons not Subjects of each other
by Bonds of Allegiance or Fidelity, should
be allowed as one of the lawful Titles of
acquiring Dominion over the Persons,
Places and Things so conquer'd

But whatever be the real Truth or Justice
of this Position, yet we are much at a Loss,
touching the Thing in *Hypothesi*, viz. Whether this be the Effect of every Kind of
Conquest? Whether the War be Just or
Unjust? What are the Requisites to the
Constituting of a just War? Who are the
Persons that may acquire? And what are
the

the Solemnities requisite for that Acqueft?
But above all, the greateft Difficulty is,
when there fhall be faid, Such a Victory as
acquires this Right? Indeed, if there be a
total Deletion of every Perfon of the Op-
pofing Party or Country, then the Victory
is compleat, becaufe none remains to call
it in queftion. But fuppofe they are beaten
in one Battle, may they not rally again?
Or if the greater Part be fubdued, may not
the leffer keep their Ground? Or if they do
not at the prefent, may they not in the
next Age regain their Liberty? Or if they
be quiet for a Time, may they not, as they
have Opportunity, renew their Pretenfions?
And altho' the Victor, by his Power, be able
to quell and fupprefs them, yet he is be-
holding to his Sword for it, and the Right
that he got by his Victory before, would
not be fufficient without a Power and Force
to eftablifh and fecure him againft new
Troubles. And on the other Side, if thofe
few fubdu'd Perfons can by Force regain
what they once had a Pretence to, a former Victory will be but a weak Defence;
and if it would, they would have the like
Pretence to a Claim of Acqueft by Victory
over him, as he had over them

It feem therefore a difficult Thing to
determine in what indivifible Moment this
Victory is fo compleat, that *Jure Belli* the
Acqueft of Dominion is fully gotten, and
the efore Victors ufe to fecure themfelves
againft Difputes of that Kind, and as it
were to under-pin their Acqueft *Jure Belli*,
that

that they might not be loft by the fame
Means, whereby they were gained by the
Continuation of External Forces of Standing-
Armies, Caftles, Garifons, Munitions, and
other Acts of Power and Force, fo as thereby to over-bear and prevent an ordinary
Poffibility of the Prevailing of the conquered or fubdued People, againft the
Conqueror or Victor. He that lays the
Weight of his Title upon Victory or Conqueft, rarely refts in it as a compleat Conqueft, till he has added to it fomewhat of
Confent or Faith of the Conquered, fub-
mitting voluntarily to him, and then, and
not till then, he thinks his Title fecure, and
his Conqueft compleat: And indeed, he has
no Reafon to think his Title can be otherwife fecure, for where the Title is meerly
Force or Power, his Title will fail, if the
Conquered can with like Force or Power
overmatch his, and fo regain their former
Intereft or Dominion.

Now this Confent is of Two Kinds, either Confent
Exprefs'd, or Imply'd   An Exprefs Confent 1 Expref-
is, when after a Victory the Party con- fed
quered do exprefly fubmit themfelves to the
Victors, either fimply or abfolutely, by Dedition, yielding themfelves, giving him
their Faith and their Allegiance, or elfe
under certain Pacts, Conventions, Agreements, or Capitulations, as when the fubdued Party, either by themfelves, or by
Subftitutes, or Delegates by them chofen,
do yield their Faith and their Allegiance to
the Victor upon certain Pacts or Agreements

ments between them; as for holding or
continuing their Religion, their Laws, their
Form of Civil Adminiſtration, &c.

And thus, tho' Force were perhaps the
Occaſion of this Conſent, yet in truth 'tis
Conſent only that is the true proximate
and fix'd Foundation of the Victor's Right,
which now no longer reſts barely upon external Force, but upon the expreſs Conſent
and Pact of the ſubdu'd People, and conſequently this Pact or Convention is that
which is to be the immediate Foundation of
that Dominion; and upon a diligent Obſervation of moſt Acqueſts gotten by Conqueſt, or ſo called, we ſhall find this to be
the Concluſion of almoſt all Victories, they
end in Deditions and Capitulations, and
Faith given to the Conqueror, whereby
oftentimes the former Laws, Privileges,
and Poſſeſſions are confirmed to the Subdued, without which the Victors ſeldom
continue long or quiet in their New Acqueſts, without extream Expence, Force,
Severity and Hazard

2 Impli-
ed.
An implied Conſent is, when the Subdued do continue for a long Time quiet
and peaceable under the Government of
the Victor, accepting his Government, ſub-
mitting to his Laws, taking upon them the
Offices and Employments under him, and
obeying and owning him as their Governor, without oppoſing him, or claiming
their former Right This ſeems to be a
tacite Acceptance of, and Aſſent to him;
and tho' this is gradual, and poſſibly no

4

detect-

determinate Time is ftinted, wherein a Man can fay, this Year, or this Month, or this Day, fuch a tacite Confent was compleated and concluded; for Circumftances may make great Variations in the Sufficiency of the Evidence of fuch an Affent, yet by a long and quiet Tract of peaceable Submiffion to the Laws and Government of the Victor, Men may reafonably conjecture, that the Conquered have relinquifhed their Purpofe of regaining by Force what by Force they loft.

But ftill all this is intended of a lawful Conqueft by a Foreign Prince or State, and not an Ufurpation by a Subject, either upon his Prince or Fellow Subject; for feveral Ages and Defcents do not purge the Unlawfulnefs of fuch an Ufurpation.

Secondly, Concerning the feveral Kinds of Conquefts, and their Effects, as to the Alteration of Laws by the Victor. There feems to be a double kind of Conqueft, which induces a various Confideration touching the Change of Laws, *viz Victoria in Regem & Populum, & Victoria in Regem tantum.* The Conqueft over the People or Country, is when the War is denounced by a Prince or State Foreign, and no Subject, and when the Intention and Denunciation of the War is againft the King and People or Country, and the Pretenfion of Title is by the Sword, or *Jure Belli*; fuch were moft of the Conquefts of ancient Monarchs, *viz* The *Affyrian, Perfian, Græcian,* and *Roman* Conquefts; and in fuch Cafes, the Acquifitions of the Victor

2 The Kinds and Effects of Conqueft

Victor were abſolute and univerſal, he gain'd the Intereſt and Property of the very Soil of the Country ſubdued; which the Victor might, at his Pleaſure, give, ſell or arrent: He gain'd a Power of aboliſhing or changing their Laws and Cuſtoms, and of giving New, or of impoſing the Law of the Victor's Country. But although this the Conqueror might do, yet a Change of the Laws of the conquered Country was rarely univerſally made, eſpecially by the *Romans*. Who, though in their own particular Colonies, planted in conquered Countries, they obſerved the *Roman* Law, which poſſibly might by Degrees, without any rigorous Impoſition, gain and inſinuate themſelves into the conquered People, and ſo gradually obtain, and inſenſibly conform them, at leaſt ſo many of them as were conterminous to the Colonies and Gariſons to the *Roman* Laws, yet they rarely made a rigorous and univerſal Change of the Laws of the conquered Country, unleſs they were ſuch as were foreign and barbarous, or altogether inconſiſtent with the Victor's Government: But in other Things, they commonly indulged unto the Conquered, the Laws and Religion of their Country upon a double Account, *viz*

Firſt, On Account of Humanity, thinking it a hard and over-ſevere Thing to impoſe preſently upon the Conquered a Change of their Cuſtoms, which long Uſe had made dear to them. And, 2*dly*, Upon the Account

I   of

of Prudence; for the *Romans* being a wise
and experienced People, found that those
Indulgences made their Conquests the more
easy, and their Enjoyments thereof the more
firm, when as a rigorous Change of the Laws
and Religion of the People would render
them in a restless and unquiet Condition,
and ready to lay hold of any Opportunity
of Defection or Rebellion, to regain their
ancient Laws and Religion, which ordinary
People count most dear to them; (though
at this Day the Indulgence of a *Paganish*
Religion is not used to be allowed by any
Christian Victor, as is observed in *Calvin's*
Case in the Seventh Report,) and to give
One Instance for all, it was upon this Account, That though the *Romans* had wholly
subdued *Syria* and *Palestina*, yet they allow'd
to the Inhabitants the *Jews, &c.* the Use of
their Religion and Laws, so far forth as
consisted with the Safety and Security of
the Victor's Interest. And therefore, though
they reserved to themselves the Cognizance
of such Causes as concern'd themselves,
their Officers or Revenues, and such Cases
as might otherwise disturb the Security of
their Empire, as Treasons, Insurrections,
and the like, yet 'tis evident they indulged
the People of the *Jews, &c.* to judge by
their own Law, not only of some Criminal
Proceedings, but even of Capital in some
Cases, as appears by the History of the
Gospels, and Acts of the Apostles.

The Romans indulged the vanquish'd in their Laws and Religion

G

But

Conqueſt upon Terms and Capitulations.

But ſtill this was but an Indulgence, and therefore was reſumable by the Victor, unleſs there intervened any Capitulation between the Conqueror and the Conquered to the contrary ; which was frequent, eſpecially in thoſe Caſes, when it was not a compleat Conqueſt, but rather a Dedition upon Terms and Capitulations, agreed between the Conqueror and the Conquered ; wherein uſually the yielding Party ſecured to themſelves, by the Articles of their Dedition, the Enjoyment of their Laws and Religion; and then by the Laws of Nature and of Nations, both which oblige to the Obſervation of Faith and Promiſes, thoſe Terms and Capitulations were to be obſerved Again, 2*dly*, When after a full Conqueſt, the conquered People reſumed ſo much Courage and Power as began to put them in a Capacity of regaining their former Laws and Liberties. This commonly was the Occaſion of Terms and Capitulations between the Conquerors and Conquered. Again, 3*dly*, When by long Succeſſion of Time, the Conquered had either been incorporated with the conquering People, whereby they had worn out the very Marks and Diſcriminations between the Conquerors and Conquered, and if they continued diſtinct, yet by a long Preſcription, Uſage and Cuſtom, the Laws and Rights of the conquered People were in a manner ſettled, and the long Permiſſion of the Conquerors amounted to a tacite Conceſſion

ceffion or Capitulation, for the Enjoyment
of their Laws and Liberties.

But of this more than enough is faid, be-
caufe it will appear in what follows, That
William I never made any fuch Conqueft of
England.

Secondly, Therefore I come to the Second
Kind of Conqueft, *viz*. That which is only *Victoria in Regem* · And this is where the
Conqueror either has a real Right to
the Crown or chief Government of a
Kingdom, or at leaft has, or makes
fome Pretence of Claim thereunto ; and,
in Purfuance of fuch Claim, raifes War,
and by his Forces obtains what he fo pretends a Title to   Now this kind of Conqueft does only inftate the Victor in thofe
Rights of Government, which the conquered Prince, or that Prince to whom the
Conqueror pretends a Right of Succeffion,
had, whereby he becomes only a Succeffor
Jure Belli, but not a Victor or Conqueror
upon the Peeple ; and therefore has no more
Right of altering their Laws, or taking
away their Liberties or Poffeffions, than
the conquered Prince, or the Prince to
whom he pretends a Right of Succeffion,
had ; for the Intention, Scope and Effect
of his Victory extends no further than the
Succeffion, and does not at all affect the
Rights of the People.   The Conqueror is,
as it were, the Plaintiff, and the conquered
Prince is the Defendant, and the Claim is

(side note: Conqueft over the King, but not the People.*)*

a Claim

a Claim of Title to the Crown; and becaufe each of them pretends a Right to the Sovereignty, and there is no other competent Trial of the Title between them, they put themfelves upon the great Trial by Battle, wherein there is nothing in Queftion touching the Rights of the People, but only touching the Right of the Crown, and that being decided by the Victory, the Victor comes in as a Succeffor, and not *Jure Victoriæ*, as in relation to the Peoples Rights; the moft Sacred whereof are their Laws and Religion.

Indeed, thofe that do voluntarily affift the conquered Prince, commonly undergo the fame Hazard with him, and do, as it were, put their Intereft upon the Hazard and Iffue of the fame Trial, and therefore commonly fall under the fame Severity with the Conquered, at leaft *de facto*, becaufe, perchance the Victor thinks he cannot be fecure without it: But yet Ufage, and indeed common Prudence, makes the Conquerors ufe great Moderation and Difcrimination in relation to the Affiftants of the conquered Prince; and to extend this Severity only to the eminent and bufy Affiftants of the Conquered, and not to the *Gregarii*, or fuch as either by Conftraint or by Neceffity were enforced to ferve againft him; and as to thofe alfo, on whom they exercife their Power, it has been rarely done *Jure Belli aut Victoriæ*, but by a judiciary Proceeding, as in Cafes of Treafon, becaufe now the great Trial by Battle has pronounced for the Right of the Conqueror,

queror, and at beſt no Man muſt' dare to
ſay otherwiſe now, whatſoever Debility
was in his Pretenſion or Claim We ſhall ſee
the Inſtances hereof in what follows

Thirdly, As to the Third Point, How the
Laws of *England* ſtood at the Entry of King
William I. And it ſeems plain, that at the
Time of his Entry into *England*, the Laws,
commonly call'd, *The Laws of* Edward *the
Confeſſor*, were then the ſtanding Laws of
the Kingdom. *Hoveden* tells us, in a Di-
greſſion under his Hiſtory of King *Henry* II
that thoſe Laws were originally put together
by King *Edgar*, who was the Confeſſor's
Grandfather, *viz. Verum tamen poſt mortem
ipſius Regis* Edgari *uſq; ad Coronationem Sancti
Regis* Edvardi *quod Tempus Continet Sexaginta &
Septem Annos prece (vel pretio) Leges ſopitæ ſunt &
tus prætermiſſæ ſed poſtquam Rex* Edvardus *in
Regno fuit ſublimatus Concilio Baronum Angliæ
Legem Annos Sexaginta & Septem Sopitam, exci-
tavit & confirmavit, & ea Lex ſic confirmata
vocata eſt Lex Sancti* Edvardi, *non quod ipſe
prius inveniſſet eam ſed cum prætermiſſa fuiſſet &
oblivioni penitus dedita a morte avi ſui Regis*
Edgari *qui primus inventor ejus fuiſſe dicitur
uſque ad ſua Tempora, viz. Sexaginta & Septem
Annos.* And the ſame Paſſage in *totidem Verbis* is in the Hiſtory of *Lichfield*, cited in
Sir *Robert Twiſden*'s Prologue to the Laws of
King *William* I. But although poſſibly thoſe
Laws were collected by King *Edgar*, yet it
is evident, by what is before ſaid, they were
augmented by the Confeſſor, by that Ex-

3d Que-
ſtion
How the
Laws
ſtood at
W I's
Entry

G 3   -tract

tract of Laws before-mentioned, which he made out of that Threefold Law, that obtain'd in feveral Parts of *England*, *viz.* The *Danish*, the *Mercian*, and the *Weſt-Saxon* Laws.

This Manual (as I may call it) of Laws, ſtiled, *The Confeſſor's Laws*, was but a ſmall Volume, and contains but few Heads, being rather a Scheme or Directory touching ſome Method to be obſerved in the Diſtribution of Juſtice, and ſome particular Proceedings relative thereunto, eſpecially in Matters of Crime, as appears by the Laws themſelves, which are now printed in Mr *Lambart's Saxon* Laws, *p* 133. and other Places; yet the *Engliſh* were very zealous for them, no leſs or otherwiſe than they are at this Time for the *Great Charter*; infomuch, that they were never ſatisfied till the ſaid Laws were reinforced and mingled for the moſt Part with the Coronation Oath of King *William* I and ſome of his Succeſſors

And this may ſerve ſhortly touching this Third Point, whereby we ſee that the Laws that obtain'd at the Time of the Entry of King *William* I. were the *Engliſh* Laws, and principally thoſe of *Edward* the Confeſſor

_th Queſtion.

What kind of Conqueſt *William* I made:
Fourthly, The Fourth Particular is, The Pretenſions of King *William* I to the Crown of *England*, and what kind of Conqueſt he made; and this will be beſt rendered and underſtood by producing the Hiſtory of that Buſineſs, as it is delivered over to us by the ancient Hiſtorians that lived in or near that

that Time: The Sum, or *Totum* whereof,
is this

King *Edward* the Confeffor having no
Children, nor like to have any, had Three
Perfons related to him, whom he principal-
ly favoured, *viz.* 1*ft*, *Edgar Ætheling*, the
Son of *Edward*, the Son of *Edmond Ironfide*,
Mat Paris, *Anno* 1066. *Edmundus autem latus
ferreum Rex naturalis de ftirpe Regum genuit* Ed-
wardum *&* Edwardus *genuit* Edgarum *cui de
jure debebatur Regnum Anglorum.* 2*dly*, Ha-
rold, the Son of *Goodwin*, Earl of *Kent*, the
Confeffor's Father-in-Law, he having married
Earl *Goodwin*'s Daughter. And, 3*dly*, *William*
Duke of *Normandy*, who was allied to the
Confeffor thus, *viz William* was the Son of
Robert, the Son of *Richard* Duke of *Nor-
mandy*, which *Richard* was Brother unto the
Confeffor's Mother *Vide* Hoveden, *fub initio
Anni primi Willielmi primi.*

There was likewife a great Familiarity,
as well as this Alliance, between the Confeffor and Duke *William*, for the Confeffor
had often made confiderable Refidencies
in *Normandy*. And this gave a fair Expectation to Duke *William* of fucceeding him in
this Kingdom: And there was alfo, at leaft
pretended, a Promife made him by the *Confeffor*, That Duke *William* fhould fucceed
him in the Crown of *England*, and becaufe
Harold was in great Favour with the King,
and of great Power in *England*, and therefore the likelieft Man by his Affiftance to
advance, or by his Oppofition to hinder or
emperate the Duke's Expectation, there

G4 was

Three Competitors for the Crown of England

was a Contract made between the Duke and *Herold* in *Normandy* in the *Confessor's* Lifetime, That *Harold* should, after the *Confessor's* Death, assist the Duke in obtaining the Crown of *England* (*Vide Brompton, Hoveden, &c*) Shortly after which the *Confessor* died, and then step'd up the Three Competitors to the Crown, *viz*

1. *Edgar Ætheling*, who was indeed favoured by the Nobility, but being an Infant, was overborn by the Power of *Harold*, who thereupon began to set up for himself: Whereupon *Edgar*, with his Two Sisters, fled into *Scotland*; where he, and one of his Sisters, dying without Issue, *Margaret*, his other Sister and Heir, married *Malcolm*, King of *Scots*; from whence proceeded the Race of the *Scottish* Kings, *and from whom Her present Majesty Queen* Anne *is derived in a direct and uninterrupted Line*

2. *Harold*, who having at first raised a Power under Pretence of supporting and preserving Duke *William's* Title to this Kingdom, and having by Force suppress'd *Edgar*, he thereupon claimed the Crown to himself, and pretending an Adoption or Bequest of the Kingdom unto him by the Confessor, he forgot his Promise made to Duke *William*, and usurped the Crown, which he held but the Space of 9 Months and 4 Days, *Hoveden*.

3. *William*, Duke of *Normandy*, who pretended a Promise of Succession by the *Confessor*, and a Capitulation or Stipulation by *Harold* for his Assistance, and had, it seems,

so

so far interested the Pope in Favour of his Pretensions, that he pronounced for *William* against both the others.

Hereupon the Duke makes his Claim to the Crown of *England*, gathered a powerful Army, came over, and upon the 14th of *October*, *Anno* 1067. gave *Harold* Battle, and overthrew him at that Place in *Sussex*, where *William* afterwards founded *Battle-Abbey*, in Memory of that Victory.; and then he took upon him the Government of the Kingdom, as King thereof, and upon *Christmas* following was solemnly crown'd at *Westminster* by the Archbishop of *York*; and he declared at his Coronation, That he claimed the Crown not *Jure Belli*, but *Jure Successionis*; and *Brompton* gives us this Account thereof, *Cum nomen Tyranni exhorresceret & nomen legitimi principis induere vellet petiit consecrari*, and accordingly, says the same thor, the Archbishop of *York*, in respect of some present Incapacity in the Archbishop of *Canterbury, Munus hoc adimplevit ipsumq, Gulielmum Regem ad jura Ecclesiæ Anglicanæ tuenda & conservanda populumque suum recte regendum, & Leges rectas Statuendum, Sacramento solemniter adstrinxit*, and thereupon he took the Homage of the Nobility.

This being the true, though short Account of the State of that Business, there necessarily follows from thence those plain and unquestionable Consequences

First, That the Conquest of King *William* I was not a Conquest upon the Country

1.

try or People, but only upon the King of it, in the Person of *Harold*, the Usurper; for *William* I. came in upon a Pretence of Title of Succession to the *Confessor*; and the Prosecution and Success of the Battle he gave to *Harold* was to make good his Claim of Succession, and to remove *Harold*, as an unlawful Usurper upon his Right; which Right was now decided in his Favour, and determined by that great Trial by Battle

2.   *Secondly*, That he acquired in Consequence thereof no greater Right than what was in the *Confessor*, to whom he pretended a Right of Succession; and therefore could no more alter the Laws of the Kingdom upon the Pretence of Conquest, than the *Confessor* himself might, or than the Duke himself could have done, had he been the true and rightful Successor to the Crown, in Point of Descent from the *Confessor*; neither is it material, whether his Pretence were true or false, or whether, if true, it were available or not, to entitle him to the Crown; for whatsoever it was, it was sufficient to direct his Claim, and to qualify his Victory so, that the *Jus Belli* thereby acquired could be only *Victoria in Regem, sed non in Populum*, and put him only in the State, Capacity and Qualification of a Successor to the King, and not as Conqueror of the Kingdom

3.   *Thirdly*, And as this his antecedent Claim kept his Acquest within the Bounds of a Successor, and restrained him from the unlimited

limited Bounds and Power of a Conqueror; fo his fubfequent Coronation,
and the Oath by him taken, is a further unqueftionable Demonftration, that
he was reftrain'd within the Bounds of
a Succeffor, and not enlarged with the
Latitude of a Victor; for at his Coronation, he binds himfelf by a Solemn Oath
to preferve the Rights of the Church, and
to govern according to the Laws, and not
abfolutely and unlimittedly according to
the Will of a Conqueror.

Fourthly, That if there were any Doubt 4.
whether there might be fuch a Victory as
might give a Pretenfion to him, of altering
Laws, or governing as a Conqueror; yet
to fecure from that poffible Fear, and to
avoid it, he ends his Victory in a Capitulation; namely, he takes the ancient Oath
of a King unto the People, and the People
reciprocally giving or returning him that
Affurance that Subjects ought to give their
Prince, by performing their Homage to
him as their King, declared by the Victory
he had obtain'd over the Ufurper, to be the
Succeffor of the *Confeffor* And confequently,
if there might be any Pretence of Conqueft
over the Peoples Rights, as well as over
Harold's, yet the Capitulation or Stipulation
removes the Claim or Pretence of a Conqueror, and enftates him in the regulated
Capacity and State of a Succeffor And upon all this it is evident, That King *William* I.
could not abrogate or alter the ancient
Laws of the Kingdom, any more than if
he

he had ſucceeded the *Confiſſor* as his lawful
Heir, and had acquir'd the Crown by the
peaceable Courſe of Deſcent, without any
Sword drawn.

And thus much may ſuffice, to ſhew that
King *William* I did not enter by ſuch a
Right of Conqueſt, as did or could alter
the Laws of this Kingdom.

§ de-
f. r
Whether
W I al-
ter'd the
Laws

Therefore I come to the laſt Queſtion I
propoſed to be conſidered, *viz.* Whether *de
Facto* there was any Thing done by King
William I. after his Acceſſion to the Crown,
in reference either to the Alteration or
Confirmation of the Laws, and how and
in what Manner the ſame was done · And
this being a Narrative of Matters of Fact,
I ſhall divide into thoſe Two Inquiries,
Viz 1ſt What was done in relation to the
Lands and Poſſeſſions of the *Engliſh* And
2*dly* What was done in relation to the
Laws of the Kingdom in general , for both
of theſe will be neceſſary to make up a
clear Narrative touching the Alteration or
Suſpenſion, Confirmation or Execution of
the Laws of this Kingdom by him

1. *Firſt*, Therefore touching the former,
viz What was done in relation to the
Lands and Poſſeſſions of the *Engliſh* Thoſe
Two Things muſt be premiſed, *viz* Firſt, a
Matter of Right, or Law , which is this,
That in caſe this had been a Conqueſt
upon the Kingdom, it had been at the Plea-
ſure of the Conqueror to have taken all the
Lands of the Kingdom into his own Poſſeſ-
ſion, to have put a Period to all former
Titles,

Titles, to have cancelled all former Grants, and to have given, as it were, the Date and Original to every Man's Claim, so as to have been no higher nor ancienter than such his Conquest, and to hold the same by a Title derived wholly from and under him. I do not say, that every absolute Conqueror of a Kingdom will do thus, but that he may if he will, and have Power to effect it.

Secondly, The Second Thing to be premised is, a Matter of Fact, which is this; That Duke *William* brought in with him a great Army of Foreigners, that would have expected a Reward of their Undertaking, and therefore were doubtless very craving and importunate for Gratifications to be made them by the Conqueror *Again,* it is very probable, that of the *English* themselves there were Persons of very various Conditions and Inclinations; some perchance did adhere to the Duke, and were Assistant to him openly, or at least under-hand, towards the bringing him in; and those were sure to enjoy their Possessions privately and quietly when the Duke prevailed. *Again,* some did without all Question adhere to *Harold,* and those in all probability were severely dealt with, and dispossess'd of their Lands, unless they could make their Peace. *Again,* possibly there were others who assisted *Harold,* partly out of Fear and Compulsion, yet those possibly, if they were of any Note or Eminence, fared little better than the rest. *Again,* there were some that pro-

probably ftood Neuters, and medled not; and thofe, though they could not expect much Favour, yet they might in Juftice expect to enjoy their own. *Again*, it muft needs be fuppofed, That the Duke having fo great an Army of Foreigners, fo many Ambitious and Covetous Minds to be fatisfied, fo many to be rewarded in Point of Gratitude; and after fo great a Concuffion as always happens upon the Event of a Victory, it muft needs, upon thofe and fuchlike Accounts, be evident to any Man that confiders Things of this Nature, that there were great Outrages and Oppreffions committed by the Victor's Soldiers and their Officers, many falfe Accufations made againft innocent Perfons, great Difturbances and Evictions of Poffeffions, many right Owners being unjuftly thrown out, and confequently many Occupations and Ufurpations of other Men's Rights and Poffeffions, and a long while before thofe Things could be reduced to any quiet and regular Settlement.

What was done after the Conqueft   Thefe general Obfervations being premifed, we will now fee what *de Facto* was done in relation to Men's Poffeffions, in Confequence of this Victory of the Duke.

1.   *Firft*, It is certain that he took into his Hands all the Demefn Lands of the Crown which were belonging to *Edward the Confeffor* at the Time of his Death, and avoided all the Difpofitions and Grants thereof

I   made

made by *Harold*, during his short Reign; and this might be one great End of his making that Noble Survey in the Fourth Year of his Reign, called generally *Doomſ-day-Read*, in some Records, as *Rot. Winton*, *&c.* thereby to ascertain what were the Possessions of the Crown in the Time of the *Confeſſor*, and those he entirely re-sumed: And this is the Reason why in some of our old Books it is said, *Ancient Demeaſn* is that which was held by King *William* the Conqueror, and in others 'tis said, *Ancient Demeaſn* is that which was held by King *Edward the Confeſſor*, and both true in their Kind, and in this Respect, *viz.* That whatsoever appeared to be the *Confeſſor's* at the Time of his Death, was assumed by King *William* into his own Posses-sion.

Secondly, It is also certain, That no Per-son simply, and *quatenus* an *Engliſh* Man, was dispossess'd of any of his Possessions, and consequently their Land was not pre-tended unto as acquired *Jure Belli*, which appears most plainly by the following Evi-dences, *viz.*

Firſt, That very many of those Persons that were possessed of Lands in the Time of *Edward* the Confessor, and so returned up-on the Book of *Doomſday*, retain'd the same unto them and their Descendants, and some of their Descendants retain the same Possessions to this Day, which could not have been, if presently *Jure Belli ac Victoriæ universalis*, the Lands of the *English* had been vested in the Conqueror And again,

Secondly, We do find, that in all Times, even suddenly after the Conquest, the Charters of the ancient *Saxon* Kings were pleaded and allowed, and Titles made and created by them to Lands, Liberties, Franchises, and Regalities, affirm'd and adjudged under *William* I Yea, when that Exception has been offered, That by the Conquest those Charters had lost their Force, yet those Claims were allowed as in 7 *E.* 3. *Fines*, as mentioned by Mr. *Selden*, in his Notes upon *Eadmerus*, which could not be, if there had been such a Conquest as had vested all Mens Rights in the Conqueror

Thirdly, Many Recoveries were had shortly after this Conquest, as well by Heirs as Successors of the Seizin of their Predecessors before the Conquest We shall take one or two Instances for all, namely, that famous Record *apud Pinerdon*, by the Archbishop of *Canterbury*, in the Time of King *William* I. of the Seizin and Title of his Predecessors before the Conquest : See the whole Process and Proceedings thereupon in the End of Mr. *Selden's* Notes upon *Eadmerus*; and see *Spelman's Glossary*, Title *Drenches* Upon these Instances, and much more that might be added, it is without Contradiction, That the Rights and Inheritances of the *English qua Tales*, were not abrogated or impeach'd by this Conquest, but continued notwithstanding the same; for, as is before observ'd, it was *Jure Belli quoad Regem, sed non quoad Populum*.

3   But

But to defcend to fome Particulars: The
Englifh Perfons that the Conqueror had to
deal with, were of Three Kinds, *viz. Firft,*
Such as adhered to him againft *Harold* the
Ufurper; and, without all Queftion, thofe
continued the Poffeffion of their Lands,
and their Poffeffions were rather encreafed
by him, than any way diminifhed. *Secondly,* Such as adhered to *Harold,* and oppofed
the Duke, and fought againft him; and
doublefs, as to thofe, the Duke after his
Victory ufed his Power, and difpoffefs'd
them of their Eftates : Which Thing is ufual
upon all Conclufions and Events of this
Kind, upon a double Reafon; 1*ft,* To fecure
himfelf againft the Power of thofe that oppos'd him, and to weaken them in their
Eftates, that they fhould not afterwards be
enabled to make Head againft him. And,
2*dly,* To gratifie thofe that affifted him,
and to reward their Services in that Expe-
dition; and to make them firm to his Intereft, which was now twifted with their
own : For it can't be imagined, but that the
Conqueror was affifted with a great Com-
pany of Foreigners, fome that he favour'd,
fome that had highly deferved for their
Valour, fome that were neceffitous Soldiers
of Fortune, and others that were either
ambitious or covetous : All whofe Defires,
Deferts, or Expectations, the Conqueror
had no other Means to fatisfie, but by the
Eftates of fuch as had appeared open Ene-
mies to him, and doubtlefs, many innocent
Perfons fuffered in this Kind, under falfe

H Sug-

Suggestions and Accusations, which occafioned great Exclamations by the Writers of
thofe Times againft the Violencies and Oppreffions which were ufed after this Victory And, *Thirdly*, Such as ftood Neuters, and
meddled not on either Side during the Controverfie: And doubtlefs, for fome Time
after this great Change, many of thofe fuffered very much, and were hardly ufed in
their Eftates, efpecially fuch as were of the
more Eminent Sort.

Gervafius Tilburienfis, who wrote in the
Time of *Hen.* II *Libro* 1° *Cap. Quid Mur-
drum & quare fic dictum*, gives us a large
Account of what he had traditionally learned touching this Matter, to this Effect, *viz.
Poft Regni* Conquifitionem & *Perduellium Sub-
jectionem*, &c *Nomine autem Succeffionis à tem-
poribus* fubactæ Gentis *nihil fibi Vendicarent*, &c.
i e After the Conqueft of the Kingdom,
and Subjection of the Rebels, when the
King himfelf and his great Men had fur-
veyed their new Acquifitions; and ftrict
Inquiry was made, who there were that,
fighting againft the King, had faved themfelves by Flight From thefe, and the Heirs
of fuch as were flain in Battle, fighting
againft him, all hopes of Succeffion, or of
poffeffing their Eftates; for the People being fubdued, they held their Lives as a
Favour, &c

But *Gerv fe*, as he fpeaks fo liberally in
relation to the Conqueft, and the *Subacta
Gens* as he terms us; fo it fhould feem, he
was in great Meafure miftaken in this Relation:

lation : For it is moſt plain, That thoſe that
were not engaged viſibly in the Aſſiſtance
of *Harold*, were not, according to the Rules
of thoſe Times, diſabled to enjoy their Poſſeſſions, or make Title of Succeſſion to their
Anceſtors, or tranſmit to their Poſterity
as formerly, tho' poſſibly ſome Oppreſſions
might be uſed to particular Perſons here
and there to the contrary. And this appears by that excellent Monument of Antiquity, ſet down in Sir *H. Spelman's Gloſſary*,
in the Title of *Drenches* or *Drenges*, which
I ſhall here tranſcribe, *viz.*

Lands of Neuters not Forfeited

Edwinus *de* Sharborne, *Et quidam alii qui
ejecti fuerunt & Terris ſuis abierunt ad conque-
ſtorem & dixerunt ei, quod nunquam ante conqueſtum nec in conqueſtum nec poſt, fuerunt contra Regem ipſum in Concilio aut in auxilio ſed
tenuerunt ſe in pace, Et hoc parati ſunt probare
qualiter Rex vellet Ordinare, Per quod idem Rex
facit Inquiri per totam Angliam ſi ita fuit, quod
quidem probatum fuit, propter quod idem Rex
præcepit ut omnes illi qui ſic tenuerunt ſe in pace
in forma prædicta quod ipſi rehaberent omnes
Terras & Dominationes ſuas adeo integre & in
pace ut unquam habuerunt vel tenuerunt ante conqueſtum ſuum, Et quod ipſi in poſterum vocaren-
tur Drenges.*

But it ſeems the Poſſeſſions of the Church
were not under this Diſcrimination, for
they being held not in Right of the Perſon, but of the Church, were not ſubject to
any Confiſcation by the Adherence of the

Church Lands not Confiſcated.

H 2 Poſ-

Poffeffor to *Harold* the Ufurper: And therefore, tho' it feems *Stigand* Archbifhop of
Canterbury, at the coming in of *William* I.
had been in fome Oppofition againft him,
which probably might be the true Caufe
why he perform'd not the Office of his
Coronation, which of Right belonged to
him, tho' fome other Impediments were
pretended, *Vide Eadmerus in initio Libri*, and
might alfo poffibly be the Reafon why a
confiderable part of his Poffeffions were
granted to *Odo* Bifhop of *Bayonne*, but were
afterwards recovered by *Lanfrank*, his Succeffor, at *Pinendon*, *in pleno Comitatu, ubi Rex
præcepit* totum Comitatum *abfque mora confi-
dere, & homines Comitatûs omnes Francigenos &
præcipue Anglos in antiquis Legibus & Confuetu-
dinibus peritos, in unum convenire.*

To this may be added thofe feveral Grants
and Charters made by King *William* I. mentioned in the Hiftory of *Ely*, and in *Eadmerus*, for Reftoring to Bifhopricks and Abbies
fuch Lands, or Goods, as had been taken
away from them, *viz.*

Charters
for re-
ftoring
Lands to
Churches
&c

*Willielmus Dei gratia Rex Anglorum, Lan-
franco Archiepifcopo Cantuar' & Galfrido Epif-
copo Conftantiarum & Roberto Comiti de ou &
Richardo filio Comitis Gileberti & Hugoni de
Monteforti, fuifque aliis proceribus Regni Angliæ
falutem Summonete Vicecomites meos ex meo præ-
cepto, & ex parte mea eis dicite ut reddant Epi-
fcopatibus meis & Abbatiis totum Dominium om-
nefque Dominicas terras quas de Dominio Epifco-
patuum meorum, & Abbatiarum, Epifcopi mei &*
Abbates

Abbates eis vel lenitate vel timore vel cupiditate dederunt vel habere consenserunt vel ipsi violentia sua inde abstraxerunt, & quod hactenus injuste possiderunt de Dominio Ecclesiarum mearum. Et nisi reddiderint sicut eos ex parte mea summonebitis, vos ipsos velint nolint, constringite reddere; Et quod si quilibet alius vel aliquis vestrum quibus hanc Justitiam imposui ejusdem querelæ fuerit reddat similiter quod de Domino Episcopatuum vel Abbatiarum mearum habuit ne propter illud quod inde aliquis vestrum habebit, minus exerceat super meos Vicecomites vel alios, quicunque teneant Dominium Ecclesiarum mearum, quod Præcipio, &c.

Willielmus Rex Anglorum omnibus suis fidelibus suis & Vicecomitibus in quorum Vicecomitatibus Abbatia de Heli Terras habet salutem. Præcipio ut Abbatia pred. habeat Omnes consuitudines suas scilicet Saccham & Socham Toll & Team & Infanganetheof, Hamsocua & Grithbrice Fithwite & Ferdwite infra Burgum & extra & omnes alias forisfacturas in terra sua super suos homines sicut habuit Die qua Rex Edwardus *fuit* vivus & mortuus, *& sicut mea jussione* dirationatæ *apud* Keneteford *per* plures Scyras *ante meos* Barones, viz. Galfridum Constantientem Ep. & Baldewine Abbatem, &c. Teste Rogero Bigot.*

Willielmus Rex Angl. Lanfranco Archiepo, *&* Rogero Comiti Moritoniæ, *&* Galfrido Constantien Epo. *salutem. Mando vobis & Præcipio ut iterum faciatis congregari omnes Scyras quæ interfuerunt placito habito de Terris Ecclesia de Heli, antequam mea conjux in Normaniam novissime veniret, cum quibus etiam sint de Baronibus meis, qui competenter adesse poterint &*

H 3 *prædicto*

prædicto placito interfuerint & qui terras ejuſdem Eccleſiæ tenent, Quibus in unum congregatis eligantur plures de illis Anglis *qui ſciunt quomodo Terræ jacebant præfatæ Eccleſiæ* Die *qua Rex Edwardus Obiit, & quod inde dixerint ibidem jure jurando teſtentur; quo facto reſtituentur Eccleſiæ terræ quæ in Dominico ſuo erant die obitus Regis Edwardi; Exceptis his quæ homines clamabant me ſibi dediſſe; illas vero Literis mihi ſignificate quæ ſint, & qui eas tenent; Qui autem tenent Theinlandes quæ proculdubio debent teneri de Eccleſia faciant concordiam cum Abbate quam Meliorem poterint, & ſi noluerunt terræ remaneant ad Eccleſiam, Hoc quoque detinentibus* Socham & Saccam *fiat, &c*

Willielmus Rex Anglorum, Lanfranco Archiepiſc', & G. Epiſc. & R. Comiti M. ſalutem, &c. Defendite ne Remigius Epiſcopus novas conſuetudines requirat *infra Inſulam de Heli, Nolo enim quod ibi habeat* niſi illud quod Anteceſſor ejus habebat Tempore Regis Edwardi *Scilicet qua die ipſe Rex mortuus eſt. Et ſi Remig Epiſcopus inde* Placitare voluerit placitet inde ſicut feciſſet tempore *Regis Edw &* placitum iſtum ſit in veſtra *præſentia; De cuſtodia de Norguic Abbatem Simeonem quietum eſſe demittite; Sed ibi municionem ſuam conduci faciat & cuſtodiri. Facite* remanere placitum de Terris *quas Calumniantur Willielmus de ou, & Radulphus filius Gualeranni, & Robertus Gernon, ſi inde* placitare noluerint *ſicut* inde placitaſſent tempore Regis Edwardi, *& ſicut in eodem tempore Abbatia* conſuetudines ſuas *habebat, Volo ut eas omnino faciatis* habere *ſicut Abbas per* Chartas

tas suas, *& per* Testes *suos eas* deplacitare
poterit.

I might add many more Charters to the
foregoing, and more especially those famous Charters in *Spelman's* Councils, *Vol* 2.
Fol. 14. *&* 165. whereby it appears, That
King *William* I. *Communi Concilio, & Concilio*
Archiepiscoporum, Episcoporum & Abbatum, &
omnium Principum & Baronum Regni, instituted
the Courts for holding Pleas of Eccle-
siastick Causes, to be separate and distinct
from those Courts that had Jurisdiction of
Civil Causes. *Sed de his plusquam satis.*

And thus I conclude the Point I first
propounded, *viz* How King *William* I.
after his Victory, dealt with the Possessions
of the *English,* whereby it appears that there
was no Pretence of an Universal Conquest,
or that he was a Victor *in Populum*; neither
did he claim the Title of *English* Lands upon
that Account, but only made use of his
Victory thus far, to seize the Lands of such
as had oppos'd him · Which is universal in
all Cases of Victories, tho' without the Pretence of Conquest

Secondly, Therefore I come to the Second
general Question, *viz* What was done in
relation to the Laws ? It is very plain, that
the King, after his Victory, did, as all wise
Princes would have done, endeavour to
make a stricter Union between *England* and
Normandy; and in order thereunto, he endeavoured to bring in the *French* instead of the
Saxon Language, then used in *England*: *De-*

*Ecclesia-
stical Ju-
risdiction
seperated
from the
Temporal*

*2d Que-
stion.*

H 5   *liberavit*

liberavit (says *Holcot*) *quomodo Linguam Saxoni-*

cam possit destruere, & Anglicam & Normani-
cam idiomate concordare & ideo ordinavit quod
nullus in Curia Regis placitaret nisi in Lingua
Gallica, &c From whence arose the Practice
of Pleading in our Courts of Law in the
Norman or *French* Tongue, which Custom
continued till the Statute of 36 *E.* 3. *c.* 15.

And as he thus endeavoured to make a
Community in their Language, so possibly
he might endeavour to make the like in their
Laws, and to introduce the *Norman* Laws
into *England,* or as many of 'em as he thought
convenient; and it is very probable, that
after the Victory, the *Norman* Nobility and
Soldiers were scattered through the whole
Kingdom, and mingled with the *English,*
which might possibly introduce some of the
Norman Laws and Customs insensibly into
this Kingdom; and to that End, the Conqueror did industriously mingle the *English*
and *Normans* together, shuffling the *Normans*
into *English* Possessions here, and putting the
English into Possessions in *Normandy,* and
making Marriages among them, especially
between the Nobility of both Nations.

This gave the *English* a Suspicion, that
they should suddenly have a Change of their
Laws before they were aware of it. But it
fell out much better: For first, there arising
some Danger of a Defection of the *English,*
countenanced by the Archbishop of *York* in
the *North,* and *Frederick,* Abbot of St. *Albans*
in the *South,* the King, by the Perswasions of
Lanfrank, Archbishop of *Canterbury, Pro bono*
pacis

pacis apud Berkhamstead juravit super Animas reliquias Sancti Albani tactisque Sacrosanctis Evangeliis (ministrante juramento Abbate Frede- rico) ut bonas & approbatas antiquas Regni Leges quas sancti & pii Angliæ Reges ejus Antecessores, & maxime Rex Edvardus statuit inviolabiliter observaret; Et sic pacificati ad propria læti reces- serunt. Vide Mat. Paris in Vita Frederici Ab- batis Sancti Albani The Englifh Laws Confirm- ed.

But altho' now, upon this Capitulation, the ancient *Englijh* Laws were confirm'd, and namely, the Laws of St. *Edward* the *Confeffor*, yet it appeared not what thofe Laws were: And therefore, in the Fourth Year of his Reign, we are told by *Hoveden*, in a Digreffion he makes in his Hiftory under the Reign of King *Hen.* II and alfo in the Chronicle of *Litchfield.*

Willielmus Rex, Anno quarto Regni sui Consilio Baronum suorum fecit Summonari per Universos Consulatos Angliæ, Anglos Nobiles & Sapientes & sua Lege eruditos ut eorum jura & consuetudines ab ipsis audiret, Electis igitur de singulis totius Patriæ Comitatibus viri duodecim, jurejurando confirmaverunt ut quoad possint recto tramite neque ad Dextram neque ad Sinistram partem divertentes Legum suarum consuetudinem & san- citam patefacerent nihil prætermittentes nihil ad- dentes, nihil prævaricando mutantes, &c And then fets down many of thofe ancient Laws approv'd and confirm'd by the King, and *Commune Concilium*; wherein it appears, that he feems to be moft pleafed with thofe Laws that came under the Title of *Lex Danica,* as moft confonant to the *Norman* Cuftoms.

Quo

Qua auditu mox universi compatrioti qui Leges dixerint Tristes effecti, uno ministerio deprecati sunt quatenus permitteret Leges sibi proprias & consuetudines antiquas habere in quibus vixerunt Patres, & ipsi in iis nati & nutriti sunt, quia durum Valde sibi foret suscipere Leges igno- tas, & judicare de iis quæ nesciebant; Rege vero ad flectendum ingrato existente, tandem eum persecuti sunt deprecantes quatenus pro Anima Regis Edvardi qui eas sub diem suum eis concesserat Báro- nes & Regnum & cujus orant Leges non aliorum extraneorum cogere quam sub Legibus perseverare patris; Unde Consilio habito Præcatur Baronum tandem acquievit, &c.

The Con- fessors Laws Confirm- ed. *Gervasius Tilburiensis,* who lived nearer that Time, speaks shortly, and to the Purpose, thus: *Propositis Legibus Anglicanis secundum triplicitam earum Distinctionem, i. e.* Merchen- lage, Westsaxon-lage, *&* Dane-lage *quas- dam earum reprobans quasdam autem appro- bans, illis transmarinas Leges Neustriæ quas ad Regni Pacem tuendam efficacissime videbantur, adjecit.*

So that by this, there appears to have been a double Collection of Laws, *viz*

First, The Laws of the *Confessor,* which were granted and confirmed by King *Wil- liam,* and are also called the Laws of King *William,* which are transcribed in Mr. *Sel- den's* Notes upon *Eadmerus,* Page 173. the Title whereof is thus, *viz Hæ sunt Leges & Consuetudines quas Willielmus Rex concessit universo populo Angliæ post subactam Terram eadem sunt quas Edvardus Rex cognatus ejus observavit ante eum:* And these seem to be the
very

very same that *Ingulfus* mentions to have been brought from *London*, and placed by him in the Abbey of *Crowland* in the Fifteenth Year of the same King *William*, *attuli eadem Vice mecum Londini in meum Monasterium Legum Volumen*, &c.

Secondly, There were certain additional Laws at time establish'd, which *Gervasius Tilburiensis* calls, *Leges Neustriæ quæ efficacissimæ videbantur ad tuendam Regni pacem*; which seems to be included in those other Laws of King *William* transcribed in the same Notes upon *Eadmerus*, Page 189, 193, &c. which indeed were principally designed for the Establishment of King *William* in the Throne, and for the securing of the Peace of the Kingdom, especially between the *English* and *Normans*, as appears by these Instances, *viz.* And others added.

The Law *de Murdro*, or the Common Fine for a *Norman* or *Frenchman* slain, and the Offender not discovered: The Law for the Oath of Allegiance to the King: The Introduction of the Trial by single Combat, which many Learned Men have thought was not in Use here in *England* before *William* I. And the Law touching Knights Service, which *Bracton*, *Lib.* 2. supposes to be introduced by the Conqueror, *viz. Quod omnes Comites Milites & Servientes & universi liberi homines totius Regni habeant & teneant se semper bene in Armis & in Equis ut decet & quod sint semper prompti & bene parati ad Servitium suum integrum nobis explendum & peragendum cum semper Opus affuerit secundum quod nobis de Feodo debent & Tenementis suis de Jure facere*

cere & ficut illis ftatuimus per Commune Concilium totius Regni noftri prædicti, & illis dedimus & conceffimus in Feodo jure hæreditario. Wherein we may obferve, that this Conftitution feems to point at Two Things, *viz.* The affizing of Men for Arms, which was frequent under the Title *De affidenda ad Arma,* and is afterwards particularly enforc'd and rectified by the Statute of *Winton,* 13 *E.* 1. and next of Conventional Services referved by *Tenures* upon Grants made out of the Crown or Knights Service, called in Latin, *Forinfecum,* or *Regale Servitium.*

And *Note,* That thefe Laws were not impofed *ad Libitum Regis,* but they were fuch as were fettled *per Commune Concilium Regni,* and poffibly at that very Time when Twelve out of every County were return'd to afcertain the *Confeffor's* Laws, as before is mentioned out of *Hoveden,* which appears to be as fufficient and effectual a Parliament as ever was held in *England.*

By all which it is apparent, *Firft,* That *William* I did not pretend, nor indeed could he pretend, notwithftanding this Nominal Conqueft, to alter the Laws of this Kingdom without common Confent *in Communi Concilio Regni,* or in Parliament. And, *Secondly,* That if there could be any Pretence of any fuch Right, or if in that turbulent Time fomething of that Kind had happened; yet by all thofe folemn Capitulations, Oaths, and Conceffions, that Pretence was wholly avoided, and the ancient Laws of the Kingdom fettled, and were not to be altered, or

added

added unto, at the Pleasure of the Conqueror, without Consent in Parliament.

In the Seventeenth Year of his Reign, (or as some say, the Fifteenth) he began that great Survey, recorded in Two Books, called, *The Great Doomsday Book*, and *Little Doomsday Book*, and finished it in the Twentieth Year of his Reign, *Anno Domini* 1086. as appears by the learned Preface of Mr. *Selden* to *Eadmerus*, and indeed by the Books themselves. The Original Record of which is still extant, remaining in the Custody of the Vice-Chamberlains of Her Majesties *Exchequer*. This Record contains a Survey of all the ancient Demeasn Lands of the Kingdom, and contains in many Manors, not only the Tenants Names, with the Quantity of Lands and their Values, but likewise the Number and Quality of the Resients or Inhabitants, with divers Rights, Privileges, and Customs claimed by them; and being made and found by Verdict or Presentment of Juries in every Hundred or Division upon their Oaths, there was no Receeding from, or Avoiding what was written in this Record : And therefore as *Gervasius Tilburiensis* says, Page 41. *Ob hoc nos eundem Librum* Judiciarium *Nominamus* ; *Non quod in eo de propositis aliquibus dubiis feratur sententia, sed quod ab eo sicut ab ultimo Die Judicii non licet ulla ratione discedere.*

And thus much shall suffice touching the Fifth General Head; namely, of the Progress made after the Coming in of King

William,

William, relating to the Laws of *England*, their Establishment, Settlement, and Alteration If any one be minded to see what this Prince did in reference to Ecclesiasticks, let him consult *Eadmerus*, and the Learned Notes of Mr. *Selden* upon it, especially Page 167, 168, &c where he shall find how this King divided the Episcopal Consistory from the County Court, and how he restrain'd the Clergy and their Courts from exercising Ecclesiastical Jurisdiction upon Tenants in *Capite*

CHAP.

CHAP. VI.

Concerning the Parity or Similitude of the Laws of England *and* Normandy, *and the Reasons thereof.*

THE great Similitude that in many Things appears between the Laws of England, and those of *Normandy*, has given some Occasion to such as consider not well of Things, to suppose that this happened by the Power of the Conqueror, in Conforming the Laws of this Kingdom to those of *Normandy*; and therefore will needs have it, that our *English* Laws still retain the Mark of that Conquest, and that we received our Laws from him as from a Conqueror; than which Assertion, (as it appears even by what has before been said) nothing can be more untrue. Besides, if there were any Laws derived from the *Normans* to us, as perhaps there might be some, yea, possibly many, yet it no more concludes the Position to be true, that we received such Laws *per Modum Conquestus*, than if the Kingdom of *England* should at this Day take some of the Laws of *Persia*, *Spain*, *Egypt*, or *Assyria*, and by Authority of Parliament settle them here. Which tho' they were for their Matter Foreign, yet their obligatory Power, and their formal Nature

Our Laws not derived from the Normans.

3 or

or Reason of becoming Laws here, were not at all due to thofe Countries, whofe Laws they were, but to the proper and intrinfical Authority of this Kingdom by which they were received as, or enacted into, Laws: And therefore, as no Law that is Foreign binds here in *England*, till it be received and authoritatively engrafted into the Law of *England*; fo there is no Reafon in common Prudence and Underftanding for any Man to conclude, that no Rule or Method of Juftice is to be admitted in a Kingdom tho' never fo Ufeful or Beneficial, barely upon this account, That another People entertain'd it, and made it a Part of their Laws before us.

But as to the Matter it felf I fhall confider, and enquire of the following Particulars, *viz.*

1. How long the Kingdom of *England* and Dutchy of *Normandy* ftood in Conjunction under one Governor.

2. What Evidence we have touching the Laws of *Normandy*, and of their Agreement with ours

3. Wherein confifts that Parity or Difparity of the *Englifh* and *Norman* Laws.

4. What might be reafonably judged to be the Reafon and Foundation of that Likenefs, which is to be found between the Laws of both Countries.

1. *Firft*, Touching the Conjunction under one Governor of *England* and *Normandy*, we

are to know, That the Kingdom of *England*
and Dutchy of *Normandy* were *de facto* in
Conjunction under thefe Kings, *viz. Willi-*
am I *William* II *Henry* I King *Stephen,*
Henry II and *Richard* I who, dying without
Iffue, left behind him *Arthur* Earl of *Bri-*
tain, his Nephew, only Son of *Geoffry* Earl
of *Britain,* fecond Brother of *Richard* I and
John the youngeft Brother to *Richard* I.
who afterward became King of *England* by
ufurping the Crown from his Nephew *Ar-*
thur But the Princes of *Normandy* ftill adhered to *Arthur, ficut Domino Ligeo fuo dicentes*
Judicium & Confuetudinem effe illarum Regionum
ut Arthurus Filius Fratris Senioris in Patrimon o
fibi debito & hæreditate Avunculo fuo fuccedat
eodem jure quod Gaulfridus Pater ejus effet habi-
turus fi Regi Richardo defuncto fupervixiffet

And therein they faid true, and the Laws
of *England* were the fame, Witnefs the Succeffion of *Richard* II to *Edward* III alfo
the Laws of *Germany,* and the ancient *Saxons*
were accordant hereunto, and it was accordingly decided in a Trial by Battle, under *Otho* the Emperor, as we are told by
Radulphus, de Diceto fub Anno 9 5 And fuch
are the Laws of *France* to this Day, *Vide*
Chopinus de Domanio Francia, Lib 2 *Tit* 12
And fuch were the ancient Cuftoms of the
Normans, as we are told by the *Grand Con-*
tumier, cap 99. And fuch is the Law of
Normandy, and of the Ifles of *Jerfey* and
Guernfey (which fome time were Parcel
thereof) at this Day, as is agreed by *Terrien,*
the beft Expofitor of their Cuftoms, *Liv.* 2

Elder Brother dying in Life of the Father, his Son to inherit.

I

cap 2 And so it was adjudg'd within my Remembrance in the Isle of *Jersey*, in a Controverse there, between *John Perchard* and *John Rowland*, for the Goods and Estate of *Peter Perchard*

But nevertheless, *John* the Uncle of *Arthur* came by Force and Power, *Et Rotomagum Gladio Ducatus Normanniæ accinctus est per Masterium Rotomagensis Archiepiscopi,* as *Mat Par's* says, and shortly after also usurped the Crown of *England*, and imprisoned his Nephew *Arthur*, who died in the Year 1202 being as was supposed Murthered by his said Uncle, *Vide Mat Paris in fine Regni Regis Rici' Primi*, and *Walsingham* in his *Ypodigma Neustriæ sub eodem Anno* 1202.

And to countenance his Usurpation in *Normandy*, and to give himself the better Pretence of Title, he by his Power so far prevailed there, that he obtained a change of the Law there, purely to serve his Turn, by transferring the Right of Inheritance from the son of the elder Brother to the younger Brother, as appears by the *Grand Coutumier*, *cap 9*. But withal, the *Gloss* takes notice of it as an Innovation, and brought in by Men of Power, tho' it mentions not the particular Reason, which is as aforesaid

The King of *France* (of whom the Dutchy of *Normandy* was holden) highly resented the Injury done by King *John* to his Nephew *Arthur*, who as was strongly suspected came to his end by his means. He summoned King *John* as Duke of *Normandy* into *France*, to give an Account of his Actions and upon

his

his Default of appearing, he was by King *Philip* of *France* forejudged of the said Duchy, *Vide Mat Paris, in initio Regni Joh nnis*; and this Sentence was so effectually put in Execution, that in the Year 1204 *M t Paris* tells us, *Tota Normanni , Turania Andegavi , & Pictevia cum Civitatibus & Castellis & Rebus aliis pr æter Rupellam, Toar, & Mir Castellam sunt in Regis b nconi a Dominium devoluta*

But yet he retained, tho' with much Difficulty, the Islands of *Jerse* and *Guernsey*, and the uninterrupted Possession of some Parts of *Normand* for some time after, and both he and his Son King *H n* III kept the Stile and Title of Dukes of *Norman d*, &c till the 43d Year of King *Hen* III. at which time for 3000 *I v es 7 v no s*, and upon some other Agreements, he resigned *Normand* and *Anjou* to the King of *F nce*, and never afterwards used that Title as appears by the Continuation of *M t Paris*, *sub Anno* 1260 only the four Islands, so ne time Parcel of *Normandy*, were still, and to this Day, are enjoyed by the Crown of *England*, viz *Jersey, Guernsey S rke*, and *Alderney*, tho' they are still governed under their ancient *Norman Laws*

Secondly, As to the Second Inquiry, What Evidence we have touching the Laws of *Normandy* The best, and indeed only common Evidence of the ancient Customs and Laws of *Normand*, is that Book which is called, *The Grand Customer of Normandy*, which in later Years has been illustrated,

I

Normandy resigned by King

2

The Customer of Normandy

not only with a *Latin* and *French* Glofs, but
alfo with the Commentaries of *Terrien*, a
French Author

This Book does not only contain many
of the ancienter Laws of *Normandy*, but
moft plainly it contains thofe Laws and Cuftoms which were in Ufe here in the Time
of King *Hn.* II King *Rich* I and King *John*,
yea, and fuch alfo as were in Ufe and Practice in that Country after the Separation
of *Normandy* from the Crown of *England*,
for we fhall find therein, in their Writs and
Proceffes, frequent Mention of King *Rich* I
and the entire Text of the 110th Chapter
thereof is an Edict of *Philip* King of *France*,
after the Severance of *Normandy* from the
Crown of *England* (I fpeak not of thofe
additional Edicts which are annex'd to that
Book of a far later Date) So that we are
not to take that Book as a Collection of the
Laws of *Normandy*, as they ftood before the
Acceffion or Union thereof to the Crown
of *England*, but as they ftood long after,
under the Time of thofe Dukes of *Normandy*
that fucceeded *William* I and it feems to
be a Collection made after the Time of
K. *Hn.* III or at leaft after the Time of
K *John*, and confequently it ftates their Laws
and Cuftoms as they ftood in Ufe and Practice about the Time of that Collection
made, which Obfervation will be of Ufe
in the enfuing Difcourfe.

3   *Thirdly*, Touching the Third Particular,
viz The Agreement and Difparity of the
Laws of *England* and *Normandy* It is very

Np,

true, we shall find a great Suitableness in their Laws, in many Things agreeing with the Laws of *England*, especially as they stood in the Time of King *Hen.* II the best Indication whereof we have in the Collection of *Glanville*, the Rules of Descents, of Writs, of Process, of Trials, and some other Particulars, holding a great Analogy in both Dominions, yet not without their Differences and Disparities in many Particulars, *viz.*

First, Some of those Laws are such as were never used in *England*, for Instance, There was in *Normandy* a certain Tribute paid to the Duke, called *Monya, id est,* a certain Sum yielded to him (in Consideration that he should not alter their Coin) payable every three Years, *Vide Contumier, cap* 15 But this Payment was never admitted in *England*; indeed it was taken for a Time, but was ousted by the first Law of King *Hen* I. as an Usurpation Again, by the Custom of *Normandy*, the Lands descended to the Bastard Eigne, born before Marriage of the same Woman, by whom the same Man had other Children after Marriage, *Contumier, cap* 27 But the Laws of *England* were always contrary, as appears by *Glanville, Lib* 7°. *cap* 12 And the Statute of *Merton*, which says, *Nolumus Leges Anglicanas Mutare, &c.* Again, by the Laws of *Normandy*, if a Man died without Issue, or Brother, or Sister, the Lands did descend to the Father, *Contumier, cap.* 15. *Terrier, cap* 2 But in

Difference between the *Contumier* and the Laws of *England.*

I 3

Eng-

England, this Law seems never to have been used, *Sed Quære*, *Granville*, *Lib* 7. *cap* 1

2*dly*, Again, Some Laws were used in *Normandy*, which were in Use in *England* long before the supposed *Norman* Conquest, and therefore could in no Possibility have their original Force, or any binding Power here upon that Pretence. For Instance, it appears by the *Custumes* of *Normandy*, that the Sheriff of the County was an *Annual* Officer, and so 'tis evident he was likewise in *England* before the Conquest. And among the Laws of *Edward* the *Confessor*, it is provided, *Quod Aldermanni in Civitatibus eandem habeant Dignitatem quolem habent Ballivi hundredorum in Ballivis suis sub Vicecomitem*. Again, Wreck of the Sea, and Treasure *Trove* was a Prerogative belonging to the Dukes of *Normandy*, as appears by the *Custumar, cp* 17, & 18 and so it was belonging to the Crown of *England* before the Conquest, as appears by the Charter of *Edward* the *Confessor* to the Abby of *Ramsey* of the Manor of *Ringstede, cum toto ejectu Maris quod Wreccum dicitur*, and the like *vide* also of Treasure *Trove, & vide* the Laws of *Edward* the *Confessor, cap* 14 So Fealty, Homage, and Relief, were incident to Tenures by the Laws of *Normandy, Vide Custumar, c p* 29. And so they were in *England* before the Conquest, as appears by the Laws of *Edward* the *Confessor, c p* 35 and the Laws of *Carnus*, mentioned by *Brompton, c p* 8. So the Trial by Jury of Twelve Men was the usual Trial among the *Normans* in most

moft Suits, efpecially in Affizes, & *Juris
Utrums*, as appears by the *Contumier*, cap 92,
93, & 94 and that Trial was in Ufe here in
England before the Conqueft, as appears in
Brompton among the Laws of King *Etheldred*,
cap 3. which gives fome Specimen of it,
viz. *Habeant placita in fingulis* Wapentachiis
& exean: Seniores duodecim Thani *vel Præ-
pofitus cum iis & jurent quod neminem innocen-
tem accufare nec Noxium concelare.*

3*dly*, Again, In fome Things, tho' both
the Law of *Normandy* and the Law of
England agreed in the Fact, and in the
manner of Proceeding, yet there was an
apparent Difcrimination in their Law from
ours As for Inftance, The Husband feized
in Right of the Wife, having Iffue by her,
and fhe dying, by the Cuftom of *Normandy*
he held but only during his Widowhood,
Contumier, cap 119. But in *England*, he
held during his Life by the Curtefy of
England

4*thly* But in fome Things, the Laws of
Normandy agreed with the Laws of *England*,
efpecially as they ftood in the Times of
Hen II and *Richard* I fo that they feem
to be as it were Copies or Counterparts
one of another, tho' in many Things, the
Laws of *England* are fince changed in a great
Meafure from what they then were For
Inftance, at this Day in *England*, and for
very many Ages paft, all Lands of Inheritance, as well *Socage Tenures*, as of Knights
Service, defcend to the eldeft Son, unlefs
in *Kent* and fome other Places where the

Cuftom

Custom directs the Descent to all the Males, and in some Places to the youngest, but the ancient Law used in *England*, though it directed Knights Services and Serjeanties to descend to the eldest Son, yet it directed Vassalagies and Socage Lands to descend to all the Sons, *Glanvil*, *Lib* 7 *cap* 2. and so does the Laws of *Normandy* to this Day *Vide Conturier*, *cap* 26 *& post hic*, *cap* 11

Again, *Leprosy* at this Day does not impede the Descent, but by the Laws in Use in *England*, in the elder Times, unto the Time of King *John*, and for some Time afterwards, *Leprosy* did impede the Descent, as *Placito quarto Johannis*, in the Case of *W Fulch*, a Judge of that Time, and accordingly were the Laws of *Normandy*, *Vide Le Conturmier*, *cap* 27

Old Law of Trials by Jury   *Again*, At this Day, by the Law of *England*, in Cases of Trials by Twelve Men, all ought to agree, and any one dissenting, no Verdict can be given ; but by the Laws of *Normandy*, though a Verdict ought to be by the concurring Consent of Twelve Men, yet in case of Dissent or Disagreement of the Jury, they used to put off the lesser Number that were Dissenters, and added a kind of *Tales* equal to the greater Number so agreeing, until they had got a Verdict of Twelve Men that concurred, *Contumier*, *c* 95. And we may find some ancient Footsteps of the like Use here in *England*, though long since antiquated, *Vide Bratton*, *Lib* 4 *cap* 19. where he speaks thus, *Contingit etiam multoties quod Juratores in veritate dicenda sunt*

fib

fibi contrarii ita quod in unam concordare non poſſunt ſententiam, Quo caſu de Conſilio Curiæ aſſortietur Aſſiſa, ita quod apponantur alii juxta numerum majoris partis quæ diſſenſerit, vel ſaltem qtatuor vel ſex & adjungantur aliis, vel etiam per ſeipſos ſine aliis, de veritate diſcutiant & judicent, & per ſe reſpondeant & eorum veredittum allocabitur & tenebitur cum quibus ipſi convenirent

Again, at this Day, by the Laws of *England,* a Man may give his Lands in Fee-simple, which he has by Descent, to any one of his Children, and diſinherit the reſt: But by the ancient Laws uſed here, it ſeems to be otherwiſe, as *Mich.* 10 *Johannis Glanv. Lib* 7. *cap* 2 the Caſe of *William de Cauſeia.* And accordingly were the Laws of *Normandy,* as we find in the *Grand Contumier, cap* 36. *Quand le Pere avoit pluſieurs fills, ils ne peut faire de ſon Heritage le un Meilleur que le auter,* and yet it ſeems to this Day, in *England,* it holds ſome Reſemblance in Caſes of Frank-Marriage, *viz* That the *Doneſs,* in caſe ſhe will have any Part of her Father's other Lands, ought to put her Lands in *Hochpot.*

Again, By the Law of *England,* the younger Brother ſhall not exclude the Son of the elder, who died in the Life-time of the Father. And this was the ancient Law of *Normandy,* but received ſome Interruption in Favour of King *John's* Claim, *Vide Contumier, cap* 25 *& hic ante,* and indeed, generally the Rule of Deſcents in *Normandy* was the ſame in moſt Caſes with that of

And of Deſcents.

Difcents with us at this Day, as for Inftance, That the Defcent of the Line of
the Father fhall not refort to that of the
Mother, *Et e converfo*, and that the Courfe
was otherwife in Cafes of Purchafes But
in moft Things the Law of *Normandy* was
confonant to the Law with us, as it was in
the Time of King *Richard* I and King
John, except in Cafes of Defcents to *Baftard eigne*, excluding *Mulier puifne*, as afore-
faid.

Their
Writs.

Again, at this Day there are many Writs
now in Ufe which were anciently alfo in
Ufe here, as well as in *Normandy* As Writs
of Right, Writs of Dower, Writs *De novel
Differfin*, *de Mortdanceftor*, *Juris utrum*, *Dar-
rein prefentment*, &c And fome that are now
out of Ufe, though anciently in Ufe here
in *England*, as Writs *De Feodo vel vado*, *De
Feodo vel Warda*, &c. All which are taken
Notice of by *Glanvil*, *Lib* 13. *cap* 28, 29.
And the very fame Forms of Writs in Effect
were in Ufe in *Normandy*, as appears by the
Contumier per Totum, and the Writ *De Feodo
vel Vado*, (*ib d cap* 1) according to *Glanville*, *Lib* 13 *cap* 27 runs thus, *viz* *Rex
Viccecomiti falutem Summone per bonos fummoni-
tores duodecim liberos & legales homines de vi-
cineto quod fint coram me vel Jufticiariis eo die
per ti Sacramento Recognofcere utrum N tenent
unam Carucatam Terræ in illa villa quæ R cla-
mat verfus eum per Breve meum in Feodo an in
vadio, invidictam ei b ipfi R vel ab H ante-
ceffore ejus. (vel aliter) fi fit Feod in vel hære-
d. . . ipfis N an in vadio vadiatio ii ab ipfa
R vel*

R vel ab H &c. Et interim Terram illam videant, &c. Vide ibid

And according to the *Grand Contumier,* that Writ runs thus, viz. *Si Rex fecerit te securum de clamore suo prosequend' summoneas Recognitores de Viceneto quod sint ad primas Assisas Ballivæ, ad cognoscendum utrum Carucata Terræ in B quod G deforceet R sit Feodum tenentis vel vadium novum dictum per Manus G. post Coronationem Regis* Richardi *& pro quanta, & utrum sit propinquior Hæres ad redimendum vadium, & videatur interim Terræ, &c* So that there seems little Variance, either in the Nature or in the Form of those Writs used here, in the Time of *Henry* II And those used in *Normandy* when the Contumier was made

Again, The Use was in *England* to limit certain notable Times, within the Compass of which those Titles which Men design'd to be relieved upon, must accrue. Thus it was done in the Time of *Henry* III by the Statute of *Merton, cap* 8 at which Time the Limitation in a Writ of Right was from the Time of King *Henry* I. and by that Statute it is reduced to the Time of King *Henry* II and for Assizes of *Mortdancestor* they were thereby reduced from the last Return of King *John* out of *Ireland,* which was 12 *Johannis,* and for Assizes of *Novel Disseisin, a prima Transfretatione Regis in Normanniam,* which was 5 *Hen* 3 and which before that had been *post ultimum redditum* Henricus III *d. Britannia,* as appears by *Bracton* And this Time of Limitation was also

Times of Limitation

also afterwards, by the Statute of *West.* 1
cap 39 and *West.* 2. *cap* 2 46. reduced
unto a narrower Scantlet, the Writ of Right
being limitted to the First Coronation of
King *Richard* I.

But before the Limitation set by that
Statute of *Merton*, there were several Limitations set for several Writs ; for we find
among the Pleas of King *John's* Time, the
Limitation of Writs, *De Tempore quo Rex*
Henricus *avus noster fuit vivus & Mortuus* ;
and in a Writ of Aile, *Die quo Rex* Henricus *obiit* in the Time of *Henry* II as appears by *Glanville, Lib.* 13 *cap* 3 there
were then divers Limitations in Use, as in
*Mortdancestors, post prima Coronationem no-
stram, viz. Henrici secundi, Glanvil Lib* 1.
cap 1. and touching Assizes of *Novel Dif-
seisin, Vide ibid cap* 32 where he tells us,
Cum quis intra Assisam, &c. And the Time of
Limitation in an Assize, was then *post ultimam
meam Transfretationem,* (*viz* Henrici *primi*) *in
Normanniam, Lib* 13 *cap* 33 But in a Writ
of Right, as also in a Writ of Customs and
Services, it was *de tempore Regis* Henrici *avi
mei, viz. Hen* 1 *vid ib Lib* 12 *cap* 10, 16.
And it seems very apparent, that the Limi-
tations anciently in *Normandy*, for all Actions
Ancestrel was *post primum Coronationem Regis*
Henrici *secundi*, as appears expresly in the
Contumies, cap 111 *De Foefe & Gage*

So that aneiently the Time of Limitation in *Normandy* was the same as in *England*,
and indeed borrowed from *England, viz.* In
all Actions Ancestrel from the Coronation
of

of *Henry* II. And thus in thofe Actions wherein the Limitation was anciently from the Coronation of King *Richard* I. was fub-ftituted as in the Writ *De Feofe & Gage*, in the *Contumier*, *cap* 111 *De Feofe & Forme*, *cap.* 112. In the Writ *De Ley Apparifan, ib. cap.* 24. *& cap* 22. *Afcun Gage ne peut eftre requife en* Normandy, *fi il ne fuit engage poft le Coronement de Roy* Richaid *ou deins quarante annus* So that the old Limitation, as well for the Redemption of Mortgages, as for bringing thofe Writs above-mentioned, was *poft Coronationem Regis* Henrici *Secundi*, but altered, as it feems, by King *Philip*, the Son of *Lewis* King of *France*, after King *John*'s Ejectment out of *Normandy*, and fince the Time from the Coronation of King *Richard* I. is eftimated to bear Proportion to 40 Years. It is probable this Change of the Limitation by King *Philip* of *France*, was about the beginning of the Reign of King *Henry* III. or about 30 or 40 Years after the Coronation of *Richard* I. from whofe Coronation about 30 Years were elapfed, 5 *aut* 6 Henrici 3 for anciently the Limitation in this Cafe was 30 Years

Fourthly, I now come to the Fourth In-quiry, *viz.* How this great Parity between the Laws of *England* and *Normandy* came to be effected; and before I come to it, I fhall premife Two Obfervables, which I would have the Reader to carry along with him through the whole Difcourfe, *viz.* *Firft*, That this Parity of Laws does not at all infer a Neceffity, that they fhould be

impofed

impoſed by the *Conqueror*, which is ſuffi-
ciently ſhewn in the foregoing Chapters;
and in this it will appear, that there were
divers other Means that cauſed a Similitude
of both Laws, without any Suppoſition of
impoſing them by the *Conqueror* *Secondly*, That the Laws of *Normandy* were in the
greater Part thereof borrowed from ours,
rather than ours from them, and the Similitude of the Laws of both Countries did
in greater Meaſure ariſe from their Imitation of our Laws, rather than from our Imitation of theirs, though there can't be denied a Reciprocal Imitation of each others
Laws was, in ſome Meaſure at leaſt, had
in both Dominions. And theſe Two Things
being premiſed, I deſcend to the *Means*
whereby this Parity or Similitude of the
Laws of both Countries did ariſe, as follow, *viz.*

Cauſes of a congrui-ty of Laws

Firſt, Mr *Camden* and ſome others have
thought, there was ever ſome Congruity between the ancient Cuſtoms of this Iſland
and thoſe of the Country of *France*, both
in Matters Religious and Civil; and tells
us of the ancient *Druids*, who were the
common Inſtructors of both Countries
Galli Cauſidicos docut ferunda Britannos.
And ſome have thought, that anciently
both Countries were conjoined by a ſmall
Neck of Land, which might make an eaſier
Tranſition of the Cuſtoms of either Country to the other, but thoſe Things are too
remote Conjectures, and we need them not

to folve the Congruity of Laws between *England* and *Normandy*. Therefore,

Secondly, It feems plain, that before the Commerce,&c between the *Englifh* and *Normans*.
Normans coming in Way of Hoftility, there was a great Intercourfe of Commerce and Trade, and a mutual Communication, between thofe Two Countries, and the Confanguinty between the Two Princes gave Opportunities of feveral Interviews between them and their Courts in each others Countries. And it is evident by Hiftory, that the *Confeffor*, before his Acceffion to the Crown, made a long Stay in *Normandy*, and was there often, which of Confequence muft draw many of the *Englifh* thither, and of the *Normans* hither, all which might be a Means of their mutual Underftanding of the Cuftoms and Laws of each others Country, and gave Opportunities of incorporating and engrafting divers of them into each other, as they were found ufeful or convenient, and therefore the Author of the Prologue to the *Grand Cuftumier* thinks it more probable, That the Laws of *Normandy* were derived from *England*, than that ours were derived from thence

Thirdly, 'Tis evident, that when the Duke of *Normandy* came in, he brought over a great Multitude, not only of ordinary Soldiers, but of the beft of the Nobility and Gentry of *Normandy*, hither they brought their Families, Language and Cuftoms, and the Victor ufed all Art and Induftry to incorporate them into this Kingdom And the more effectually to make both People

become

become one Nation, he made Marriages between the *English* and *Normans*, transplantmaingny *Norman* Families hither, and many *English* Families thither ; he kept his Court sometimes here, and sometimes there , and by those Means insensibly derived many *Norman* Customs hither, and *English* Customs thither, without any severe Imposition of Laws on the *English* as Conqueror : And by this Method he might easily prevail to bring in, even without the People's Consent, some Customs and Laws that perhaps were of Foreign Growth ; which might the more easily be done, considering how in a short Time the People of both Nations were intermingled ; they were mingled in Marriages, in Families, in the Church, in the State, in the Court, and in Councils, yea, and in Parliaments in both Dominions, though *Normandy* became, as it were, an Appendix to *England*, which was the nobler Dominion, and received a greater Conformity of their Laws to the *English*, than they gave to it.

Fourthly, But the greatest Means of the Assimilation of the Laws of both Kingdoms was this The Kings of *England* continued Dukes of *Normandy* till King *John*'s Time, and he kept some Footing there notwithstanding the Confiscation thereof by the King of *France*, as aforesaid, and during all this Time, *England*, which was an absolute Monarchy, had the Prelation or Preference before *Normandy*, which was but a Feudal Dutchy, and a small Thing in respect of

England,

England, and by this Means *Normandy* became, as it were, an Appendant to *England*, and succeſſively received its Laws and Government from *England*, which had a greater Influence on *Normandy* than that could have on *England*, inſomuch, that oftentimes there iſſued Precepts into *Normandy* to ſummon Perſons there to anſwer in Civil Cauſes here, yea, even for Lands and Poſſeſſions in *Normandy*; as *Placito* 1 *Johannis*, a Precept iſſued to the Seneſchal of *Normandy*, to ſummon *Robert Jeronymus*, to anſwer to *John Marſhal*, in a Plea of Land, giving him 40 Days Warning; to which the Tenant appeared, and pleaded a Recovery in *Normandy* And the like Precept iſſued for *William de Boſco*, againſt *Jeoffry Ruſham*, for Lands in *Corbeſpine* in *Normandy*.

And on the other Side, *Trin* 14 *Johannis*, in a Suit between *Francis Borne* and *Thomas Adorne*, for certain Lands in *Ford* The Defendant pleaded a Concord made in *Normandy* in the Time of King *Richard* I upon a Suit there before the King, for the Honour of *Bonn* in *Normandy*, and for certain Lands in *England*, whereof the Lands in Queſtion were Parcel before the Seneſchal of *Normandy*, *Anno* 1099 But it was excepted againſt, as an inſufficient Fine, and varying in Form from other Fines, and therefore the Defendant relied upon it as a Releaſe.

By theſe, and many the like Inſtances, it appears as follows, *viz.*

K   *Firſt*,

First, That there was a great Intercourse between *England* and *Normandy* before and after the Conqueror, which might give a great Opportunity of an Assimilation and Conformity of the Laws in both Countries. *Secondly,* That a much greater Conformation of Laws arose after the Conqueror, during the Time that *Normandy* was enjoyed by the Crown of *England,* than before. And *Thirdly,* That this Similitude of the Laws of *England* and *Normandy* was not by Conformation of the Laws of *England* to those of *Normandy,* but by Conformation of the Laws of *Normandy* to those of *England,* which now grew to a great Height, Perfection and Glory; so that *Normandy* became but a Perquisite or Appendant of it.

And as the Reason of the Thing speaks it, so the very Fact it self attests it For,

First, It is apparent, That in Point of Limitation in Actions Ancestrel, from the Time of the Coronation of King *Henry* II it was anciently so here in *England* in *Glanvil*'s Time, and was transmitted from hence into *Normandy*; for it is no way reasonable to suppose the Contrary, since *Glanville* mentions it to be enacted here, *Concilio procerum*; and though this be but a single Point, or Instance, yet the Evidence thereof makes out a Criterion, or probable Indication, that many other Laws were in like Manner so sent hence into *Normandy.*

Secondly, It appears, That in the Succession of the Kings of *England*, from King *William* I. to King *Henry* II the Laws of *England* received a great Improvement and Perfection, as will plainly appear from *Glanvil's* Book, written in the Time of King *Henry* II especially if compared with those Sums or Collections of Laws, either of *Edward* the Confessor, *William* I. or *Henry* I. whereof hereafter.

So that it seems, by Use, Practice, Commerce, Study and Improvement of the *English* People, they arrived in *Henry* II.'s Time to a greater Improvement of the Laws, and that in the Time of King *Richard* I. and King *John*, they were more perfected, as may be seen in the Pleadings, especially of King *John*'s Time ; and tho' far inferior to those of the Times of Succeeding Kings, yet they are far more regular and perfect than those that went before them. And now if any do but compare the *Coutumier* of *Normandy*, with the Tract of *Glanville*, he will plainly find that the *Norman* Tract of Laws followed the Pattern of *Glanvil*, and was writ long after it, when possibly the *English* Laws were yet more refined and more perfect ; for it is plain beyond Contradiction, that the Collection of the Customs and Laws of *Normandy* was made after the Time of King *Henry* II for it mentions his Coronation, and appoints it for the Limitation of Actions Ancestrel, which must at least be 30 Years after ; nay, the *Coutumier* appears to have been

made

made after the Act of Settlement of *Normandy* in the Crown of *France*; for therein is specified the Institution of *Philip* King of *France*, for appointing the Coronation of King *Richard* I. for the Limitation of Actions, which was after the said *Philip's* full Possession of *Normandy*.

Indeed, if those Laws and Customs of *Normandy* had been a Collection of the Laws they had had there before the coming in of King *William* I. it might have been a Probability that their Laws, being so near like ours, might have been transplanted from thence hither; but the Case is visibly otherwise, for the *Coutumier* is a Collection after the Time of King *Richard* I. yea, after the Time of King *John*, and possibly after *Henry* III's Time, when it had received several Repairings, Amendments and Polishings, under the several Kings of *England*, *William* I. *William* II. *Henry* I. King *Steven*, *Henry* II. *Richard* I. and King *John*; who were either knowing themselves in the Laws of *England*, or were assisted with a Council that were knowing therein

And as in this Tract of Time the Laws of *England* received a great Advance and Perfection, as appears by that excellent Collection of *Glanville*, written even in *Henry* II's Time, when yet there were near 30 Years to acquire unto a further Improvement before *Normandy* was lost; so from the Laws of *England* thus modelled, polished and perfected, the same Draughts were drawn upon the Laws of

Nor-

Normandy, which received the faireſt Lines from the Laws of *England,* as they ſtood at leaſt in the beginning of King *John's* Time, and were in Effect in a great Meaſure the Defloration of the *Engliſh* Laws, and a Tranſcript of them, though mingled and interlarded with many particular Laws and Cuſtoms of their own, which altered the Features of the Original in many Points.

K 3   CHAP.

CHAP. VII.

Concerning the Progreſs of the Laws of England after the Time of King William I. until the Time of King Edward II.

THAT which precedes in the Two foregoing Chapters, gives us ſome Account of the Laws of *England*, as they ſtood in and after the great Change which happened under King *William* I commonly called, *The Conqueror* I ſhall now proceed to the Hiſtory thereof in the enſuing Times, until the Reign of King *Edward* II.

K W 2.   *William* I. having Three Sons; *Robert* the eldeſt, *William* the next, and *Henry* the youngeſt, diſpoſed of the Crown of *England* to *William* his ſecond Son, and the Dutchy of *Normandy* to *Robert* his eldeſt Son; and accordingly *William* II commonly called, *William Rufus*, ſucceeded his Father in this Kingdom. We have little memorable of him in relation to the Laws, only that he ſeverely preſs'd and extended the *Foreſt Laws*.

K H 1.   *Henry* I. Son of *William* I and Brother of *William* II. ſucceeded his ſaid Brother in the Kingdom of *England*, and afterwards expelled his eldeſt Brother *Robert* out of the Dutchy of *Normandy* alſo. He proceeded

ceeded much in the Benefit of the Laws, *viz.*

Firft, He reftored the Free-Election of Bifhops and Abbots, which before that Time he and his Predeceffors invefted, *per Annulum & Bacculum* , yet referving thofe Three Enfigns of the Patronage thereof, *viz. Conge d'Eflire,* Cuftody of the Temporalties, and Homage upon their Reftitution. *Vide Hoveden, in Vita fua.*

But *Secondly,* The great Effay he made, was the compofing an Abftract or Manual of Laws, wherein he confirm'd the Laws of *Edward* the Confeffor, *Cum illis Emendationibus quibus eam Pater meus emendavit Baronum fuorum Concilio;* and then adds his own Laws, fome whereof feem to tafte of the Canon Law The whole Collection is tranfcribed in the Red Book of the *Exchequer;* from whence it is now printed in the End of *Lambard's Saxon* Laws, and therefore not needful to be here repeated.

They, for the moft Part, contain a Model of Proceedings in the County Courts, the Hundred Courts, and the Courts Leet , the former to be held Twelve Times in the Year, the latter twice; and alfo of the Courts Baron. Thefe were the ordinary ufual Courts, wherein Juftice was then, and for a long Time after, moft commonly adminiftred; alfo they concern Criminal Proceedings, and the Punifhment of Crimes, and fome few Things touching Civil Actions and Interefts, as in Chapter 70, directing Defcents, *viz.*

K 4   S

Si quis sine Liberis decesserit Pater aut Mater ejus in Hereditatem succedant, vel Frater vel Soror, si Pater & Mater desint, si nec hos habeat, Frater vel Soror Patris vel Matris, & deinceps in quintum Genealium, qui cum propiores in parentela sint hereditario Jure succedant, Et dum virile sexus extiterit & hæreditas ab inde sit Femina non hæreditetur; primum Patris Feodum primogenitus Filius habeat, Emptiones vero & deinceps Acquisitiones det cui magis velit, sed si Bockland habeat quam ei Parentes dederint, non Mittat eam extra cognationem suam

☞   I have obferv'd and inferted this Law, for Two Reafons, *viz. First*, To juftify what I before faid, That the Laws of *Normandy* took the *English* Laws for their Pattern in many Things, *Vide le Coutumier, cap* 25, 26, 36, *&c.* And *Secondly*, To fee how much the Laws of *England* grew and increafed in their Particularity and Application between this Time and the Laws of *William* I. which in Chapter 36, has no more touching Defcents but this, *viz. Si quis intestatus obierit, liberi ejus hæreditatem equaliter dividant.* But Procefs of Time grafted thereupon, and made particular Provifions for particular Cafes, and added Diftributions and Subdivifions to thofe General Rules.

These Laws of King *Henry* I are a kind of Mifcellany, made up of thofe ancient Laws, called, *The Laws of the Confessor*, and King *William* I. and of certain Parts of the Canon and Civil Law; and of other Provifions, that Cuftom and the Prudence

of

of the King and Council had thought upon, chofen, and put together.

King *Stephen* fucceeded, by Way of Ufur- King *Ste-* pation, upon *Maud* the Sole Daughter and *phen.* Heir of King *Hen* I. The Laws of *Hen.* I. grew tedious and ungrateful to the People, partly becaufe new, and fo not fo well known, and partly becaufe more difficult and fevere than thofe ancient Laws, called, *The Confeffor's* , for *Walfingham*, in his *Ypodigma Neuftriæ*, tells us, That the *Londoners* petitioned Queen *Maud, ut liceret eis uti Legibus fancti Edvardi & non legibus Patris fui Henrici, quia graves erant* ; and that her Refufal gave Occafion to their Defection from her, and ftrenthened *Stephen* in his Ufurpation; who, according to the Method of Ufurpers, to fecure himfelf in the Throne, was willing and ready to gratifie the Defires of the People herein , and furthermore, took his Oath, 1*ft,* That he would not retain in his Hands the Temporalties of the Bifhops , 2*dly,* That he would remit the Severity of the *Foreft* Laws , and 3*dly,* That he would alfo remit the Tribute of *Danegelt:* But he performed nothing

His Times were troublefome, he did little in relation to the Laws, nor have we any Memorial of any Record touching his Proceedings therein, only there are fome few *Pipe Rolls* of his Time, relating to the Revenue of the Crown.

Henry II. the Son of *Maud*, fucceeded K. H II. *Stephen*, he Reigned long, *viz* about Thirty Five Years; and tho' he was not without

great

great Troubles and Difficulties, yet he built up the Laws and the Dignity of the Kingdom to a great Height and Perfection. For,

Settles Peace, and reforms the Coin. *First*, In the Entrance of his Government he settled the Peace of the Kingdom; he also reformed the Coin, which was much adulterated and debased in the Times and Troubles of King *Stephen*, *Et Leges Henrici avi sui præcepit per totum Regnum inviolabiliter observari.* Hoveden.

Constitutions of Clarendon's. *Secondly*, Against the Insolencies and Usurpations of the Clergy; he by the Advice of his Council or Parliament at *Clarendon*, enacted those Sixteen Articles mentioned by *Mat. Paris*, *sub Anno* 1164 They are long, and therefore I remit you thither for the Particulars of them.

'Tis true, *Thomas Becket*, Archbishop of *Canterbury*, boldly and insolently took upon him to declare many of those Articles void, especially those Five mentioned in his Epistle to his Suffragans, recorded by *Hoveden*, *viz.* 1*st*, That there should be no Appeal to the Bishop without the King's *Licence* 2*dly*, That no Archbishop or Bishop should go over the Seas at the *Pope's* Command without the King's *Licence*. 3*dly*, That the Bishop should not excommunicate the King's Tenants *in Capite* without the King's *Licence*. 4*thly*, That the Bishop should not have the Conuzance of Perjury, or *Fidei Læsionis*. And, 5*thly*, That the Clergy should be convened before Lay Judges, and that the King's

Courts

Courts fhould have Conuzance of Churches
and of Tythes.

Thirdly, He raifed up the Municipal Laws *Improv'd*
of the Kingdom to a greater Perfection, *the Laws.*
and a more orderly and regular Adminiftration than before, 'tis true, we have no
Record of judicial Proceedings fo ancient
as that Time, except the Pipe Rolls in the
Exchequer, which are only Accounts of his
Revenue. But we need no other Evidence
hereof than the Tractate of *Glanville*, which
tho' perhaps it was not written by that
Ranulphus de Glanvilla, who was *Juftitiarius
Angliæ* under *Hen.* II. yet it feems to be
wholly written at that Time, and by that
Book, tho' many Parts thereof are at this
Day antiquated and altered, and in that
long Courfe of Time, which has elapfed
fince that King's Reign, much enlarged,
reformed, and amended, yet by comparing
it with thofe Laws of the *Confeffor* and Con-
qeror, yea, and the Laws of his Grandfather King *Hen* I. which he confirmed; it
will eafily appear, that the Rule and Order,
as well as the Adminiftration of the Law,
was greatly improved beyond what it was
formerly, and we have more Footfteps of
their Agreement and Concord herein with
the Laws, as they were ufed from the Time
of *Edw.* I. and downwards, than can be
found in all thofe obfolete Laws of *Hen.* I
which indeed were but diforderly, confufed
and general Things, rather the Cafes and
Shells of directing the way of Adminiftration

tion than Inftitutions of Law, if compared with *Glanville*'s Tractate of our Laws

Fourthly, The Adminiftration of the Common Juftice of the Kingdom, feems to be wholly difpenfed in the County Courts, Hundred Courts, and Courts Baron, except fome of the greater Crimes reformed by the Laws of King *Hen* I. and that Part thereof which was fometimes taken up by the *Juftitiarius Angliæ* This doubtlefs bred great Inconvenience, Uncertainty, and Variety in the Laws, *viz.*

Inconveniencies in the Laws

Firft, By the Ignorance of the Judges, which were the Freeholders of the County: For altho' the Alderman or Chief Conftable of every Hundred was always to be a Man learned in the Laws; and altho' not only the Freeholders, but the Bifhops, Barons, and great Men, were by the Laws of King *Hen* I appointed to attend the County Court, yet they feldom attended there, or if they did, in Procefs of Time they neglected the Study of the *Englifh* Laws, as great Men ufually do

Secondly, Another Inconvenience was, That this alfo bred great Variety of Laws, efpecially in the feveral Counties· For the Decifion or Judgments being made by divers Courts, and feveral Independent Judges and Judicatories, who had no common Intereft among them in their feveral Judicatories, thereby in Procefs of Time every feveral County would have feveral Laws, Cuftoms, Rules, and Forms of Proceeding, which is always the Effect of feveral Independent

dependent Judicatories adminiftred by feveral Judges

Thirdly, A Third Inconvenience was, That all the Bufinefs of any Moment was carried by Parties and Factions: For the Freeholders being generally the Judges, and Converfing one among another, and being as it were the Chief Judges, not only of the Fact, but of the Law; every Man that had a Suit there, fped according as he could make Parties, and Men of great Power and Intereft in the County did eafily overbear others in their own Caufes, or in fuch wherein they were interefted, either by Relation of Kindred, Tenure, Service, Dependance, or Application.

And altho' in Cafes of falfe Judgment, the Law, even as then ufed, provided a Remedy by Writ of falfe Judgment before the King or his Chief Juftice, and in cafe the Judgment was found to be fuch in the County Court, all the Suitors were confiderably amerced, (which alfo continued long after in Ufe with fome Severity) yet this proved but an ineffectual Remedy for thofe Mifchiefs. *Remedied, By Ordaining*

Therefore the King took another and a more effectual Courfe; for in the 22d Year of his Reign, by Advice of his Parliament held at *Northampton*, he inftituted Juftices *itinerant*, dividing the Kingdom into Six Circuits, and to every Circuit allotting Three Judges, Knowing or Experienced in the Laws of the Realm. Thefe Juftices *Juftices Itinerant.*

with

with their several Circuits are declared by *Hoveden, sub eodem Anno, i.e.* 22 H 2 viz.

1 *Hugo Cressy, Walterus filius Roberti, & Robertus Maunsel,* for *Norfolk, Suffolk, Cambridge, Huntingdon, Bedford, Buckingham, Essex,* and *Hartford* Counties.

2. *Hugo de Gundevilla, W filius Radulphi, & W. Basset,* for *Lincoln, Nottingham, Derby, Stafford, Warwick, Northampton,* and *Leicester* Counties.

3 *Robertus filius Bernardi, Richardus Giffard, & Rogerus filius Ramfrey,* for *Kent, Surrey, Sussex, Hampshire, Berks,* and *Oxon* Counties.

4. *W filius Stephani, Bertein de Verdun, & Turstavi filius Simonis,* for *Hereford, Gloucester, Worcester,* and *Salop* Counties.

5. *Radulphus filius Stephani, W Ruffus, & Gilbertus Pipard,* for the Counties of *Wilts, Dorset, Somerset, Devon,* and *Cornwall.*

6. *Robertus de Watts, Radulphus de Glanvilla, & Robertus Picknot,* for the Counties of *York, Richmond, Lancaster, Copland, Westmerland, Northumberland,* and *Cumberland.*

Hi, (*Consilio Archiepiscoporum Episcoporum Comitum & Baronum Regni,* &c. *apud Nottingham existentium*) *missi sunt per singulos Angliæ Comitatus & juraverunt quod cuilibet jus suum conservarent illæ sum Hoveden fo.* 313. & *Mat. Paris, in Anno* 1176. And that these Men were well known in the Law, appears by their Companion *Radulphus de Glanvilla,* who seems to be the Author of the Treatise *De Legibus*

Legibus Angliæ, and was afterwards made *Justitiarius Angliæ*

To those Justices, was afterwards committed the Conuzance of all Civil and Criminal Pleas happening within their Divisions, and likewise Pleas of the Crown, Pleas touching Liberties, and the King's Rights; and the better to acquaint them with their Business, there were certain Assises which were first enacted at *Clarendon*, and afterwards confirmed at *Northampton*; they were not much unlike the *Capitula Itineris* mentioned in our old *Magna Charta*, but not so perfect, and are set down by *Hoveden*, *Ubi supra*, and are too long to be here inserted: I shall only take Notice of this one, *viz.* Establishing Descents, because I shall hereafter have Occasion to use it, *Si quis obierit Francus Tenens hæredes ipsius remaneant in talem Seisina qualem Pater suus, &c*

* But besides those Courts in *Eyre*, there were two great standing Courts, *viz.* The *Exchequer*, and the Court of *Queen's-Bench*, *Vel Curiam coram ipso Rege, vel ejus Justiciario*; and it was provided by the above-mentioned *Assisa*, *Quod Justiciæ faciant omnes Justicias & Rectitudines, Spectantes ad Dominium Regis, & ad Coronam suam, per breve Domini Regis vel illorum qui in ejus Loco erunt de Feodo dimidii Militis & infra, Nisi tam grandis sit quærela quod non possit deduci sine Domino Rege vel talis quam Justiciæ ei reponunt pro dubitatione sua, vel ad illos qui in Loco ejus erunt, &c.*

Neither do I find any distinct Mention of the Court of *Common Bench* in the Time of

I

* *Note, Notwithstanding what our Author here writes, it appears by Glanville and others, That the Common-Pleas was then also in being, and Magna Charta has only fix'd thatCourt to a certain Place which before was moveable and uncertain.*

this

this King, tho' in the Time of King *John*
there is often Mention made thereof, and
the Rolls of that Court of King *John*'s Time
are yet extant upon Record, *& vide poſt.
ſub Richardi Primi*

Limita-
tion.
　　The Limitation of the Aſſiſe of *Novel Diſ-
ſeiſin*, is by thoſe Aſſiſes appointed to be,
*a tempore quo Dominus Rex venit in Angliam
proximam poſt Pacis factam inter ipſum, & Regem filium ſuum.*

Juſtices
itinerant.
　　The ſame King afterwards, in the Twenty
fifth Year of his Reign, divided the Limits
of his *Itinerant Juſtices* into Four Circuits or
Diviſions, and to each Circuit aſſigned a
greater Number of Juſtices, *viz.* Five at
leaſt, which are thus ſet down in *Hoveden,
Folio* 337. *viz.*

Anno 1179. 25 H 2. *Magno Concilio cele-
brato apud Windeſhores, Communi Conſilio Archie-
piſcoporum Comitum & Baronum & coram Rege
Filio ſuo, Rex diviſit Angliam in quatuor Partes,
& unicuique partium præfecit viros ſapientes
ad ficiendum Juſtitiam in Terra ſua in hunc
Modum*

　1. *Ricardus Epiſcopus Winton, Ricardus The-
ſaurarius Regis, Nicholaus filius Turoldi, Thomas Baſſet & Robertus de Whitefield*, for the
Counties of *Southampton, Wilts, Glouceſter,
Somerſet, Devon, Cornwall, Berks* and *Oxon*
　2 *Galfridus Elienſis Epiſcopus, Nicholaus Capellanus Regis, Gilbertus Pipard, Reginald de
Wiſebeck Capellanus Regis & Gaulfridus Hoſce*,
for the Counties of *Cambridge, Huntingdon,*
Nor-

3

Northampton, Leicester, Warwick, Winchester, Hereford, Stafford and *Salop*

3 *Johannes Episcopus Norwcensis, Hugo Murdac Clericus Regis, Michael Bellet, Richardus de le Pec, & Radulphus Brito,* for *Norfolk, Suffolk, Essex, Hartford, Middlesex, Kent, Surrey, Sussex, Bucks* and *Bedford.*

4 *Galfredus de Luci, Johannes Comyn, Hugo de Gaerst, Radulphus de Glanvilla, W de Bendings, Alanus de Furnellis,* for the Counties of *Nottingham, Derby, York, Northumberland, Westmerland, Cumberland,* and *Lancaster.*

Isti sunt Justiciæ in Curia Regis constituti ad audiendum clamores Populi.

This Prince did these Three notable Things, *viz*

First, By this Means, he improved and perfected the Laws of *England,* and doubtless transferred over many of the *English* Laws into *Normandy,* which, as before is observed, caused that great Suitableness between their Laws and ours; so that the Similitude did arise much more by a Conformation of their Laws to those of *England,* than by any Conformation of the *English* Laws to theirs, especially in the Reigns of King *Hen.* II. and his Two Sons, King *Richard,* and King *John,* both of whom were also Dukes of *Normandy.* _{He improv'd the Laws.}

Secondly, He check'd the Pride and Insolence of the *Pope* and the *Clergy,* by those Constitutions made in a Parliament at *Clarendon,* whereby he restrained the Exorbitant _{Check'd the Pope}

L Power

Power of the Ecclesiasticks, and the Exemption they claimed from Secular Jurisdiction. And,

Conquered *Ireland* *Thirdly*, He subdued and conquered *Ireland*, and added it to the Crown of *England*, which Conquest was begun by *Richard* Earl of *Strigule* or *Strongbow*, 14 H 2 But was perfected by the King himself in the Seventeenth Year of his Reign, and for the greater Solemnity of the Business, was ratified by the Fealties of the Bishops and Nobles of *Ireland*, and by a *Bull* of Confirmation from *Pope Alexander*, who was willing to interest himself in that Business, to ingratiate himself with the King, and to gain a Pretence for that arrogant Usurpation of disposing of Temporal Dominions. *Vide Hoveder*, *Anno* 14 H 2

K. R ch I *Richard* I eldest Son of King *Henry* II succeeded his Father. I have seen little of Record touching the Juridical Proceedings, either of him, or his said Father, other than what occurs in the *Pipe-Rolls* in the *Excheqrer*, which both in the Time of *Hen* II *Rich* I and King *John*, and all the succeeding Kings, are fairly preserved; and the best Remembrances that we have of this King's Reign, in relation to the Law, are what *Roger Hoveden's Annals* have delivered down to us, *viz.*

His Naval Laws, &c *First*, He instituted a Body of Naval Laws in his Return from the *Holy Land*, in the Island of *Oleron*, which are yet extant with some Additions, *De quibus*, *Vide* Mr. *Selden's Mare Clausum*, *Lib* 2 *cap.* 24. and I suppose
they

they are the fame which are attributed to him by *Mrt Parts, Anno* 1196 and he conftituted Juftices to put them in Execution

Secondly, He obferved the fame Method of diftributing Juftice as his Father had begun, by Juftices *Itinerant per fingulos Angliæ Comitatus,* to whom he delivered two Kinds of Extracts or Articles of Inquiry, *viz Capitula Coronæ,* much reformed and augmented from what they were before, and *Capituli de Judæis,* the whole may be read in *Hoveden, fo* 423 *fub Anno* 5 R 1 and by thofe Articles it appears, That at that Time there was a fettled Court for the *Common-Pleas,* as well as for the *Queen's-Bench,* tho' it feems that Pleas of Land were then indifferently held in either, as appears by the firft and fecond Articles thereof, where we have, *Placita per breve Domini Regis, vel per breve Capitalis Jufticiæ, vel a Capitali Curia Regis coram eis (Jufticiis) miffa:* The former whereof feems to be the *Common Pleas,* which held Pleas by Original Writ, which Writ was under the King's Tefte when he was in *England,* but when he was beyond the Seas, it was under the Tefte of the *Jufticiarius Angliæ,* as the *Cuftos Regni* in the King's Abfence.

The Power which the Juftices *Itinerant* had to hold Plea in Writs of Right, or the Grand Affize, was fometimes limited, as here by the *Articuli Coronæ* under *Hen.* II to half a Knight's Fee, or under For here in thefe Articles it is, *De Magnis Affifs quæ funt de*

Articles of Juftices Itinerant

J 2   *centum*

centum Solidis & infra But in the next Commiffions, Inftructions, or *Capitula Coronæ*, it is, *De Magnis Affifis ufque ad Decem Libratas Terre & infra.*

Weights and Meafures

In his Eighth Year, he eftablifhed a Common Rule for *Weights and Meafures* throughout *England*, called *Affifa de Menfuris*, wherein we find the Meafure of Woollen Cloths was then the fame with that of *Magna Charta*, 9 H 3. VIZ. *De duobus ulnis infra Lifuras*

In the Year before his Death, the like Juftices Errant went through many Counties of *England*, to whom Articles, or *Capitula placitorum Coronæ*, not much unlike the former were delivered *Vide Hoveden, fub Anno* 1198 *fo* 445.

And in the fame Year, he iffued Commiffions in the *Trent, Hugh de Neville* being Chief Juftice, and to thofe were alfo delivered Articles of Inquiry, commonly called *Affifæ de Forefta*, which may be read at large in *Hoveden, fub eodem Anno.* Thefe gave great Difcontent to the Kingdom, for both the Laws of the Foreft, and their Execution were rigorous and grievous

K John.

King *John* fucceeded his faid Brother, both in the Kingdom of *England*, and Dutchy of *Normandy*; the Evidence that we have, touching the Progrefs of the Laws of his Time, are principally Three, *viz First*, His Charters of Liberties. 2*dly*, The Records of Pleadings and Proceedings in his Courts; And 3*dly*, The Courfe he took for fettling the *English* Laws in *Ireland*.

1. Touch-

1 Touching the fiift of thefe, his Charters of the Liberties of *England*, and of the *Foreft*, were hardly, and with Difficulty, gained by his Baronage at *Stanes*, *Anno Dom* 1215 The Collection of the former was, as *Mat. Paris* tells us, upon the View of the Charter or Laws of King *Hen* I. which fays, he contained *quafdam Libertates & Leges a Rege Edvardo Sancto, Ecclefiæ & Magnatibus concefsas, exceptis quibufdam Libertatibus quas idem Rex de fuo adjecit*; and that thereupon the Baronage fell into a Refolution to have thofe Laws granted by King *John*. But as it is certain, that the Laws added by King *Hen* I. to thofe of the *Confeffor* were many more, and much differing from his; fo the Laws contained in the Great Charter of King *John*, differed much from thofe of King *Hen* I. Neither are we to think, that the Charter of King *John* contained all the Laws of *England*, but only or principally fuch as were of a more comprehenfive Nature, and concerned the common Rights and Liberties of the Church, Baronage and Commonalty which were of the greateft Moment, and had been moft invaded by King *John*'s Father and Brother.

The leffer Charter, or *De Forefta*, was to reform the Exceffes and Encroachments which were made, efpecially in the Time of *Rich* I. and *Hen* II. who had made New Afforeftations, and much extended the Rigour of the Foreft Laws. And both thefe Charters do in Subftance agree with that

Magna

Magna Charta, & *de Foresta*, granted and confirm'd in 9 *Hen* 3 I shall not need to recite them, or to make any Collections or Inferences from them, they are both extant in the *Red Book* of the *Exchequer*, and in *Mat Paris*, *sub Anno* 1215 and the Record and the Historian do *Verbatim* agree

2

Records, &c.

As to the Second Evidence we have of the Progress of the Laws in King *John*'s Time, they are the Records of Pleadings and Proceedings which are still extant: But altho' this King endeavoured to bring the Law, and the Pleadings and Proceedings thereof, to some better Order than he found it, for saving his Profits whereof, he was very studious, and for the better Reduction of it into Order and Method, we find frequently in the Records of his Time, Fines imposed, *pro Stultiloquio*, which were no other than Mulcts imposed by the Court for barbarous and disorderly Pleading: From whence afterwards that Common Fine arose, *Pro pulchre placitando*, which was indeed no other than a Fine for want of it, and yet for all this, the Proceeding in his Courts were rude, imperfect, and defective, to what they were in the ensuing Times of *Edw* I &c But some few Observables I shall take Notice of upon the Perusal of the Judicial Records of the Time of King *John*, *viz*

His Courts, &c

1*st*, That the Courts of *King's-Bench* and *Common-Pleas* were then distinct Courts, and distinct-

diſtinctly held from the Beginning to the End
of King *John*'s Reign

2dly, That as yet, neither one nor both
of thoſe Courts diſpatch'd the Buſineſs of the
Kingdom, but a great Part thereof was diſpatch'd by the *Juſtices Itinerant*, which were
ſometimes in Uſe, but not without their Inter-
miſſions, and much of the Publick Buſineſs
was diſpatch'd in the County Courts, and in
other inferior Courts, and ſo it continued,
tho' with a gradual Decreaſe till the End of
King *Edw* I and for ſome Time after:
And hence it was, That in thoſe elder Times,
the Profits of thoſe County Courts for which
the Sheriff anſwered in his Farm, *de Proficuis
Comitatus*, alſo Fines were levied there, and
poſt Fines, and Fines *pro licentia concordandi*,
and great Fines there anſwered ; Fines *pro
Inquiſitionibus habendi*, Fines for Miſdemeanors,
tho' called Amerciaments, aroſe to great
Sums, as will appear to any who ſhall per-
uſe the ancient *Viſcontiels*

But, as I ſaid before, the Buſineſs of Inferior Courts grew gradually leſs and leſs,
and conſequently their Profits and Buſineſs
of any Moment came to the Great Courts,
where they were diſpatch'd with greater
Juſtice and Equality Beſides, the greater
Courts obſerving what Partiality and Bro-
cage was uſed in the Inferior Courts, gave a
pretty quick Ear to Writs of falſe Judgment,
which was the Appeal the Law allowed
from erroneous Judgments in the County
Courts; and this, by Degrees, waſted the
Credit and Buſineſs of thoſe inferior Courts

3dly,

3*dly*, That the Diſtinction between the *King's-Bench* and *Common-Bench*, as to the Point of *Communia placita*, was not yet, nor for ſome Time after, ſettled, and hence it is, that frequently in the Time of King *John*, we ſhall find that *Common Pleas* were held in B R yea, in *Mich* & *Hill* 13 *Johannis*, a Fine is levied *coram ipſo Rege*, between *Gilbert Fitz Roger* and *Helwiſe* his Wife, Plaintiffs, and *Robert Barpyard* Tenant of certain Lands in *Kirby*, &c.

And again, whereas there was frequently a Liberty granted anciently by the Kings of *England*, and allowed, *Quod non implacite-tur niſi coram Rege*; I find *inter Placita de diverſis Terminis ſecundo Johannis*, That upon a Suit between *Henry de Rachola*, and the Abbot of *Leiceſter* before the Juſtices *de Banco*, the Abbot pleaded the Charter of King *Richard* I. *Quod idem Abbas pro nullo reſpondeat niſi coram ipſo Rege vel Capitali Juſtitiario ſuo*, and it is ruled againſt the Abbot, *Quia omnia Placita quæ coram* Juſtic de Banco *tenentur, coram Domino Regi vel ejus Capitali Juſtitiario teneri intelliguntur* But this Point was afterwards ſettled by the Statute of *Magna Charta, Quod Communia placita non ſequantur Curiam noſtram*

4*thly*, That the four Terms were then held according as was uſed in After-times with little Variance, and had the ſame Denominations they ſtill retain

5*thly*, That there were oftentimes conſiderable Sums of Money, or Horſes, or other Things given to obtain Juſtice; ſometimes
'tis

'tis said to be, *pro habenda Inquisitione ut supra*, and *inter placita incerti temporis Regis Johannis*. The Men of *Yarmouth* against the Men of *Hastings* and *Winchelsea*, *Afferunt Domino Regi tres Palfridos, & sex Asturias Narenses ad Inquisitionem habendam per Legales*, &c. and frequently the same was done, and often accounted for in the *Pipe-Rolls*, under the Name of *Oblata*; and to remedy this Abuse, was the Provision made in King *John's* and King *Hen* III d's Charters, *Nulli Vendemus Justitiam vel Rectum*. But yet Fines upon Originals being certain, have continued to this Day, notwithstanding that Provision; but those enormous *Oblata* before-mentioned, are thereby remedied and taken away.

6thly, That in all the Time of King *John*, the Purgation *per Ignem & Aquam*, or the Trial by *Ordeal*, continued, as appears by frequent Entries upon the Rolls; but it seems to have ended with this King, for I do not find it in Use in any Time after · Perchance the Barbarousness of the Trial, and Perswasives of the Clergy, prevailed at length to antiquate it, for many Canons had been made against it.

7thly, In this King's Time, the Descent of Socage as well as Knight's Service Lands to the eldest Son prevailed in all Places, unless there were a special Custom, that the Lands were partible *inter Masculos*; and therefore, *Mich secundo Johannis*, in *a rationabili parte Bonorum*, by *Gilbert Beville* against *William Beville* his elder Brother for Lands in *Gunthorpe*, the Defendant pleaded,

Quod

Quod nunquam partita vel partibilia fuere; and becaufe the Defendant could not prove it, Judgment was given for the Demandant: And by degrees it prevail'd fo, that whereas at this Time the Averment came on the Part of the Heir at Law, that the Land *nunquam partita vel partibilis extetit*, in a little Time after the Averment was turn'd on the other Hand, *viz.* That tho' the Land was Socage, yet unlefs he did aver and prove that it was *partita & partibilis*, he failed in his Demand.

Thirdly, The third Inftance of the *Progrefs* of King *John*'s Reign, in relation to the Common Law, was his fettling the fame in *Ireland,* which he made his more immediate and particular Bufinefs: But hereof we fhall add a particular Chapter by it felf, when we have fhewn you what Proceedings and Progrefs was made therein in the Time of *Edw.* I. The many and great Troubles that fell upon King *John* and the whole Kingdom, efpecially towards the later End of his Reign, did much hinder the good Effect of fettling the Laws of *England,* and confequently the Peace thereof, which might have been bottom'd, efpecially upon the *Great Charter* But this Unfortunate Prince and Kingdom were fo intangled with inteftine Wars, and with the Invafion of the *French,* who affifted the *Englifh* Barons againft their King, and by the Advantages and Ufurpations that the *Pope* and the *Clergy* made

made by thofe Diftempers, that all ended
in a Confufion with the King's Death

I come therefore to the long and trouble- **K** *Hen* **III.**
fome Reign of *Hen* III who was about
Nine Years old at his Father's Death, he
being born *in Fefto fancti Rem gii*, 1207 and
King *John* died *in Fefto fancti Lucæ*, 1216. Hiftory
and the young King was crowned the 28th of his
of *October*, being then in the Tenth Year of Charters
his Age, and was under the Tutelage of
William Earl Marfhal

The *Nobility* were quick and earneft, not-
withftanding his Minority, to have the Li-
berties and Laws of the Kingdom confirm'd,
and Preparatory thereto, in the Year 1223,
Writs iffued to the feveral Counties to inquire, by Twelve good and lawful Knights,
Quæ fuerunt Libertates in Anglia tempore Regni
Henrici avi fui, returnable *quindena Pafchæ*.
What Succefs thofe Inquifitions had, or what
Returns were made thereof, appears not.
But in the next Year following, the young
King ftanding in Need of a Supply of Money
from the Clergy and Laity, none would be
granted, unlefs the Liberties of the Kingdom were confirm'd as they were exprefs'd
and contain'd in the Two Charters of King
John, which the King accordingly granted
in his Parliament at *Weftminfter*, and they
were accordingly proclaimed, *Ita quod Chartæ*
utrorumque Regum in nulla inveniatur diffimiles,
Mat Paris, Anno 1224.

In the Year 1227 The King holding his
Parliament at *Oxford*, and being now of full
Age.

Age; by ill Advice caufes the Two Charters he had formerly granted to be cancell'd, *Hanc cccafionem prætenden quod Chartæ illæ conceffæ fueruut & Libertates fcriptæ & fignitæ dum ipfe erat fub Cuftodia nec fui Corporis aut fgill. aliqu m poteftatem habuit, unde viribus carere debuit, &c* Which Fact occafioned a great Difturbance in the Kingdom: And this Inconftancy in the King, was in Truth the Foundation of all his future Troubles, and yet was ineffectual to his End and Purpofe, for thofe Charters were not avoidable for the King's Nonage, and if there could have been any fuch Pretence, that alone would not avoid them, for they were Laws confirm'd in Parliament

But the Great Charter, and the Charter of the *Foreft*, did not expire fo; for in 1253, they were again fealed and publifhed. And becaufe after the Battle of *Evefham*, the King had wholly fubdued the Barons, and thereby a Jealoufie might grow, that he again meant to infringe it, in the Parliament at *Marlbridge, cap 5.* they are again confirm'd. And thus we have the great Settlement of the Laws and Liberties of the Kingdom eftablifhed in this King's Time: The Charters themfelves are not every Word the fame with thofe of King *John*, but they differ very little in Subftance.

This Great Charter, and *Charta de Forefta*, was the great Bafis upon which this Settlement of the *Englifh* Laws ftood in the Time of this King and his Son, there were alfo fome additional Laws of this King yet extant, which

which much polifhed the Common Law, *viz* The Statutes of *Merton* and *Marlbridge*, and fome others.

We have likewife Two other principal Monuments of the great Advance and Perfection that the *Englifh* Laws attained to under this King, *viz* The Tractate of *Bracton*, and thofe Records of Plea, as well in both Benches, as before the *Juftices Itinerant*, the Records whereof are ftill extant.

Touching the former, *viz.* *Bracton*'s Tractate, it yields us a great Evidence of the Growth of the Laws between the Times of *Henry* II and *Hen.* III. If we do but compare *Glanville*'s Book with that of *Bracton*, we fhall fee a very great Advance of the Law in the Writings of the later, over what they are in *Glanville*. It will be Needlefs to inftance Particulars; fome of the Writs and Procefs do indeed in Subftance agree, but the Proceedings are much more regular and fettled, as they are in *Bracton*, above what they are in *Glanville* The Book it felf in the Beginning feems to borrow its Method from the Civil Law; but the greateft part of the Subftance is either of the Courfe of Proceedings in the Law known to the Author, or of Refolutions and Decifions in the Courts of *King's-Bench* and *Common-Bench*, and before *Juftices Itinerant*, for now the inferior Courts began to be of little Ufe or Efteem

As to the Judicial Records of the Time of this King, they were grown to a much greater Degree of Perfection, and the Pleadings

Bracton's Treatife.

Records, Temp Hen III

dings more orderly, many of which are extant But the great Troubles, and the Civil Wars, that happened in his Time, gave a great Interruption to the legal Proceedings of Courts, they had a particular Commission and Judicatory for Matters happening in Time of War, stiled, *Placita de Tempore Turbationis*, wherein are many excellent Things They were made principally about the Battle of *Evesham*, and after it, and for settling of the Differences of this Kingdom, was the *Dictum*, or *Edictum de Kenelworth* made which is printed in the old *Magna Charta*

We have little extant of Resolutions in this King's Time, but what are either remembred by *Britton*, or some few broken and scattered Reports collected by *Fitzherbert* in his Abridgment There are also some few Sums or Constitutions relative to the Law, which tho' possibly not Acts of Parliament, yet have obtained in Use as such, as *De districtione Scaccarii*, *Statutum Pan. & Cervisiæ*, *Dies Communes in Banco*, *Statutum Hiberniæ*, *Stat. de Scaccario*, *Judicium Collistrigii*, and others

K Edw I We come now to the Time of *Edw.* I who is well stiled our *English Justinian*, for in his Time the Law *qua si per Saltum*, obtained a very great Perfection The Pleadings are short indeed, but excellently good and perspicuous And altho' for some Time some of those Imperfections and ancient inconvenient Rules obtain'd, as for Instance, in point of Descents where the middle Brother held

of

of the Eldeſt, and dying without Iſſue, the Lands deſcended to the Youngeſt, upon that old Rule in the Time of *Hen* II *Nemo poteſt eſſe Dominus & Hæres,* mentioned in *Glanville,* at leaſt if he had once received Homage, 13 *E.* 1. *Fitz Avowry* 225 Yet the Laws did never in any one Age receive ſo great and ſudden an Advancement, nay, I think I may ſafely ſay, all the Ages ſince his Time have not done ſo much in reference to the orderly ſettling and eſtabliſhing of the diſtributive Juſtice of this Kingdom, as he did within a ſhort Compaſs of the Thirty five Years of his Reign, eſpecially about the firſt Thirteen Years thereof

Indeed, many Penal Statutes and Proviſions, in relation to the Peace and good Government of the Kingdom, have been ſince made But as touching the Common Adminiſtration of Juſtice between Party and Party, and accommodating of the Rules, and of the Methods and Orders of Proceeding, he did the moſt, at leaſt of any King ſince *William* I and left the ſame as a fix'd and ſtable Rule and Order of Proceeding, very little differing from that which we now hold and practice, eſpecially as to the Subſtance and Principal Contexture thereof.

It would be the Buſineſs of a Volume to ſet down all the Particulars, and therefore I ſhall only give ſome ſhort Obſervations touching the ſame

Firſt,

1   *First*, He perfectly settled the Great Charter, and *Charta de Foresta*, not only by a Practice consonant to them in the Distribution of Law and Right, but also by that solemn Act passed 25 *E.* 1 and stiled *Confirmationes Chartarum*.

2   *Secondly*, He established and distributed the several Jurisdictions of Courts within their proper Bounds And because this Head has several Branches, I shall subdivide the same, *viz.*

1. He check'd the Incroachments and Insolencies of the *Pope* and the *Clergy*, by the Statute of *Carlisle*

2. He declared the Limits and Bounds of the Ecclesiastical Jurisdiction, by the Statute of *Circumspecte Agatis & Articuli Cleri* For *note*, Tho' this later Statute was not published till *Edw* II. yet was compiled in the Beginning of *Edw.* I.

3 He established the Limits of the Court of *Common-Pleas*, perfectly performing the Direction of *Magna Charta, Quod Communia placita non sequentur Curia nostra*, in relation to *B. R.* and in express Terms, extending it to the Court of *Exchequer* by the Statute of *Articuli super Chartas*, cap. 4 It is true, upon my first reading of the *Placita de Banco* of *Edw* I. I found very many Appeals of Death, of Rape, and of Robbery therein; and therefore I doubted, whether the same were not held at least by Writ in the *Common Pleas* Court: But upon better Inquiry, I found many of the Records before *Justices*

3

Itinerants were enter'd or fill'd up among the Records of the *Common-Pleas*, which might occasion that Mistake

4 He establish'd the Extent of the Jurisdiction of the Steward and Marshal *Vide Articuli supe, Chartas*, *cap.* 3. And,

5. He also settled the Bounds of Inferior Courts, not only of Counties, Hundreds, and Courts Baron, which he kept within their proper and narrow Bounds, for the Reasons given before, and so gradually the Common Justice of the Kingdom came to be administred by Men knowing in the Laws, and conversant in the Great Courts of *B R.* and *C B* and before *Justices Itinerant*; and also by that excellent Statute of *Westminster* 1 *cap* 35 he kept the Courts of Great Men within their Limits under several Penalties, wherein ordinarily very great Incroachments and Oppressions were exercised

The *Third* general Observation I make is, He did not only explain, but excellently enforc'd, *Magna Charta*, by the Statute *De Tallagio non concedendo*, 34 *E* 1

Fourthly, He provided against the Interruption of the Common Justice of the Kingdom, by Mandates under the Great Seal, or Privy Seal, by the Statute of *Articuli supe, Chartas*, *cap* 6 which, notwithstanding *Magna Charta*, had formerly been frequent in Use

Fifthly, He settled the Forms, Solemnities, and Efficacies of Fines, confining them to

M   the

the *Common-Pleas*, and to *Justices Itinerant*, and appointed the Place where they brought the Records after their Circuits, whereby one common Repository might be kept of Affurances of Lands; which he did by the Statute *De modo levandi Fines*, 18 E. 1.

6.   *Sixthly*, He settled that great and orderly Method for the Safety and Preservation of the Peace of the Kingdom, and surpreffing of Robberies, by the Statute of *Winton*.

7   *Seventhly*, He settled the Method of Tenures, to prevent Multiplicity of Penalties, which grew to a great Inconvenience, and remedied it by the Statute of *Quia Emptores Terrarum*, 18 E 1.

8   *Eighthly*, He settled a speedier Way for Recovery of Debts, not only for Merchants and Tradefmen, by the Statutes of *Acton, Burnel, & de Mercatoribus*, but also for other Perfons, by granting an Execution for a Moiety of the Lands by *Elegit*

9.   *Ninthly*, He made effectual Provision for Recovery of Advowfons and Prefentations to Churches, which was before infinitely lame and defective, by Statute *Weftminfter* 2. *cap.* 1.

10   *Tenthly*, He made that great Alteration in Eftates from what they were formerly, by Statute *Weftminfter* 2. *cap.* 1 whereby Eftates of Fee-Simple, conditional at Common Law, were turn'd into Eftates-Tail, not removable from the Iffue by the ordinary Methods of Alienation, and upon this Statute, and for the Qualifications hereof, are the Super-

                       structures

ftructures built of 4 *H* 7. *cap.* 32. 32 *H.* 8. *cap.* and 33 *H.* 8.

Eleventhly, He introduced quite a new 11 Method, both in the Laws of *Wales*, and in the Method of their Difpenfation, by the Statute of *Rutland*.

Twelfthly, In brief, partly by the Learn- 12. ing and Experience of his Judges, and part-ly by his own wife Interpofition, he filent-ly and without Noife abrogated many ill and inconvenient Ufages, both in his Courts of Juftice, and in the Country He recti-fied and fet in Order the Method of collect-ing his Revenue in the *Exchequer*, and re-moved obfolete and illeviable Parts thereof out of Charge; and by the Statutes of *Weftminfter* 1 and *Weftminfter* 2 *Gloucefter* and *Weftminfter* 3 and of *Articuli fuper Chartas*, he did remove almoft all that was either grievous or impractical out of the Law, and the Courfe of its Adminiftration, and fub-ftituted fuch apt, fhort, pithy, and effectual Remedies and Provifions, as by the Length of Time and Experience, had of their Con-venience, have ftood ever fince without any great Alteration, and are now as it were incorporated into, and become a Part of the Common Law it felf.

Upon the whole Matter, it appears, That the very Scheme, Mold and Model of the Common Law, efpecially in relation to the Adminiftration of the Common Juftice be-tween Party and Party, as it was highly rectified and fet in a much better Light and

Order

Order by this King than his Predeceffors left it to him, fo in a very great Meafure it has continued the fame in all fucceeding Ages to this Day; fo that the Mark or *Epocha* we are to take for the true Stating of the Law of *England*, *what it is*, is to be confidered, ftated and eftimated, from what it was when this King left it. Before his Time it was in a great Meafure rude and unpolifh'd, in comparifon of what it was after his Reduction thereof, and on the other Side, as it was thus polifhed and ordered by him, fo has it ftood hitherto without any great or confiderable Alteration, abating fome few Additions and Alterations which fucceeding Times have made, which for the moft part are in the fubject Matter of the Laws themfelves, and not fo much in the Rules, Methods, or Ways of its Adminiftration

As I before obferved fome of thofe many great Acceffions to the Perfection of the Law under this King, fo I fhall now observe fome of thofe Boxes or Repofitories where they may be found, which are of the following Kinds, *viz*

Repofitories of the Law

1   *Firft*, The Acts of Parliament in the Time of this King are full of excellent Wifdom and Perfpicuity, yet Brevity; but of this, enough before is faid.

2   *Secondly*, The Judicial Records in the Time of this King. I fhall not mention thofe of the *Chancery*, the Clofe-Patent and Charter Rolls, which yet will very much evidence the

the Learning and Judgment of that Time, but I fhall mention the Rolls of Judicial Proceedings, efpecially thofe in the *King's-Bench* and *Common-Pleas*, and in the *Eyres*. I have read over many of them, and do generally obferve.

1. That they are written in an excellent Hand

2. That the Pleading is very fhort, but very clear and perfpicuous, and neither loofe or uncertain, nor perplexing the Matter either with Impropriety, Obfcurity, or Multiplicity of Words. They are clearly and orderly digefted, effectually reprefenting the Bufinefs that they intend

3. That the Title and the Reafon of the Law upon which they proceed (which many times is exprefly delivered upon the Record it felf) is perfpicuous, clear and rational; fo that their fhort and pithy Pleadings and Judgments do far better render the Senfe of the Bufinefs, and the Reafons thereof, than thofe long, intricate, perplexed, and formal Pleadings, that oftentimes of late are unneceffarily ufed.

Thirdly, The Reports of the Terms and Years of this Kings Time, a few broken Cafes whereof are in *Fitzherbert's* Abridgment, but we have no fucceffive Terms or Years thereof, but only ancient Manufcripts perchance, not running through the whole Time of this King, yet they are very good, but very brief Either the Judges then fpoke lefs, or the Reporters were not fo ready handed as to take all they faid And hence

M

this Brevity makes them the more obscure. But yet in those brief Interlocutions between the Judge and the Pleaders, and in their Definitions, there appears a great deal of Learning and Judgment. Some of those Reports, tho' broken, yet the best of their Kind, are in *Lincolns-Inn* Library. *Quære, if those Reports are not now published.*

4 *Fourthly,* The Tracts written or collected in the Time of this wise and excellent Prince, which seem to be of Two Kinds, *viz.* such as were only the Tractates of private Men, and therefore had no greater Authority than private Collections, yet contain much of the Law then in Use, as *Fleta* the Mirror, *Britton* and *Thornton*; or else, 2*dly*, They were Sums or Abstracts of some particular Parts of the Law, as *Novæ Narrationes, Hengam Magna & Parva, Cadit assisa Summa, De Bastardia Summa*; by all which, compared even with *Bracton*, there appears a Growth and a Perfecting of the Law into a greater Regularity and Order.

And thus much shall serve for the several Periods or Growth of the Common Law untill the Time of *Edw.* I inclusively, wherein having been somewhat prolix, I shall be the briefer in what follows, especially seeing that from this Time downwards, the Books and Reports printed give a full Account of the ensuing Progress of the Law.

C H A P.

C H A P. VIII.

A Brief Continuation of the Progress of the
Laws, from the Time of King Edward II.
inclusive, down to these Times.

HAving in the former Chapter been somewhat large in Discoursing of the Progress of the Laws, and the incidental Additions they received in the several Reigns of
King *William* II King *Hen.* I King *Stephen,*
King *Hen* II. King *Richard* I. King *John,*
King *Hen.* III. and King *Edw.* I. I shall
now proceed to give a brief Account of the
Progress thereof in the Time of *Edw.* II.
and the succeeding Reigns, down to these
Times.

Edward II. succeeding his Father, tho' he   K. *Ed* II.
was an Unfortunate Prince, and by reason
of the Troubles and Unevenness of his
Reign, the very Law it self had many In-
terruptions, yet it held its Current in a great
Measure according to that Frame and State
that his Father had left it in

Besides the Records of Judicial Proceedings in his Time, many whereof are still
extant, there were some other Things that
occurr'd in his Reign which give us some
kind of Indication of the State and Condition of the Law during that Reign: As,

First,

1   *First*, The Statutes made in his Time, and especially that of 7 E. 2. stiled *De Prærogativa Regis*, which tho' it be called a Statute, yet for the most part is but a Sum or Collection of certain of the King's Prerogatives that were known Law long before; as for Instance, The King's Wardship of Lands *in Capite* attracting the Wardship of Lands held of others, The King's Grant of a Manor not carrying an Advowson Appendant unless named; The King's Title to the Escheat of the Lands of the *Normans*, which was in Use from the first Defection of *Normandy*, under King *John*, The King's Title to Wreck, Royal Fish, Treasure-Trove, and many others, which were ancient Prerogatives to the Crown

2   *Secondly*, The Reports of the Years and Terms of this King's Reign, these are not printed in any one entire Volume, or in any Series or Order of Time, only some broken Cases thereof in *Fitzherbert's* Abridgment, and in some other Books dispersedly, yet there are many entire Copies thereof abroad very excellently reported, wherein are many Resolutions agreeing with those of *Edw* I.'s Time. The best Copy of these Reports that I know now extant, is that in *Lincolns-Inn Library*, which gives a fair Specimen of the Learning of the Pleaders and Judges of that Time. *Quære*, If Maynard's *Edw*. II. was not printed from that Copy.

Edw. II   King *Edw* III. succeeded his Father, his Reign was long, and under it the Law was improved to the greatest Height. The Judges

and Pleaders were very learned · The Pleadings are fomewhat more polifhed than thofe
in the Time of *Edw* I yet they have neither
Uncertainty, Prolixity, nor Obfcurity They
were plain and skilful, and in the Rules of
Law, efpecially in relation to real Actions,
and Titles of Inheritance, very learned and
excellently polifhed, and exceeded thofe
of the Time of *Edw* I So that at the latter
End of this King's Reign the Laws feemed
to be near its *Meridian*

The Reports of this King's Time run
from the Beginning to the End of his
Reign, excepting fome few Years between
the 10th and 17th, and 30th and 33d Years
of his Reign, but thofe Omitted Years are
extant in many Hands in old Manufcripts.
And *Quære, If they are not all printed in* Maynard's *Edw*. III

The Book of Affizes is a Collection of
the Affizes that happened in the Time of
Edw III being from the Beginning to the
End extracted out of the Books and Affizes
of thofe that attended the Affizes in the
Country

The *Juftices Itinerant* continued by intermit-
ting Viciffitudes till about the 4th of *Edw* 3
and fome till the 10th of *Edw* 3 Then Jurifdiction extended to Pleas of the Crown,
or Criminal Caufes, Civil Suits and Pleas of
Liberties, and *Quo Warrantos*, the Reports
thereof are not printed, but are in many
Hands in Manufcript, both of the Times of
Edw I *Edw* II and *Edw* III full of excellent Learning Some few broken Reports of
thofe

those *Eyres*, especially of *Cornwall, Nottingham, Northampton,* and *Derby*, are collected by *Fitzherbert* in his Abridgment.

After the 10th of *Edw.* III. I do not find any Justices Errant *ad Communia Placita,* but only *ad Placita Forestæ* ; other Things that concerned those *Justices Itinerant* were supplied and transacted in the *Common Bench,* for *Communia placita,* in the *King's-Bench* and *Exchequer* for *Placita de Libertatibus,* and before Justices of Assize, *Nisi prius, Oyer* and *Terminer,* and Goal Delivery for Assises and Pleas of the Crown

And thus much for the Law in the Time of *Edw.* III.

E. Rich II.   *Richard* II succeeding his Grandfather, the Dignity of the Law, together with the Honour of the Kingdom, by reason of the Weakness of this Prince, and the Difficulties occurring in his Government, seem'd somewhat to decline, as may appear by comparing the Twelve last Years of *Edw.* III. commonly called *Quadragesms,* with the Reports of King *Richard* II. wherein appears a visible Declination of the Learning and Depth of the Judges and Pleaders

It is true, we have no printed continued Report of this King's Reign , but I have seen the entire Years and Terms thereof in a Manuscript, out of which, or some other Copy thereof, I suppose *Fitzherbert* abstracted those broken Cases of this Reign in his Abridgment.

In

In all those former Times, especially from the End of *Edw* III. back to the Beginning of *Edw* I the Learning of the Common Law consisted principally in Assizes and real Actions; and rarely was any Title dermined in any personal Action, unless in Cases of Titles to Rents, or Services by Replevin; and the Reasons thereof were principally these, *viz*

First, Because these ancient Times were great Favourers of the Possessor, and therefore if about the Time of *Edw* II a Disseisor had been in Possession by a Year and a Day, he was not to be put out without a Recovery by Assize. Again, If the Disseisor had made a Feoffment, they did not countenance an Entry upon the Feoffee, because thereby he might lose his Warranty, which he might save if he were Impleaded in an Assize or Writ of Entry; and by this Means real Actions were frequent, and also Assizes

Secondly, They were willing to quiet Men's Possessions, and therefore after a Recovery or Bar in an Assize or real Action, the Party was driven to an Action of a higher Nature

Thirdly, Because there was then no known Action wherein a Person could recover his Possession, other than by an Assize or a real Action, for till the End of *Edw*. IV. the Possession was not recovered in an *Ejectione firmæ*, but only Damages.

Fourthly, Because an Assize was a speedy and effectual Remedy to recover a Possession,

fion, the Jury being ready Impannell'd,
and at the Bar the firſt Day of the Return.
And altho' by Diſuſage, the Practiſers of the
Law are not ſo ready in it, yet the Courſe
thereof in thoſe Times was as ready and
as well known to all Profeſſors of the Law
as the Courſe of *Ejectione firmæ* is now.

K Hen IV   Touching the Reports of the Years and
K Hen V   Terms of *Hen* IV and *Hen* V I can only
ſay, They do not arrive either in the Nature of the Learning contained in them, or
in the Judiciouſneſs and Knowledge of the
Judges and Pleaders, nor in any other Reſpect ariſe to the Perfection of the laſt
Twelve Years of *Edw* III.

K Hen VI   But the Times of *Hen* VI. as alſo of
K Ed IV   *Edw* IV. *Edw* V and *Hen* VII were
K Ed V   Times that abounded with learned and ex-
and
K Hen VII cellent Men There is little Odds in the
Uſefulneſs or Learning of theſe Books, on-
ly the firſt Part of *Hen* VI is more barren,
ſpending it ſelf much in Learning of little
Moment, and now out of Uſe, but the ſe-
cond Part is full of excellent Learning

In the Times of thoſe Three Kings, *Hen* VI.
Edw IV and *Hen* VII the Learning ſeems
to be much alike But theſe two Things
are obſervable in them, and indeed generally in all Reports after the Time of
Edw. III *viz.*

Firſt, That real Actions and Aſſizes were
not ſo frequent as formerly, but many
Titles of Land were determined in perſo-

nal Actions; and the Reasons hereof seem to be,

1st, Because the Learning of them began by little and little to be less kown or underftood.

2dly, The ancient Strictnefs of preferving Poffeffions to Poffeffors till Eviction by Action began not to be fo much in Ufe, unlefs in Cafes of Difcents and Difcontinuances, the latter neceffarily drove the Demandant to his *Formedon*, or his *Cui in Vita*, &c. But the Defcents that toll'd Entry were rare, becaufe Men preferved their Rights to enter, &c by continual Claims

3dly, Becaufe the Statute of 8 *H* 6. had helped Men to an Action to recover their Poffeffions by a Writ of Forcible Entry, even while the Method of Recovery of Poffeffions by Ejectments was not known or ufed.

The *Second* Thing obfervable is, That tho' Pleadings in the Times of thofe Kings were far fhorter than afterwards, efpecially after *Hen* VIII yet they were much longer than in the Time of King *Edw*. III and the Pleaders, yea and the Judges too, became fomewhat too curious therein, fo that that Art or Dexterity of Pleading, which in its Ufe, Nature and Defign, was only to render the Fact plain and intelligible, and to bring the Matter to Judgment with a convenient Certainty, began to degenerate from its primitive Simplicity, and the true Ufe and End thereof, and to become a Pice of Nicety and Curiofity, which how thefe later Times have improved, the Length of the Pleadings, the many and unneceffary Repetitions,

the

the many Miscarriages of Causes upon small and trivial Niceties in Pleading, have too much witnessed.

I should now say something touching the Times since *Hen* VII to this Day, and therefore shall conclude this Chapter with some general Observations touching the Proceedings of Law in these later Times.

And First I shall begin where I left before, touching the Length and Nicety of Pleadings, which at this Day far exceeds not only that short yet perspicuous Course of Pleading which was in the Time of *Hen* VI. *Edw.* IV. and *Hen.* VII. but those of all Times whatsoever, as our vast Presses of Parchment for any one Plea do abundantly witness

And the Reasons thereof seem to be these, *viz.*

First, Because in ancient Times the Pleadings were drawn at the Bar, and the Exceptions (also) taken at the Bar, which were rarely taken for the Pleasure or Curiosity of the Pleader, but only when it was apparent that the Omission or the Matter excepted to was for the most part the very Merit and Life of the Cause, and purposely omitted or mispleaded because his Matter or Cause would bear no better : But now the Pleadings being first drawn in Writing, are drawn to an excessive Length, and with very much Labourousness and Care enlarged, lest it might afford an Exception not intended by the Pleader, and

I

which

which could be eafily fupplied from the Truth of the Cafe, left the other Party fhould catch that Advantage which commonly the adverfe Party ftudies, not in Contemplation of the Merits or Juftice of the Caufe, but to find a Slip to faften upon, tho' in Truth, either not material to the Merits of the Plea, or at leaft not to the Merits of the Caufe, if the Plea were in all Things conform to it

Secondly, Becaufe thofe Parts of Pleading which in ancient Times might perhaps be material, but at this Time are become only mere Styles and Forms, are ftill continued with much Religion, and fo all thofe ancient Forms at firft introduced for Convenience, but now not neceffary, or it may be antiquated as to their Ufe, are yet continued as Things wonderfully material, tho' they only fwell the Bulk, but contribute nothing to the Weight of the Plea.

Thirdly, Thefe Pleas being moftly drawn by Clerks, who are paid for Entries and Copies thereof, the larger the Pleadings are, the more Profits come to them, and the dearer the Clerk's Place is, the dearer he makes the Client pay

Fourthly, An Overforwardnefs in Courts to give Countenance to frivolous Exceptions, tho' they make nothing to the true Merits of the Caufe; whereby it often happens that Caufes are not determined according to their Merits, but do often mifcarry for inconfiderable Omiffions in Pleading.

But

2.   But, *Secondly*, I shall confider what is the Reafon that in the Time of *Edw* I one Term contained not above two or three Hundred Rolls, but at this Day one Term contains two Thoufand Rolls or more.

The Reafons whereof may be thefe, *viz.*

1*ft*, Many petty Bufineffes, as Trefpaffes and Debts under 40 *s* are now brought to *Weftmnfter*, which ufed to be difpatched in the County or Hundred Courts, and yet the Plaintiffs are not to be blamed, becaufe at this Day thofe Inferior Courts are fo ill ferved, and Juftice there fo ill adminiftred, that they were better feek it (where it may be had) at *Weftminfter*, tho' at fomewhat more Expence

2*dly*, Multitudes of Attornies practifing in the Great Courts at *Weftmrfter*, who are ready at every Market to gratifie the Spleen, Spight or Pride, of every Plaintiff.

3*dly*, A great Encreafe of People in this Kingdom above what they were anciently, which muft needs multiply Suits.

4*bly*, A great Encreafe of Trade and Trading Perfons, above what there were in ancient Times, which muft have the like Effect

5*bly*, Multitudes of new Laws, both Penal and others, all which breed new Queftions, and new Suits at Law, and in particular, the Statute touching the devifing of Lands, *cum multis aliis*

6*bly*, Multiplication of Actions upon the Cafe, which were rare formerly, and thereby

thereby Wager of Law ousted, which discouraged many Suits. For when Men were sure, that in case they rested upon a bare Contract without Specialty, the other Party might wage his Law, they would not rest upon such Contracts without reducing the Debt into a Specialty, if it were of any Value, which created much Certainty, and accorded many Suits.

And herewith I shall conclude this Chapter, shewing what Progress the Law has made, from the Reign of King *Edw*. I. down to these Times.

N   C H A P.

CHAP. IX.

*Concerning the ſettling of the Common Law
of* England *in* Ireland *and* Wales:
*And ſome Obſervations touching the Iſles
of* Man, Jerſey *and* Guernſey, *&c.*

Ireland THE Kingdom of *Ireland* being conquered by *Hen* II about the Year 1171.
He in his great Council at *Oxon,* conſtitu-
ted his younger Son, *John,* King thereof,
who proſecuted that Conqueſt ſo fully, that
he introduced the *Engliſh* Laws into that
Kingdom, and ſwore all the great Men
there to the Obſervation of the ſame, which
Laws were, after the Deceaſe of King *John,*
again reinforc'd by the Writ of King *Hen.* III
reciting that of King *John, Rot. Clauſ.*
10 *H* 3. *Memb* 8, & 10 *Vide infra,* &
Pryn 252, 253, *&c.*

And becauſe the Laws of *England* were
not ſo ſuddenly known there, Writs from
Time to Time iſſued from hence, containing
divers *Capitula Legum Angliæ,* and commanding their Obſervation in *Ireland,* as *Rot Parl*
11 *H* 3 the Law concerning Tenancy by
Curteſy, *Rot. Clauſ* 20 *H* 3 *Memb* 3 *Dorſo.*
The Law concerning the Preference of the
Son born after Marriage, to the Son born
of the ſame Woman before Marriage, or
Baſtard eigne & *Mulier puiſne, Rot Clauſ.*
20 *H.*

20 *H.* 3. *Memb* 4. *in Dorso* So the Law concerning all the Parceners inheriting without doing Homage, and several Transmissions of the like Nature

For tho' King *Hen* II had done as much to introduce the *English* Laws there, as the Nature of the Inhabitants or the Circumstances of the Times would permit; yet partly for want of Sheriffs, that Kingdom being then not divided into Counties, and partly by reason of the Instability of the *Irish*, he could not fully effect his Design: And therefore, King *John*, to supply those Defects as far as he was able, divided *Leinster* and *Munster* into the several Counties of *Dublin*, *Kildare*, *Meath*, *Uriel*, *Caterlogh*, *Kilkenny*, *Wexford*, *Waterford*, *Cork*, *Limerick*, *Tiperary*, and *Kerry*; and appointed Sheriffs and other Officers to govern 'em after the Manner of *England*; and likewise caused an Abstract of the *English* Laws under his Great Seal to be transmitted thither, and deposited in the *Exchequer* at *Dublin*: And soon after, in an *Irish* Parliament, by a general Consent, and at the Instance of the *Irish*, he ordain'd, That the *English* Laws and Customs should thenceforth be observed in *Ireland*, and in order to it, he sent his Judges thither, and erected Courts of Judicature at *Dublin*

Vide 4th Inst 149.

But notwithstanding these Precautions of King *John*, yet for that the *Brenon* Law, and other *Irish* Customs, gave more of Power to the great Men, and yet did not restrain the Common People to so strict and regular

N 2

a Difcipline as the Laws of *England* did. Therefore the very *Englifh* themfelves became corrupted by them, and the *Englifh* Laws foon became of little Ufe or Efteem, and were look'd upon by the *Irifh* and the degenerate *Englifh* as a Yoke of Bondage; fo that King *Hen* III was oftentimes neceffitated to revive 'em, and by feveral fucceffive Writs to enjoin the Obfervation of them. And in the Eleventh Year of his Reign he fent the following Writ, *viz.*

ᵉ Inft
141

N B. *This Writ is curtail'd by my Lord* Cook.

Henricus Rex, &c Baronibus Militibus & aliis libere Tenentibus Lageniæ, falutem, &c. Satis ut credimus veftra audivit difcretio, quod cum bonæ memoriæ Johannes, quondam Rex Angliæ Pater Nofter venit in Hiberniam, ipfe duxit fecum viros difcretos & Legis peritos, quorum Communi Confilio, & ad inftantiam Hibernienfium Statuit & præcepit Leges Anglicanas teneri in Hibernia, ita quod Leges eafdem in fcriptis readactas reliquit fub figillo fuo ad Scaccar. Dublin *Cum igitur Confuetudo & Lex Angliæ fuerit, quod fi aliquis defponfaverit aliquam Mulierem, five Viduam five aliam hæreditatem habentem, & ipfe poftmodum ex ea prolem fufcitaverit, cujus clamor auditus fuerit infra quatuor parietes idem Vir fi fupervixerit ipfam uxorem fuam, habebit tota vita fua Cuftodiam Hæreditatis uxoris fuæ, licet ea forte habuerit Hæredem de primo viro fuo qui fuerit* Plenæ *ætatis vobis Mandamus injungentes quatenus in loquela quæ eft in Curia Willi Com Mirefc inter Mauritium Fitz Gerold Petent. & Galfridum de Marifco Ju-*

Justiciarium nostrum Hiberniæ tenentem, vel in alia Loquela quæ fuerit in Casu prædicto nullo modo Justitiam in contrar' facere præsumatis

Teste Rege apud Westin 10 De-
cemb *Anno* 11° *Regni Nostri.*

And *Note*, In the same Year another Writ was sent to the Lord Justice, Commanding him to aid the Episcopal Excommunica-tions in *Ireland* with the Secular Arm, as in *England* was used.

And about this Time, *Hubert de Burgo,* the *Chief Justice of* England, and Earl of *Kent,* was made Earl of *Connaught,* and Lord Justice of *Ireland* during Life; and be-cause he could not Personally attend, he on *March* the 10th, 1227 appointed *Richard de Burgo* to be his Deputy, or Lord Justice, to whom the King sent the following Writ:

Rex dilecto & fideli suo Richardo de Burgo Justiciario suo Hiberniæ salutem. Mandamus vobis firmiter Præcipientes, quatenus certo die & loco faciatis venire coram vobis, Archiepiscopos Episcopos Abbates Priores Comites & Barones Milites & libere Tenentes & Ballivos Singulorum Comitatuum, & coram eis publice legi faciatis Chartam Domini Johannis Regis Patris nostri Cui sigillum suum appensum est, quam fieri fecit, & jurari a Magnatibus Hiberniæ de Legibus & consuetudinibus Anglorum Observandis in Hiber-nia, & Præcipiatis eis ex parte nostra, quod Leges illas & consuetudines in Charta prædicta conten-tas de cetero firmiter teneant & observent. Et

N 3 *hoc*

*Loc idem per fingulos Comitatus Hibernæ clamari
fciatis, & teneri prohiberies firmiter ex parte
noftra & forisfactum noftram, ne quis contra
hoc Mandatum noftrum, venire præfumt Eo
excepto quod rec de Morte nec de catalis hibernen-
fium accifor m nihil ferrant ex parte noftra citra
quindecim dies a Sancti Michælis, Anno Regni
Noftri, 12°. Super quo refpectum dedimus Mag-
nat noftri de Hib ufque ad Terminum prædict.
Tefte Meipfo apud Weftm 8° die Maii, Anno
Regni Noftri, 12°.*

And about the 20th Year of *Hen* III feveral Writs were fent into *Ireland*, efpecially
directing feveral Statutes which had been
made in *England* to be put in Ufe, and to
be obferved in *Ireland*, as the Statute of
Merton in the Cafe of Baftardy, &c.

But yet it feems by the frequent Grants
that were made afterwards to particular
Native *Irifh* Men, *Qud legibus utantur Anglicanis*, That the Native *Irifh* had not the full
Priviledge of the *Englifh* Laws, in relation
at leaft to the Liberties of *Englifh* Men, till
about the Third of *Edw* III *Vide Rot Clauf.
2 E 3 Memb* 17

As the Common Law of *England* was thus
by King *John* and *Hen* III introduced into
Ireland, fo in the Tenth of *Hen* VII all the
precedent Statutes of *England* were there
fettled by the Parliament of *Ireland*. 'Tis
true, many ancient *Irifh* Cuftoms continued
in *Ireland*, and do continue there even unto
this Day, but fuch as are contrary to the
Laws

Laws of *England* are difallowed, *Vide Davis's* Reports, the Cafe of *Tanistry.*

Wales

As touching *Wales,* That was not always the Feudal Territory of the Kingdom of *England,* but having been long governed by a Prince of their own, there were very many Laws and Cuftoms ufed in *Wales,* utterly ftrange to the Laws of *England,* the Principal whereof they attribute to their King *Howell Dha*

After King *Edw* I had fubdued *Wales,* and brought it immediately under his Dominion; He firft made a ftrict Inquifition, touching the *Welfh* Laws within their feveral *Commotes* and *Seigniores,* which Inquifitions are yet of Record After which, in the 12th of *Edw* I the Statute of *Rutland* was made, whereby the Adminiftration of Juftice in *Wales* was fettled in a Method very near to the Rule of the Law of *England* The Preamble of the faid Statute is notable, *viz.*

Edvardus Dei gratia Rex Angliæ Dominus Hibernia & Dux Acquitaniæ omnibus Fidelibus fuis de Terra fua de Snodon & de aliis terris fuis in Wallia Salutem in Domino Divina providentia quæ in fua Difpofitione non fallitur, inter alia fuæ Difpenfationis Munera, quibus nos & Regnum noftrum Angliæ decorari dignata eft, Terram Walliæ cum incolis fuis prius nobis juri Feodali fubjectam, tum fui gratia in proprietatis noftræ Dominium, obftaculis quibufcunque ceffantibus, totaliter & cum integritate convertit, &

N 4 *Coro-*

Coronæ Regni p ædicti tantum partem corporis ejusdem annexuit & univit Nos, &c.

According to the Method in that Statute prescribed, has the Method of Justice been hitherto administred in *Wales*, with such Alterations and Additions therein as have been made by the several subsequent Statutes of 27 and 34 H 8 *&c*

The *Isle of Man*

Touching the *Isle of Man* This was sometimes Parcel of the Kingdom of *Norway*, and governed by particular Laws and Customs of their own, tho' many of them hold Proportion, or bear some Analogy, to the Laws of *England*, and probably were at first and originally derived from hence; seeing the Kingdom of *Norway* as well as the *Isle of Man* have anciently been in Subjection to the Crown of *England* *Vide Leges Willi. Prim.,* in *Lambard's Saxon* Laws.

Berwick

Berwick was sometimes Parcel of *Scotland*, but was won by Conquest by King *Edw* I. and after that lost by King *Edw*. II and afterwards regained by *Edw*. III It was governed by the Laws of *Scotland*, and their own particular Customs, and not according to the Rules of the Common Law of *England*, further than as by Custom it is there admitted, as in *Liber Parliamenti,* 21 E. I. in the Case of *Moyne* and *Bartlemew*, *pro Dote* in *Berwick*, yet now by Charter, they send Burgesses to the Parliament of *England*

Jersey, Guernsey, &c.

Touching the *Islands* of *Jersey*, *Guernsey*, *Sark*, and *Alderney*, They were anciently a Part of the Dutchy of *Normandy*, and in that Right, the Kings of *England* held them till the Time of King *John*, but although King *John*, as is before shewn, was unjustly deprived of that Dutchy, yet he kept the *Islands*; and when after that, they were by Force taken from him, he by the like Force regained them, and they have ever since continued in the Possession of the Crown of *England*.

As to their Laws, they are not governed by the Laws of *England*, but by the Laws and Customs of *Normandy*. But not as they are at this Day; for since the actual Division and Separation of those *Islands* from that Dutchy, there have been several New Edicts and Laws made by the Kings of *France* which have much altered the old Law of *Normandy*, which Edicts and Laws bind not in those *Islands*, they having been ever since King *John*'s Time at least under the actual Allegiance of *England*

And hence it is, that tho there be late Collections of the Laws and Customs of *Normandy*, as *Terrien* and some others, yet they are not of any Authority in those *Islands*, for the Decision of Controversies, as the *Grand Coutumier* of *Normandy* is, which is (at least in the greatest part thereof) a Collection of the Laws of *Normandy* as they stood before the Disjoining of those *Islands* from the Dutchy, viz. before the Time of King *Hen* III tho' there be in that Collection some Edicts of the Kings of *France* which were made after that Disjunction; and

and thofe Laws, as I have fhewn before, tho'
in fome Things they agree with the Laws
of *England*, yet in many Things they differ,
and in fome are abfolutely repugnant.

And hence it is, that regularly Suits arifing
in thofe *Iflands* are not to be tried or determined in the King's Courts in *England*, but
are to be heard, tried, and determined in
thofe *Iflands*, either before the ordinary
Courts of *Jufts* there, or by the *Juftices
Itinerant* there, commiffioned under the
Great Seal of *England*, to determine Matters there arifing, and the Reafon is, becaufe their Courfe of Proceedings, and their
Laws, differ from the Courfe of Proceedings and the Laws of *England*.

And altho' it be true, that in ancient
Times, fince the Lofs of *Normandy*, fome
fcattering Inftances are of Pleas moved here
touching Things done in thofe *Iflands*, yet
the general fettled Rule has been to remit
them to thofe *Iflands*, to be tried and determined there by their Law; tho' at this
Day the Courts at *Weftminfter* hold Plea of
all tranfitory Actions wherefoever they arife,
for it cannot appear upon the Record where
they did arife

The 12 E 2 Rot 45 coram Rege, A great
Complaint was made by Petition, againft
the Deputy Governor of thofe *Iflands*, for
divers Oppreffions and Wrongs done there:
This Petition was by the Chancellor delivered into the Court of *B R.* to proceed
upon it, whereupon there were Pleadings
on both Sides, but becaufe it appeared to
be

be for Things done and transacted in the said *Islands*, Judgment was thus given *Et quia Negotium prædict' in Curia hic terminari non potest, eo quod Juratores Insulæ prædict' coram Justitiariis hic venire non possunt nec de Jure debent,. Nec aliqua Negotia infra Insula præd. Et a emergentia terminari non debent nisi secundum Consuet Insulæ Predictæ Ideo Recordum retro traditur Cancellario ut inde fiat Commissio Domini Regis ad Negotia prædicta in Insula prædicta audienda & Terminanda secundum Consuet. Insulæ prædictæ.*

And accordingly 14 *Junii*, 1565 upon a Report from the Attorney General, and Advice with the two Chief Justices, a general Direction was given by the Queen and her Council, That all Suits between the *Islanders*, or wherein one Party was an *Islander*, for Matters arising within the *Islands*, should be there heard and determined

But still this is to be taken with this Distinction and Limitation, *viz.* That where the Suit is immediately for the King, there the King may make his Suit in any of the Courts here, especially in the Court of *King's-Bench* For Instance, in *a Quære Impedit* brought by the King in *B R.* here for a Church in those *Islands*; so in a *Quo Warranto* for Liberties there, so a Demand of Redemption of Lands sold by the King's Tenant within a Year and a Day according to the Custom of *Normandy*; so in an Information for a Riot, or grand Contempt against a Governor deputed by the King. These and the like Suits have been main-
tained

tained by the King in his Court of *King's-Bench* here, tho' for Matter arifing within thofe *Iflands*: This appears, *Pafchæ* 16 E. 2 *coram Rege, Rot.* 82. *Mich* 18 E. 2. *Rot* 123, 124, 125 *& Paf.* 1 E. 3. *Rot.* 59.

And for the fame Reafon it is, that a Writ of *Habeas Corpus* lies into thofe *Iflands* for one Imprifoned there, for the King may demand, and muft have an Account of the Caufe of any of his Subjects Lofs of Liberty, and therefore a Return muft be made of this Writ, to give the Court an Account of the Caufe of Imprifonment; for no Liberty, whether of a *County Palatine*, or other, holds Place againft thofe *Brevia Mandatoria*, as that great Inftance of punifhing the Bifhop of *Durham* for refufing to execute a Writ of *Habeas Corpus* out of the *King's-bench*, 33 E. 1. makes evident

And as Pleas arifing in the *Iflands* regularly, ought not in the firft Inftance to be deduced into the Courts here, (except in King's Cafe;) fo neither ought they to be deduced into the King's Courts here in the fecond Inftance; and therefore if a Sentence or Judgment be given in the *Iflands*, the Party grieved thereby, may have his Appeal to the King and his Council to reverfe the fame if there be Caufe. And this was the Courfe of Relief in the Dutchy of *Normandy*, *viz* by Appeal to the Duke and his Council; and in the fame Manner, it is ftill obferved in the Cafe of erroneous Decrees or Sentences in thofe *Iflands*, *viz*. To Appeal to the King and his Council.   But

But the Errors in fuch Decrees or Sentences are not examined by Writ of Error in the *King's-Bench*, for thefe Reafons, *viz.*

1*ft*, Becaufe the Courts there, and thofe here, go not by the fame Rule, Method, or Order of Law:

And 2*dly*, Becaufe thofe *Iflands*, though they are Parcel of the Dominion of the Crown of *England*, yet they are not Parcel of the Realm of *England*, nor indeed ever were; but were anciently Parcel of the Dutchy of *Normandy*, and are thofe Remains thereof which the Power of the Crown and Kingdom of *France* have not been able to wreft from the Kingsof *England*.

Whoever defires to know further, touching the Hiftory, Laws, Cuftoms, Religion, and Priviledges of thefe *Iflands*, may perufe the Tract, entitled *An Account of the Ifle of Jerfey*, written by Mr *Philip Falle*, and publifhed in the Year, 1694.

CHAP

CHAP. X.

Concerning the Communication of the Laws of England *unto the Kingdom of* Scotland.

BEcause this Inquiry will be of Use, not only in it self, but also as a Parallel Discovery of the Transmission of the *English* Laws into *Scotland,* as before is shewn they were into *Normandy,* I shall in this Chapter pursue and solve these several Queries, *viz.*

1*st*, What Laws of *Scotland* hold a Congruity and Suitableness with those of *England.*

2*dly,* Whether these be a sufficient Ground for us to suppose, that that Similitude or Congruity began with a Conformation of their Laws to those of *England.* And,

3*dly,* What might be reasonably judged to be the Means or Reason of the Conformation of their Laws unto the Laws of *England.*

As to the *First* of these Inquiries; It is plain, beyond all Contradiction, that many of the Laws of *Scotland* hold a Congruity and Similitude, and many of them a perfect Identity with the Laws of *England,* at least

I   as

as the *Englifh* Laws ftood in the Times of *Hen.* II. *Ruhard* I. King *John, Henry* III. and *Edw* I. And altho' in *Scotland,* Ufe hath always been made of the Civil Law, in point of Direction or Guidance, where their Municipal Laws, either Cuftomary or Parliamentary failed; yet as to their particular Municipal Laws, we fhall find a Refemblance, Parity and Identity, in their Laws with the Laws of *England,* anciently in Ufe; and we need go no further for Evidence hereof, than the *Regiam Myeftatem,* a Book publifhed by Mr. *Skeen* in *Scotland.* It would be too long to Inftance in all the Points that might be pioduced, and therefore I fhall fingle out fome few, remitting the Reader for his further Satisfaction to the Book it felf.

Dower of the Wife to be the Third Part of her Husband's Lands of Inheritance; the Writ to recover the fame, the Means of Forfeiting thereof by Treafon or Felony of the Husband, or Adultery of the Wife; are in great Meafure conformable to the Laws of *England. Vide Reg.am Majeftatem,* Lib. 2. *cap* 16, 17 and *Quoniam Attachiamento, cap.* 85

The Exclufion of the Defcent to the elder Brother by his receiving Homage, which tho' now antiquated in *England,* was anciently received here for Law, as appears by *Glanville, Lib.* 7. *cap.* 1. and *Vide Regiam Majeftatem, Lib.* 2 *cap* 22.

The Exclufion of Daughters from Inheritances by a Son: The Defcent to all the Daugh-

Daughters in Coparcenary for want of Sons; the chief House allotted to the eldest Daughter upon this Partition, the Descent to the Collateral Heirs, for want of Lineal, &c. *Ibid. cap.* 24, 25, 26, 27, 28, 33, 34. But this is now altered in some Things *per Stat. Rob cap.* 3.

The full Age of Males 21, of Females 14, to be out of Ward in Socage 16 *Ibid. cap* 42.

That the Custody of Idiots belonged to the King, *Ibid. cap* 46

The Custody of Heirs in Socage belong to the next of Kin, to whom the Inheritance can't descend. *Vide Regiam Majest. cap.* 47.

The Son born before Marriage, or *Bastard eigne*, not to be legitimate by the Marriage after, nor was he hereditable by the ancient Laws of *Scotland*, though afterward altered in Use, as it seems, *Regiam Majest. cap.* 51.

The Confiscation of *Bona Usurariorum*, after their Death, conform to the old Law here used. *Ibid. cap.* 54. tho' now antiquated.

The Laws of Escheats, for want of Heirs, or upon Attainder. *Ibid. cap.* 55

The Acquital of Lands given in *Frank-Marriage*, till the fourth Degree be past, *Ibid. cap* 57.

Homage, the Manner of making it with the Persons, by, or to whom, as in *England, Ibid cap* 61, 62, 63, &c

The Relief of an Heir in Knights Service, of full Age, *Regiam Majestatem, cap.* 17.

3   The

The Preference of the Sister of the whole Blood, before the Sister of the half Blood *Quoniam Attachiamento, cap.* 89.

The single Value of the Marriage, and Forfeiture of the double Value, precisely agree with the Statute of *Marlbridge. Ibid. cap* 91.

The Forfeiture of the Lord's disparaging his Ward in Marriage, agrees with *Magna Charta,* and the Statute of *Marlbridge. Quoniam Attachiamento, cap.* 92.

The Preference of the Lord by Priority to the Custody of the Ward *Ibid. cap* 95.

The Punishment of the Ravisher of a Ward, by two Years Imprisonment, *&c.* as here. *Ibid cap* 90

The Jurisdiction of the Lord in *Infang-theof. Ibid cap* 100.

Goods confiscate, and Deodands, as here, *Liber De Modo tenendi Cur. Baron. cap.* 62, 63, 64

And the like of Waifs. *Ibid cap.* 65.

Widows, not to marry without Consent of the Lord, Statute *Meses* 2 *cap* 23

Wreck of the Sea, defined precisely as in the Statute *Westm.* 2. *Vide Ibid cap* 25

The Division of the Deceased's Goods, one Third to the Wife, another Third to the Children, and another to the Executor, *&c.* conformable to the ancient Law of *England,* and the Custom of the *North* to this Day *Lib* 2 *cap* 37

Also the Proceedings to recover Possessions, by *Mortdancester, Juris Utrum, Assise de Novel disseisin, &c.* The Writs and Process

O   are

are much the fame with thofe in *England*, and are directed according to *Glanville*, and the old Statutes in the Time of *Edw* I and *Hen* III *Vide Regiam Majeftat Lib.* 3. *cap* 27 to 36.

Many more Inftances might be given of many of the Municipal Laws of *Scotland*, either precifely the fame with thofe in *England*, or very near, and like to them. Though it is true, they have fome particular Laws that hold not that Conformity to ours, which were introduced either by Particular or Common Cuftoms, or by Acts of their Parliaments But, by what has been faid and inftanced in, it appears, That like as between the Laws of *England* and *Normandy*, fo alfo between the Laws of *England* and *Scotland*, there was anciently a great Similitude and Likenefs.

2. Inquiry   I come therefore to the *Second* Thing I propos'd to inquire into, *viz* what Evidence there is, That thofe Laws of *Scotland* were either defumed from the *Englifh* Laws, or from *England*, tranfmitted thither in fuch a manner, as that the Laws here in *England* were as it were the Original or prime Exemplar, out of which thofe parallel or fimilar Laws of *Scotland* were copied or tranfcribed into the Body of their Laws; and this appears evident on the following Reafons, *viz*

1   *Firft*, For that *Glanville* (which, as has been obferved, is the ancienteft Collection we have of *Englifh* Laws) feems to be even

tran-

tranfcribed in many entire *Capita* of the
Laws above-mentioned, and in fome others
wheie *Glanville* doubts, that Book doubts;
and where *Glanville* follows the Piactice of
the Laws then in Ufe, tho' altered in fucceeding Times, at leaft after the Reign of
Edw I there the *Regiam Majeftatem* does
accordingly, for Inftance, *viz*

Glanville, *Lib* 7. *cap* 1 determine, That
a Man can't give away part of the Lands
which he held by Hereditary Defcent unto
his Baftard, without the Confent of his
Heir, and that he may not give all his Purchafes from his eldeft Son, and this is alfo
declared to be the Law of *Scotland* accordingly, *Regiam Majeftatem*, *Lib* 2. *cap* 19,
20 Tho' fince *Glanville's* Time, the Law
has been altered in *England*

Alfo *Glanville*, *Lib* 7 *cap* 1. makes a
great Doubt, Whether the fecond Son, being enteoffed by the Father, and dies without Iffue, whether the Land fhall return to
to the Father, or defcend to his eldeft,
or to his youngeft Brother, and at laft gives
fuch a Decifion as we find almoft in the
fame Terms and Words recited in the Queftion and Decifions laid down in *Regiam
Majeft Lib. 2 cap 22*

Again, *Glanville*, *Lib* 7 *cap*. 1. makes it
a difficult Queftion in his Time, Whether
the eldeft Son dying in the Life-time of his
Father, having Iffue, the Nephew or the
youngeft Son fhall inherit, and gives the
Arguments *pro & contra* And *Regiam Ma-*

Q 2   *jeftatem,*

jeſtatem, cap. 33. ſeems to be even a Tran-ſcript thereof out of *Glanville.*

And further, the Tract concerning Aſ-ſiſes, and the Time of Limitation, the very Form of the Writs, and the Method of the Proceſs, and the Directions touching their Proceedings are but Tranſcripts of *Glan-ville,* as appears by comparing *Regiam Ma-jeſtatem, Lib 3 cap 36.* with *Glanville, Lib 13 cap 32* and the Collector of thoſe Laws of *Scotland* in all the before-mentioned Places, and divers others, quotes *Glanville* as the Pat-tern at leaſt of thoſe Laws

2 But *Secondly,* A ſecond Evidence is, be-cauſe many of the Laws which are men-tioned in the *Regiam Majeſtatem Quoniam Attachiamento,* and other Collections of the *Scotiſh* Laws, are in Truth very Tranſlations of ſeveral Statutes made in *England* in the Times of King *Hen* III and King *Edw.* I For Inſtance, the Statute of their King *Robert* I *cap* 1 touching Alienations to Re-ligious Men, is nothing elſe but an Enacting of the Statute of *Mortmain,* 13 *E* 1 *cap.* 13 The Law above-mentioned, touching the Diſparagement of Wards, is deſumed out of *Magna Charta, cap.* 6. and the Statute of *Merton cap* 6 So the Law above ſaid, againſt Raviſhers of Wards, is taken out of *Weſtm.* 2. *cap.* 35 So the ſaid Law of the double Va-lue of Marriage, is taken out of *Weſtm.* 1. *cap* 22. The Law concerning Wreck of the Sea, is but a Tranſcript out of *Weſtm.* 1 *cap* 4 and divers other Inſtances of like Nature might be given, whereby it may appear,

appear, that very many of thofe Laws in
Scotland which are a part of their *Corpus Juris*,
bear a Similitude to the Laws of *England*,
and were taken as it were out of thofe
Common or Statute Laws here, that obtain'd
in the Time of *Edw* I and before, but
efpecially fuch as were in Ufe or Enacted
in the Time of *Edw* I and the Laws of
England, relative to thofe Matters, were as
it were the Original and Exemplar from
whence thofe Similar or Parallel Laws of
Scotland were derived or borrowed.

Thirdly, I come now to confider the Third
Particular, *viz.* By what Means, or by what
Reafon this Similitude of Laws in *England*
and *Scotland* happened, or upon what Account, or how the Laws of *England* at leaft
in many Particulars, or *Capita Legum*, came
to be communicated unto *Scotland*, and they
feem to be principally thefe Two, *viz*
Firft, The Vicinity of that Kingdom to this
And *Secondly,* The Subjection of that Kingdom unto the Kings of *England*, at leaft for
fome confiderable Time

Touching the former of thefe ; *Firft,* It
is very well known, that *England* and *Scotland* made but one Ifland, divided not by
the Sea or any confiderable Arm thereof,
but only by the Interjacency of the River
Tweed, and fome Defert Ground, which
did not hinder any eafie common Accefs of
the People of the one Kingdom to the
other And by this Means, *Firft,* The Intercourfe of Commerce between that Kingdom and this was very frequent and ufual,

O 3   efpecially

especially in the *Northern* Counties, and this Intercourse of Commerce brought unto those of *Scotland* an Acquaintance and Familiarity with our *English* Laws and Customs, which in Process of Time were adopted and received gradually into *Scotland*

Again, *Secondly*, This Vicinity gave often Opportunities of transplanting of Persons of either Nation into the other, especially in those *Northern* Parts, and thereby the *English* transplanted and carried with them the Use of their Native Customs of *England*, and the *Scots* transplanted hither, became acquainted with our Customs, which by occasional Remigrations were gradually translated and became diffus'd and planted in *Scotland*, and it is well known, that upon this Account some of the Nobility and great Men of *Scotland* had Possessions here as well as there. The Earls of *Angus* were not only Noblemen of *Scotland*, but were also Barons of Parliament here, and sate in our *English* Parliaments, as appears by the Summons to Parliament, *Tempore Edwardi Tertii*

Again, *Thirdly*, The Kings of *Scotland* had Feodal Possessions here, for Instance, The Counties of *Cumberland*, *Northumberland* and *Westmerland*, were anciently held of the Crown of *England* by the Kings of *Scotland*, attended with several Vicissitudes and Changes until the Feast of St. *Michael*, 1237. at which Time *Alexander* King of *Scotland* finally released his Pretensions thereunto, as appears by the Deed thereof enter'd into the Red-Book of the *Exchequer*, and the Parliament

liament Book of 20 *E.* 1. and in Consideration thereof, *Hen.* III gave him the Lands
of *Penreth* and *Sowby, Habend' sibi Heredibus
suis Regibus Scotiæ,* and by Vertue of that
Special Limitation, they came to *John* the
eldest Son of the eldest Daughter of *Alexander* King of *Scotland*, together with that
Kingdom, but the Land of *Tindale*, and the
Manor of *Huntingdon*, which were likewise
given to him and his Heirs, but without
that Special Limitation, *Regibus Scotiæ*, fell
in Coparcenry, one Moiety thereof to the
said *John* King of *Scotland*, as the Issue of
the eldest Daughter, and the other Moiety
to *Hastings*, who was descended from the
younger Daughter of the said *Alexander*:
But those Possessions came again to the
Crown of *England* by the Forfeiture of King
John of *Scotland*, who through the Favour
of the King of *England* he had Restitution
of the Kingdom of *Scotland*, yet never had
Restitution of those Possessions he had in
England, and forfeited and lost by his levy-
ing War against the Kingdom of *England*
as aforesaid

And thus I have shewn, that the Vicinity of the Kingdoms of *England* and *Scotland*, and the Consequence thereof, *viz.*
Translations of Persons and Families, Intercourse of Trade and Commerce, and Possessions obtained by the Natives of each
Kingdom in the other, might be one
Means for Communicating our Laws to
them.

　　　　　　　　But

2 But *Secondly*, There was another Means far more effectual for that End, *viz.* The Superiority and Interest that the Kings of *England* obtain'd over the Crown and Kingdom of *Scotland*, whereby it is no Wonder that many of our *English* Laws were transplanted thither by the Power of the *English* Kings. This Interest, Dominion, or Superiority of the Kings of *England* in the Realm of *Scotland* may be considered these Two ways, *viz.* 1*st*, How it stood antecedently to the Reign of King *Edw* I And 2*dly*, How it stood in his Time

Touching the former of those, I shall not trouble my self with collecting Arguments or Authorities relating thereto, he that Desires to see the whole Story thereof, let him consult *Walsingham, sub Anno* 18 *Edw* I. as also *Rot Parl* 12 R 2. *Pars secunda*, N° 3 *Rot Clauf* 29 E. 1 *M.* 10. *Dorso*, and the Letter of the Nobility to the *Pope* asserting it *Ib. d*

And this might be one Means, whereby the Laws of *England* in elder Times might in some Measure be introduced into *Scotland*

But I rather come to the Times of King *Edw* I who was certainly the greatest refiner of the *English* Laws, and studiously endeavoured to enlarge the Dominions of of the Crown of *England*, so to extend and propagate the Laws of *England* into all Parts subject to his Dominion. This Prince, besides the ancient Claim he made to the Superiority of the Crown of *England* over

that

that of *Scotland*, did for many Years actually
enjoy that Superiority in its full Extent,
and the Occasion and Progress thereof was
thus, as it is related by *Walfingham*, and con-
fonantly to him appears by the Records of
those Times, *viz* King *Edw.* I. having
formerly received the Homage and Fealty of
Alexander King of *Scots*, as appears *Rot. Clauf.*
5 E 1. M 5 *Dorfo*, was taken to be *Superior Dominus Scotiæ Regni.*

Alexander dying, left *Margaret* his only
Daughter, and she dying without Issue,
about 18 E. 1. there fell a Controverfie
touching the Succeffion of the Crown of
Scotland, between the King of *Norway* claiming as Tenant by the Curtefy, *Robert de
Bruce* descended from the younger Daughter of *David* King of *Scots*, and *John de
Baliol* descended from the elder Daughter,
with divers other Competitors

All the Competitors submit their Claim
to the Decifion of *Edw.* I King of *England*
as *Superior Dominus Regni Scotiæ*, who thereupon pronounced his Sentence for *John de
Baliol*, and accordingly put him in Poffeffion of the Kingdom, and required and received his Homage.

The King of *England*, notwithstanding
this, kept still the Poffeffion, *& Infignia* of
his Superiority, his Court of *Kings-Bench*
fate actually at *Roxborough* in *Scotland, Mich.* 20,
21 *Edw* I *coram Rege*, and upon Complaint
of Injuries done by the said *John* King of
Scots, now reftor'd to his Kingdom, he fum-
moned him often to anfwer in his Courts,

Mich

Mich 21, 22 *Edw* I. *Northumb Scot.* He was summoned by the Sheriff of *Northumberland* to answer to *Walbist* in the King's Court, *Paf.* 21 E. 1 *coram Rege, Rot.* 34 He was in like manner summoned to answer *John Mazune* in the *King's-Bench* for an Injury done to him, and Judgment given against the King of *Scots*, and that Judgment executed

John King of *Scots*, being not contented with this Subjection, did in the 24th Year of King *Edw* I resign back his Homage to King *Edward*, and bade Defiance to him, wherefore King *Edw* I the same Year with a powerful Army entred *Scotland*, took the King of *Scots* Prisoner, and the greatest part of that Kingdom into his Possession, and appointed the Earl *Warren* to be *Custos Regni*, *Creffingham* to be his Treasurer, and *Ormsby* his Justice, and commanded his Judges of his Courts of *England* to issue the King of *England*'s Writs into *Scotland*.

And when in the 27th Year of his Reign, the *Pope*, instigated by the *French* King, interpos'd in the Behalf of the King of *Scotland*, he and his Nobility resolutely denied the *Pope*'s Intercession and Mediation

Thus the Kingdom of *Scotland* continued in an actual Subjection to the Crown of *England* for many Years, for *Rot Clauf.* 33 E 1. *Membr* 13 *Dorfo*, and *Rot Clauf.* 34 E 1. *Memb.* 3 *Dorfo*, several Provisions are made for the better ordering of the Government of *Scotland*.

What

What Proceedings there were herein in the Time of *Edw* II and what Capitulations and Stipulations were afterwards made by King *Edw.* III upon the Marriage of his Sister by *Robert de Bruce*, touching the Relaxation of the *Superius Dominium* of *Scotland*, is not pertinent to what I aim at, which is, to shew how the *English* Laws that were in Use and Force in the Time of *Edw* I obtained to be of Force in *Scotland*, which is but this, *viz*

King *Edward* I. having thus obtained the actual Superiority of the Crown of *Scotland*, from the beginning of his Reign until his 20th Year, and then placing *John de Baliol* in that Kingdom, and yet continuing his Superiority thereof, and keeping his Courts of Justice, and exercising Dominion and Jurisdiction by his Officers and Ministers in the very Bowels of that Kingdom, and afterwards upon the Defection of this King *John*, in the 24th of *Edw* I. taking the whole Kingdom into his actual Administration, and placing his own Judges and great Officers there, and commanding his Courts of *King's-Bench* (&c) here, to Issue their Process thither, and continuing in the actual Administration of the Government of that Kingdom during Life It is no Wonder that those Laws which obtained and were in Use in *England*, in and before the Time of this King, were in a great Measure translated thither; and possibly either by being enacted in that Kingdom, or at least for so long Time, put in Use and

and Practice there, many of the Laws in Use and Practice here in *England* were in his Time so rivetted and settled in that Kingdom, that 'tis no Wonder to find they were not shaken or altered by the liberal Concessions made afterwards by King *Edw.* III upon the Marriage of his Sister; but that they remain Part of the Municipal Laws of that Kingdom to this Day.

And that which renders it more evident, That this was one of the greatest Means of fixing and continuing the Laws of *England* in *Scotland*, is this, *viz* This very King *Edw* I. was not only a Martial and Victorious, but also a very Wise and Prudent Prince, and one that very well knew how to use a Victory, as well as obtain it: And therefore knew it was the best Means of keeping those Dominions he had powerfully obtain'd, by substituting and translating his own Laws into the Kingdom which he had thus subdued Thus he did upon his Conquest of *Wales*; and doubtless thus he did upon his Conquest of *Scotland*, and those Laws which we find there so nearly agreeing with the Laws of *England* used in his Time, especially the Statutes of *Westm* 1 and *Westm.* 2. are the Monuments and Footsteps of his Wisdom and Prudence.

And, as thus he was a most Wise Prince, and to secure his Acquests, introduced many other Laws of his Native Kingdom into *Scotland*; so he very well knew the Laws of *England* were excellent Laws fitted for the due Administration of Justice to the Constitution

ftitution of the Governed, and fitted for the Prefervation of the Peace of a Kingdom, and for the Security of a Government. And therefore he was ever folicitous, by all prudent and careful Means imaginable, to graft and plant the Laws of *England* in all Places where he might, having before-hand ufed all poffible Care and Induftry for Rectifying and Refining the *Englifh* Laws to their greateft Perfection.

Again, It feems very evident, that the Defign of King *Edw* I was by all Means poffible to unite the Kingdom of *Scotland* (as he had done the Principality of *Wales*) to the Crown of *England*, fo that thereby *Britain* might have been one entire Monarchy, including *Scotland* as well as *Wales* and *England* under the fame Sceptre; and in order to the accomplifhing thereof, there could not have been a better Means than to make the Intereft of *Scotland* one with *England*, and to knit 'em as it were together in one Communion, which could never have been better done than by eftablifhing one Common Law and Rule of Juftice and Commerce among them; and therefore he did, as Opportunity and Convenience ferved, tranflate over to that Kingdom as many of our *Englifh* Cuftoms and Laws as within that Compafs of Time he conveniently could.

And thus I have given an Effay of the Reafons and Means, how and why we find fo many Laws in *Scotland* parallel to thofe in *England*, and holding fo much of Congruity and Likenefs to them.

And

And the Reafon why we have but few of their Laws that correfpond with ours of a later Date than *Edw* I. or at leaft *Edw* II. is becaufe fince the Beginning of *Edw* III. that Kingdom has been diftinct, and held little Communion with us till the Union of the two Crowns in the Perfon of King *James* I (or *rather the happy Union of the two Kingdoms under her prefent Majefty Queen* Anne) and in fo great an Interval it muft needs be, that by the Intervention and Succeffion of new Laws, much of what was fo ancient as the Times of *Edw* I. and *Edw.* II have received many Alterations : So that it is a great Evidence of the excellency of our *Englifh* Laws, that there remain to this Day fo many of them in Force in that Part of *Great Britain* continuing to bear Witnefs, that once that excellent Prince *Edw* I. exercifed Dominion and Jurifdiction there

And thus far of the Communion of the Laws of *England* to *Scotland*, and of the Means whereby it was effected, from whence it may appear, That as in *Wales, Ireland* and *Normandy*, fo alfo in *Scotland*, fuch Laws which in thofe Places have a Congruity or Similitude with the Laws of *England*, were derived from the Laws of *England* as from their Fountain and Original, and were not derived fiom any of thofe Places to *England*.

I

C H A P.

CHAP. XI.

Touching the Course of Descents in
England.

AMong the many Preferences that the Excel-
Laws of *England* have above others, lency of
I shall single out Two particular Titles which our Laws.
are of Common Use, wherein their Prefe-
rence is very visible, and the due Consideration of their Excellence therein, may give us
a handsome Indication or Specimen of their
Excellencies above other Laws in other
Parts or Titles of the same also.

Those Titles, or *Capitula Legum*, which I
shall single out for this Purpose, are these Two In-
Two, *viz.* 1*st*, The hereditary Transmission stances
of Lands from Ancestor to Heir, and the
Certainty thereof. And 2*dly*, The Manner
of Trial by Jury, which as it stands at this
Day settled in *England*, together with the
Circumstances and Appendixes thereof, is
certainly the best Manner of Trial in the
World; and I shall herein give an Account
of the successive Progress of those *Capitula
Legis*, and what Growth they have had in
Succession of Time till they arriv'd to that
State and Perfection which they have now
obtain'd.

First then touching Descents and here- First, of
ditary Transmissions. It seems by the Laws Descents
of

of the *Greeks* and *Romans*, that the same Rule was held both in relation to Lands and Goods, where they were not otherwise disposed of by the Ancestor, which the *Romans* therefore called *Succeſſio ab inteſtato*, but the Customs of particular Countries, and especially here in *England*, do put a great Difference, and direct a several Method in the Transmiſſion of Goods or Chattels, and that of the Inheritances of Lands.

Now as to hereditary Transmiſſions or Succeſſions, commonly called with us *Deſcents*, I shall hold this Order in my Diſcourſe, *viz*

1. *Firſt*, I shall give some short Account of the ancient Laws both of the *Jews*, the *Greeks*, and the *Romans*, touching this Matter

2. *Secondly*, I shall obſerve some Things wherein it may appear, how the particular Customs or Municipal Laws of other Countries varied from those Laws, and the Laws here formerly used

3. *Thirdly*, I shall give some Account of the Rules and Laws of Deſcents or hereditary Transmiſſions as they formerly stood, and as at this Day they stand in *England*, with the succeſſive Alterations, that Proceſs of Time, and the Wiſdom of our Ancestors, and certain Customs grown up, tacitely, gradually, and succeſſively have made therein

And First, touching the Laws of Succeſſion, as well of Deſcent, of Inheritances of Lands, as alſo of Goods and Chattels,

4

which among the *Jews* was the same in
both

Mr. *Selden*, in his Book *De Successionibus apud Hæbræos*, has given us an excellent Account, as well out of the holy Text as out of the Comments of the *Rabins*, or *Jew Jh* Lawyers, touching the same, which you may see at large in the 5th, 6th, 7th, 12th and 13th Chapters of that Book, and which, for so much thereof as concerns my present Purpose, I shall briefly comprise under the Eight following Heads, *v.z*

First, That in the Descending Line, the Descent or Succession was to all the Sons, only the eldest Son had a double Portion to any one of the rest, *viz* If there were three Sons, the Estate was to be divided into four Parts, of which the eldest was to have two Fourth Parts, and the other two Sons were to have one Fourth Part each

Secondly, If the Son died in his Father's Life-time, then the Grandson, and so *in Infinitum*, succeeded in the Portion of his Father, as if his Father had been in Possession of it, according to the *Jus Representationis* now in Use here.

Thirdly, The Daughter did not succeed in the Inheritance of the Father as long as there were Sons, or any Descendants from Sons in being, but if any of the Sons died in the Life-time of his Father having Daughters, but without Sons, the Daughters succeeded in his Part as if he himself had been possessed

P

Fourthly,

Fourthly, And in case the Father left only Daughters and no Sons, the Daughters equally succeeded to their Father as in Co-partnership, without any Prelation or Preference of the eldest Daughter to two Parts, or a double Portion

Fifthly, But if the Son had purchased an Inheritance and died without Issue, leaving a Father and Brothers, the Inheritance of such Son so dying did not descend to the Brothers, (unless in case of the next Brothers taking to Wife the Deceased's Widow to raise up Children to his deceased Brother) but in such case the Father inheherited to such Son entirely

Sixthly, But if the Father in that Case was dead, then it came to the Brothers, as it were as Heirs to the Father, in the same Manner as if the Father had been actually possess'd thereof, and therefore the Father's other Sons and their Descendants *in Infinitum* succeeded, but yet especially, and without any double Portion to the eldest, because tho' in Truth the Brothers succeeded as it were in Right of Representation from the Father, yet if the Father died before the Son, the Descent was *de Facto* immediately from the Brother deceased to the other Brothers, in which Case then Law gave not a double Portion, and in case the Father had no Sons or Descendants from them, then it descended to all the Sisters.

Seventhly, If the Son died without Issue, and his Father or any Descendants from him were extant, it went not to the Grand-

father or his other Descendants, but if the
Father was dead without Issue, then it descended to the Grandfather, and if he were
dead, then it went to his Sons and their
Descendants, and for want of them, then
to his Daughters or their Descendants, as if
the Grandfather himself had been actually
possess'd and had died, and so *mutatis mu-*
tandis to the *Proavus, Abavus, Atavus,* &c
and their Descendants

Eighthly, But the Inheritance of the Son
never resorted to the Mother, or to any of
her Ancestors, but both she and they were
totally excluded from the Succession.

The double Portion therefore that was *The dou-*
Jus Primogenituræ, never took Place but in *ble Por-*
that Person that was the *Primogenitus* of him *tion.*
from whom the Inheritance immediately
descended, or him that represented him;
as if *A* had two Sons *B* and *C* and *B* the
eldest had two Sons, *D* and *E* and then *B*
died, whereas *B* should have had a double
Portion, *viz* Two Thirds in case he had
survived his Father, but now this double
Portion shall be equally divided between
D and *E* and *D* shall not have Two Thirds
of the Two Thirds that descended from *A*
to them *Vide* Selden, *ut supra*
Thus much of the Laws or Rules touching Descents among the *Jews.*
Among the *Græcians,* the Laws of Descents *Descents*
in some Sort resemble those of the *Jews, among*
and in some Things they differed *Vide the Grec-*
Petit's *Leges Atticæ, Cap* 1. *Tit.* 6. *De Testa- ans*

mentis

mentis & Hereditario Jure, where the Text
of their Law runs thus, *viz.*

*Omnes legitimi Filii Hæreditatem Paternam
e æquo inter se Hærifcunto, fi quis inteſtatus
morituri relictis Filiabus qui eas in Uxores ducunt
hæredes funto, fi nullæ fuperfint, hi ab inteſtato
hæreditatem cernunto · Et primo quidem Fratres
defuncti Germani, & legitimi Fratrum Filii hæreditatem fimul adeunto, fi nulli Fratres aut Fra-
trium Filii fuperfint, iis geniti eadem Lege hæreditatem cernunto Maſculi autem iis geniti etiam
fi remotioris cognationis fint Gradu, præferuntor,
fi nulli fuperfint, Patterni proximi, ad fobrinorum
ufque Filios, Materni defuncti propinqui fimili
Lege Hæreditatem adeunto; fi e neutra cognatione fuperfint intra definitum Gradum proximus
cognatis Paternis, addito Notho Nothave; fuper-
fice Legitima Filii Nothis Hæreditatem Patris
ve adeo*

This Law is very obfcure, but the Senfe
thereof feems to be briefly this, *viz.* That all
the Sons equally fhall inherit to the Father,
but if he have no Sons, then the Husbands
of the Daughters, and if he have no Children, then his Brothers and their Children,
and if none, then his next Kindred on the
Part of his Father, preferring the Males before the Females; and if none of the Father's Line, *ad Sobrinorum ufque Filios,* then
to defcend to the Mother's Line *Vide
Petit's Glofs* thereon
   " But with all Refpect to the Memory of
" this great good Man, I fhall venture to
       " tranflate

" tranflate this Law, whereby it will ap-
" pear, what the true Senfe and Mean-
" ing thereof is, and that it is not fo dif-
" ficult or obfcure as our Author has re-
" prefented it.

" All the lawful Sons fhall inherit their
" Father's Eftate, to be equally divided be-
" tween them . If any Perfon dies Inteftate,
" leaving only Daughters, their Husbands
" fhall be his Heirs, but if none of the
" Daughters be living, they (*i e* the Huf-
" bands) fhall not inherit to the Inteftate
" But then in the firft Place, the Brothers
" of the whole Blood, and fuch Brothers
" Children, fhall inherit together, (*i e.* the
" Children, *jure reprefentationis*) and if there
" are no Brothers or Brothers Children
" living, then their Defcendants (if they
" leave any) fhall inherit by the fame Law
" of equal Diftribution; yet ftill the Males
" and their Defcendants, tho' of the more
" remote Degree of Kindred, are to be pre-
" ferr'd; but if none of the Father's Blood
" be living, of any nearer Degree than
" that of Father's Brother's Children, then
" the Inheritance fhall defcend to thofe of
" the Mother's Blood, having a like Regard
" to the Law of Diftributions, and the
" Mother's Brother's Children, but if none
" of either Line within the Degrees before
" fpecified be living, then it fhall defcend
" to any of the Father's Blood tho' an illegi-
" timate Son or Daughter; but if a legitimate
" Daughter were living, no Baftard fhall
P 3   " fucceed

" ſucceed in the Inheritance of the Father.
" *Vide* Petit's *Gloſs in h. nc Legem*

Deſcents among the Romans

Among the *Romans* it appears, that the Laws of Succeſſions or Diſcents did ſucceſſively vary, for the Laws of the Twelve Tables did exclude the Females from inheriting, and had many other Streightneſſes and Hardſhips which were ſucceſſively remedied First, by the Emperor *Claudius*, and after him by *Adrian*, in his *Senatus Conſultus Tertullianus*, and after him by *Juſtinian* in his Third Inſtitutes, *Tit. De Hæreditatibus quæ ab inteſtato deferuntur*, and the Two enſuing Titles And again, all this was further explained and ſettled by the *Novel* Conſtitutions of the ſaid *Juſtinian*, ſtiled the *Authenticæ Novellæ*, cap 18. *De Hæreditatibus ab inteſtato venientibus & agnatorum Jure ſublato* Therefore omitting the large Inquiry into the ſucceſſive Changes of the *Roman* Law in this particular, I ſhall only ſet down how, according to that Conſtitution, the *Roman* Law ſtands ſettled therein

Deſcents or Succeſſions from any Perſon are of Three Kinds, *viz* 1ſt, *In the Deſcending Line* 2dly, *The Aſcending Line.* 3dly, *The Collateral Line*; and this latter is either *in Adgnatos a Parte Patris*, or *in Cognatos a Parte Matris.*

1 Deſcending Line

I *In the Deſcending Line*, Theſe Rules are by the *Roman* Law directed, *viz*

1 The Deſcending Line, (whether Male or Female, whether immediate or remote) takes Place, and prevents the Deſcent or

Suc-

Succeffion Afcending or Collateral *in infinitum*

2 The remote Defcents of the Defcending Line fucceed *in Stipem, i e* in that
Right which his Parent fhould have had.

3 This Defcent or Succeffion is equal in
all the Daughters, all the Sons, and all the
Sons and Daughters, without preferring the
Male before the Female, fo that if the common Anceftor had three Sons and three
Daughters, each of them had a fixth Part;
and if one of them had died in the Life
of the Father, having three Sons and three
Daughters, the fixth Part that belonged to
that Party fhould have been divided equally
between his or her fix Children, and fo *in
infinitum* in the Defcending Line

II *In the Afcending Line*, there are thefe
two Rules, *viz*   2
Afcend-
ing Line

1. If the Son dies without Iffue, or any
defcending from him, having a Father and
a Mother living, both of them fhall equally
fucceed to the Son, and prevent all others
of the *Collateral Line* except Brothers and
Sifters, and if only a Father, or only a Mother, he or fhe fhall fucceed alone

2 But if the Deceafed leaves a Father and
a Mother, with a Brother and a Sifter, *ex
utrifque Parentibus conjuncti,* they all Four
fhall equally fucceed to the Son by equal
Parts without Preference of the Males.

III *In the Collateral Line*, (*i e* where the
Perfon dies without Father or Mother,   3.
Collateral
Son Line

P 4

Son or Daughter, or any deſcending from them in the Right Line) the Rules are theſe, viz

1. The Brothers and Siſters, *ex utriſque Parentibus conjuncti,* and the immediate Children of them, ſhall ſucceed equally without Preference of either Sex, and the Children from them ſhall ſucceed *in ſtirpes,* as if there be a Brother and Siſter, and the Siſter dies in the Life of the Deſcendant leaving one or more Children, all ſuch Children ſhall ſucceed in the Moiety that ſhould have come to their deceaſed Mother, had ſhe ſurvived.

2 But if there be no Brothers or Siſters, *ex utriſque Parentibus conjuncti,* nor any of their immediate Children, then the Brothers and Siſters of the half Blood and their immediate Children ſhall ſucceed *in Stirpes* to the Deceaſed without any Prerogative to the Male

3. But if there be no Brothers or Siſters of the whole or half Blood, nor any of their immediate Children (for the Grandchildren are not provided for by the Law) then the next Kindred are called to the Inheritance

(But by our Author's Leave, I think the Grandchildren are impliedly provided for, as they ſucceed their Father or Mother Jure repreſentationis)

4 And if the next Kindred be in an equal Degree, whether on the Part of the Father as *Adgnati,* or on the Part of the Mother as *Cognati,* then they are equally called to
the

the Inheritance, and fucceeded *in Capita*, and not *in Stirpes*.

Thus far of the fettled Laws of the *Jews, Greeks*, and *Romans*, but the Particular or Municipal Laws and Cuftoms of almoft every Country derogate from thofe Laws, and direct Succeffions in a much different Way For Inftance.

By the Cuftoms of *Lombardy*, according to which the Rules of the Feuds, both in their Defcents and in other Things, are much directed ; their Decents are in a much different Manner, *viz*. *Laws of Lombardy*

Leges Feudarum, Lib 1 *Tit* 1. If a Feud be granted to one Brother who dies without Iffue, it defcends not to his other Brother unlefs it be fpecially provided for in the firft Infeudation If the Donee dies, having Iffue Sons and Daughters, it defcends only to the Sons, whereas by the *Roman* Law it defcends to both: The Brother fucceeds not to the Brother unlefs fpecially provided for, *& Ibid Tit* 50. The Afcendants fucceed not, but only the Defcendants, neither does a Daughter fucceed *nifi ex Pacto, vel nifi fit Feodum Fæmmein* *Of Feuds.*

If we come nearer Home to the Laws of *Normandy*, Lands there are of Two Kinds, *viz*. Partible, and not Partible, the Lands that are partible, are Valvafories, Burgages, and fuch like, which are much of the Nature of our Socage Lands ; thefe defcend to all the Sons, or to all the Daughters. Lands not partible, are Fiefs and Dignities, *Defcents in Normandy*

they

they defcend to the eldeft Son, and not to all the Sons, but if there be no Sons, then to all the Daughters, and become partible

The Rules and Directions of their Defcents are as follow, *viz*

1 For want of Sons or Nephews, it defcends to the Daughters, if there be no Sons or Daughters, or Defcendants from them, it goes to Brothers, and for want of Brothers, to Sifters, (obferving as before the Difference between Lands partible and not partible) and accordingly the Defcent runs to the Pofterity of Brothers to the feventh Degree, and if there be no Brothers nor Sifters, nor any Defcendants from them within the feventh Degree, it defcends to the Father, and if the Father be dead, then to the Uncles and Aunts and their Pofterity, (as above is faid in the Cafe of Brothers and Sifters) and if there be none, then to the Grandfather

So that according to their Law, the Father is *poftponed* to the Brother and Sifter, and their Iffues, but is preferred before the Uncle Tho' according to the *Jewifh* Law, the Father is preferred before the Brother, by the *Roman* Law, he fucceeds together equally with the Brother; but by the *Englifh* Law, the Father cannot take from his Son by an immediate Defcent, *but may take as Heir to his Brother, who is Heir to his Son by Collateral Defcent*

2. If

2 If Lands defcended from the Part of the Father, they could never refort by a Defcent to the Line of the Mother, but in cafe of Purchafes by the Son who died without Iffue, for want of Heirs of the Part of the Father, it defcended to the Heirs of the Part of the Mother according to the Law of *England.*

3 The Son of the eldeft Son dying in the Life of the Father, is preferred before a younger Son furviving his Father as the Law ftands here now' fettled, tho' it had fome Interruption, 4 *Johannis*

4 On Equality of Degrees in *Collateral Defcents,* the Male Line is preferred before the Female.

5. Altho' by the Civil Law, *Fratres ex utroque Parente conjuncti præferuntur Fratribus confanguineis tantum vel uterinis,* yet it fhould feem by the *Coutumier* of *Normandy, Fratres confanguinei et ex eodem Patre fed diverfa Matre,* fhall take by Defcent together with the Brothers, *ex utroque conjuncti,* upon the Death of any fuch Brothers But *Quære* hereof, for this feems a Miftake, for, as I take it, the half Blood hinders the Defcent between Brothers and Sifters by their Laws as well as ours

6. Leprofy was amongft them an Impediment of Succeffion, but then it feems it ought to be firft folemnly adjudged fo by the Sentence of the Church

Upon all this, and much more that might be obferved upon the Cuftoms of feveral Countries, it appears, That the Rules of Suc-

Succeffions, or hereditary Tranfmiffions, have been various in feveral Countries according to their various Laws, Cuftoms, and Ufages.

And now, after this brief Survey of the Laws and Cuftoms of other Countries, I come to the Laws and Ufages of *England* in relation to Defcents, and the Growth that thofe Cuftoms fucceffively have had, and whereunto they are now arrived.

Defcents in Eng-land

Fjft, Touching hereditary Succeffions · It feems, that according to the ancient *Britifh* Laws, the eldeft Son inherited their Earldoms and Baronies; for they had great Dignities and Jurifdictions annex'd to them, and were in Nature of Principalities, but that their ordinary Freeholds defcended to all their Sons, and this Cuftom they carried

Among the Welfh Statute 12 Ed 1

with them into *Wales* whither they were driven This appears by *Statutum Walliæ,* 12 E. 1 and which runs thus, *viz.*

Aliter ufitatum eft in Wallia quam in Anglia quoad Succeffionem Hæreditatis, eo quod hæreditas partibilis eft inter hæredes Mafculos, & a tempore cujus non extitit Memoria partibilis extitit Dominus Rex non vult quod confuetudo illa abrogetur, fed quod hæreditates remaneant partibiles inter confimiles hæredes ficut effe Confueverunt, & fit partitio illius ficut fieri confuevit. Hoc excepto quod Baftardi non habeant de cætero hæreditates & etiam quod non habeant purpartes, cum legitimis nec fine legitimis.

Where

Whereupon Three Things are obfervable, *viz* 1*ft*, That at this Time the hereditary Succeffion of the eldeft Son was then
known to be the common and ufual Law in
England 2*dly*, That the Succeffion of all the
Sons was the ancient cuftomary Law among
the *Britifh* in *Wales*, which by this Statute
was continued to them 3*dly*, That before
this Time, Baftards were admitted to
inherit in *Wales* as well as the Legitimate
Children, which Cuftom is thereby abrogated; and although we have but few Evi-
dences touching the *Britifh* Laws before
their Expulfion hence into *Wales*, yet this
Ufage in *Wales* feems fufficiently to evidence this to have been the ancient *Britifh*
Law

Secondly, As to the Times of the *Saxons*
and *Danes*, their Laws collected by *Brompton*
and Mr. *Lambart*, fpeak not much concerning the Courfe of Defcents; yet it feems
that commonly Defcents of their ordinary
Lands at leaft, except Baronies and Royal
Inheritances, defcended alfo to all the Sons:
For amongft the Laws of King *Canutus*, in
Mr. *Lambard* is this Law, *v.z.* N° 68 *Sive
quis incurra five Morte repentina fuerit inteftato
mortuus, Dominus tamen nullam rerum fuarum
Partem (præter eam quæ jure debetur Hereoti
nomine) Sibi affumito Verum eas Judicio fuo
Uxori, Liberis & cognatione proximis jufte (pro
fuo cuique jure) diftribuito*

Upon which Law, we may obferve thefe
five Things, *viz.*

1*ft*, That

1*st*, That the Wife had a Share, as well of the Lands for her Dower, as of the Goods

2*dly*, That in reference to hereditary Succeſſions, there then ſeem'd to be little Difference between Lands and Goods, for this Law makes no Diſtinction

3*dly*, That there was a kind of ſettled Right of Succeſſion, with reference to Proximity and Remoteneſs of Blood, or Kin, *Et cognatione proximis pro ſuo cuique jure*

4*thly*, That in reference to Children, they all ſeem'd to ſucceed alike, without any Diſtinction between Males and Females

5*thly*, That yet the Anceſtor might diſpoſe of by his Will as well Lands as Goods, which Uſage ſeems to have obtained here unto the Time of *Hen* II as will appear hereafter *Vide Glanville*

Thirdly, It ſeems that, until the Conqueſt, the Deſcent of Lands was at leaſt to all the Sons alike, and for ought appears to all the Daughters alſo, and that there was no Difference in the hereditary Tranſmiſſion of Lands and Goods, at leaſt in reference to the Children. This appears by the Laws of King *Edward the Confeſſor*, confirm'd by King *William* I and recited in Mr *Lambart*, *Folio* 167 as alſo by Mr *Selden* in his Notes upon *Eadmerus*, viz. *Lege* 36 *Tit De Inteſtatorum Bonis*, *Pag* 184 *Si quis inteſtatus obierit Liberi ejus Hereditatem æqualiter dividant*

But this equal Diviſion of Inheritances among all the Children was found to be very inconvenient For,

1*st*, It

1*st*, It weakened the Strength of the Kingdom, for by frequent parcelling and subdividing of Inheritances, in Procefs of Time they became fo divided and crumbled, that there were few Perfons of able Eftates left to undergo publick Charges and Offices

2*dly*, It did by Degrees bring the Inhabitants to a low kind of Country living, and Families were broken, and the younger Sons, which had they not had thofe little Parcels of Land to apply themfelves to, would have betaken themfelves to Trades, or to Civil or Military, or Ecclefiaftical Employments, neglecting thofe Opportunities, wholly apply'd themfelves to thofe fmall Divifions of Lands, whereby they neglected the Opportunities of greater Advantage of enriching themfelves and the Kingdom

And therefore King *William* I having by his Acceffion to the Crown gotten into his Hands the Poffeffions and Demeafns of the Crown, and alfo very many and great Poffeffions of thofe that oppos'd him, or adhered to *Harold*, difpofed of thofe Lands or great Part of them to his Countrymen, and others that adhered to him, and referved certain honorary Tenures, either by Baronage, or in Knights-Service or Grand Serjeancy, for the Defence of the Kingdom, and poffibly alfo, even at the Defire of many of the Owners, changed their former Tenures into Knights-Service, which Introduction of new Tenures was neverthe-

lefs

less not done without Consent of Parliament;
as appears by the additional Laws before
mentioned, that King *William* made by Advice of Parliament, mentioned by Mr. *Selden*
in his Notes on *Eadmerus*, Page 191. amongst
which this was one, *viz*

*Statuimus etiam & firmiter præcipimus ut
cives Comites Barones Milites & Servientes &
universi liberi Homines totius Regni nostri habeant
& teneant se semper in Armis & in Equis ut
decet & oportet, & quod sint semper prompti &
bene parati ad Servitium svum integrum nobis
explendendum & peragendum, cum semper opus
fuerit secundum quod nobis de Feodis debent &
tenentur Tenementis suis de Jure facere & sicut
illis statuimus per Commune Concilium totius Regni
nostri, Et illis dedimus & concessimus in Feodo
Jure hæreditario* ——

Whereby it appears, that there were Two
Kinds of Military Provisions; one that was
set upon all Freeholds by common Consent
of Parliament, and which was usually called
Assisa Armorum, and another that was Conventional and by Tenure, upon the Infeudation of the Tenant, and which was usually called *Knights Service*, and sometimes
Royal, sometimes Foreign Service, and
sometimes *Servitium Loricæ*

And hence it came to pass, that not only
by the Customs of *Normandy*, but also according to the Customs of other Countries,
those honorary Fees, or Infeudations, became descendible to the Eldest, and not to

all the Males. And hence alfo it is, that in *Kent*, where the Cuftom of all the Males taking by Defcent generally prevails, and that pretend a Conceffion of all their Cuftoms by the Conqueror, to obtain a Submiffion to his Government, according to that Romantick Story of their *Moving Wood.* But even in *Kent* it felf, thofe ancient Tenements or Fees that are there held anciently by Knights Service, are defcendible to the Eldeft Son, as Mr *Lambard* has obferved to my Hands in his *Perambulation,* Page 533, 553. out of 9 H. 3. *Fitz Prefcription* 63. 26 H. 8 5 and the Statute of 31 H. 8. *cap* 3. And yet even in *Kent*, if Gavelkind Lands efcheat, or come to the Crown by Attainder or Diffolution of Monafteries, and be granted to be held by Knights Service, or *per Baroniam*, the Cuftomary Defcent is not changed, neither can it be but by Act of Parliament, for it is a Cuftom fix'd to the Land.

But thofe honorary Infeudations made in ancient Times, efpecially fhortly after the Conqueft, did filently and fuddenly affume the Rule of Defcents to the Eldeft, and accordingly held it, and fo altho' poffibly there were no Acts of Parliament of thofe Elder Times, at leaft none that are now known of, for altering the ancient Courfe of Defcents from all the Sons to the Eldeft, yet the Ufe of the Neighbouring Country might introduce the fame Ufage here as to thofe honorary Poffeffions.

Q   And

And becaufe thofe honorary Infeudations were many, and fcattered almoft through all the Kingdom, in a little Time they introduced a Parity in the Succeffion of Lands of other Tenures, as Socages, Valvaforics, &c. So that without Queftion, by little and little, almoft generally in all Counties of *England* (except *Kent*, who were moft tenacious of their old Cuftoms in which they gloried, and fome particular Feuds and Places where a contrary Ufage prevailed), the generalty of Defcents or Succeffions, by little and little, as well of Socage Lands as Knights Service, went to the eldeft Son, according to the Declaration of King *Edw*. I. in the Statute of *Wales* above-mentioned, as will more fully appear by what follows

In the Time of *Hen* I as we find by his 70th Law, it feems that the whole Land did not defcend to the eldeft Son, but begun to look a little that Way, *viz. Primum Patris Feudum, primogenitus Filius habeat.* And as to *Collateral Defcents*, that Law determins thus *Si quis fine Liberis decefferit Pater aut Mater ejus in hæreditatem fuccedat vel Frater vel Soror fi Pater & Mater defint, fi nec hos, habeat Soror Patris vel Matris, & deinceps in Quintum geniculum; qui cum propinquiores in parentela fint hæreditario jure fuccedant; & dum Virilis fexus extiterit & hæreditas ab inde fit, Fæmi‑ea non hæreditetur.*

Vide Ante Chap 7. and Lambard, ut fupra

By

By this Law it seems to appear;

1. The eldest Son, tho' he had *Jus primogenituræ*, the principal Fee of his Father's Land, yet he had not all the Land.

2 That for want of Children, the Father or Mother inherited before the Brother or Sister.

3. That for want of Children, and Father, Mother, Brother, and Sister, the Land descended to the Uncles and Aunts to the fifth Generation

4. That in Successions Collateral, Proximity of Blood was preferred.

5 That the Male was preferred before the Female, *i e.* The Father's Line was preferred before the Mother's, unless the Land descended from the Mother, and then the Mother's Line was preferred

How this Law was observed in the Interval between *Hen* I and *Hen* II. we can give no Account of, but the next Period that we come to is, the Time of *Hen* II. wherein *Glanville* gives us an Account how the Law stood at that Time · *Vide Glanville, Lib* 7. Wherein notwithstanding it will appear, that there was some Uncertainty and Unsettledness in the Business of Descents or Hereditary Successions, tho' it was much better polished than formerly, the Rules then of Succession were either in reference to Goods, or Lands. 1*st*, As to Goods, one Third Part thereof went to the Wife, another Third Part went to the Children, and the other Third was left to the Disposition

Q 2   of

of the Testator, but if he had no Wife, then a Moiety went to the Children, and the other Moiety was at the Deceased's Disposal And the like Rule if he had left a Wife, but no Children *Glanv lib.* 7. *cap.* 5 *& Vide lib* 2 *cap* 29.

But as to the Succession of Lands, the Rules are these.

First, If the Lands were Knights Service, they generally went to the eldest Son; and in case of no Sons, then to all the Daughters, and in case of no Children, then to the eldest Brother

Secondly, If the Lands were Socage, they descended to all the Sons to be divided; *Si fuerit Soccagium & id antiquitus divisum*; only the Chief House was to be allotted to the Purparty of the Eldest, and a Compensation made to the rest in lieu thereof: *Si vero non fuerit antiquitus divisum, tunc Primogenitus secundum quorundam Consuetudinem totam Hæreditatem obtinebit, secundum autem quorundam Consuetudinem postnatus Filius Hæres est Glanville, lib* 7 *cap* 3. So that altho' Custom directed the Descent variously, either to the eldest or youngest, or to all the Sons, yet it seems that at this Time, *Jus Commune*, or Common Right, spoke for the eldest Son to be Heir, no Custom intervening to the contrary.

Thirdly, As the Son or Daughter, so their Children *in infinitum*, are preferred in the Descent before the Collateral Line or Uncles.

Fourthly,

Fourthly, But if a Man had two Sons, and the eldeſt Son died in the Life-time of his Father, having Iſſue a Son or Daughter, and then the Father dies; it was then controverted, whether the Son or Nephew ſhould ſucceed to the Father, tho' the better Opinion ſeems to be for the Nephew, *Glanvil. lib* 7. *cap* 3.

Fifthly, A Baſtard could not inherit, *Ibid cap.* 13, or 17. And altho' by the Canon or Civil Law, if *A.* have a Son born of *B.* before Marriage, and after *A.* marries *B.* this Son ſhall be legitimate and heritable; yet according to the Laws of *England* then, and ever ſince uſed, he was not heritable, *Glanvil lib.* 7. *cap.* 15.

Sixthly, In caſe the Purchaſer died without Iſſue, the Land deſcended to the Brothers; and for want of Brothers, to the Siſters; and for want of them, to the Children of the Brothers or Siſters; and for want of them, to the Uncles; and ſo onward according to the Rules of Deſcents at this Day; and the Father or Mother were not to inherit to the Son, but the Brothers or Uncles, and their Children. *Ibid. cap.* 1. *&* 4.

And it ſeems, That in all Things elſe, the Rules of Deſcents in reference to the Collateral Line were much the ſame as now; as namely, That if Lands deſcended of the Part of the Father, it ſhould not reſort to the Part of the Mother, or *è converſo*; but in the Caſe of Purchaſers, for want of

Heirs of the Part of the Father, it resorted to the Line of the Mother, and the nearer and more worthy of Blood were preferred: So that if there were any of the Part of the Father, tho' never so far distant, it hindred the Descent to the Line of the Mother, though much nearer.

But in those Times it seems there were two Impediments of Descents or hereditary Successions which do not now obtain, *viz.*

First, Leprosy, if so adjudged by Sentence of the Church: This indeed I find not in *Glanville*; but I find it pleaded and allowed in the Time of King *John*, and thereupon the Land was adjudged from the Leprous Brother to the Sister. *Pasch.* 4 *Johannis*.

Secondly, There was another Curiosity in Law, and it was wonderful to see how much and how long it prevail'd, for we find it in Use in *Glanville*, who wrote *Temp Hen* II. in *Bracton Temp Hen* III. in *Fleta Temp Edw.* I and in the broken Year of 13 E. 1. *Fitzh. Avowry* 235. *Nemo potest esse Tenens & Dominus, & Homagium repellit Perquisitum* And therefore if there had been three Brothers, and the eldest Brother had enfeoff'd the second, reserving Homage, and had received Homage, and then the second had died without Issue, the Land should have descended to the youngest Brother and not to the eldest Brother, *Quia Homagium repellit perquisitum*, as 'tis here said, for he could not pay Homage to himself.

Vide

Vide for this, *Bratton, Lib.* 2. *cap* 30 *Glanvil. Lib* 7. *cap.* 1. *Fleta, Lib* 6. *cap.* 1

But at this Day the Law is altered, and so it has been for ought I can find ever since 13 *E.* 1. Indeed, it is antiquated rather than altered, and the Fancy upon which it was grounded has appear'd trivial, for if the eldest Son enfeoff the second, reserving Homage, and that Homage paid, and then the second Son dies without Issue, it will descend to the Eldest as Heir, and the Seigniory is extinct. It might indeed have had some Colour of Reason to have examined, whether he might not have waved the Descent, in case his Services had been more beneficial than the Land: But there could be little Reason from thence to exclude him from the Succession I shall mention no more of this Impediment, nor of that of Leprosy, for that they both are vanished and antiquated long since; and, as the Law now is, neither of these are any Impediment of Descents.

And now passing over the Time of King *John* and *Richard* I. because I find nothing of Moment therein on this Head, unless the Usurpation of King *John* upon his eldest Brother's Son, which he would fain have justified, by introducing a Law of prefering the younger Son before the Nephew descended from the elder Brother· But this Pretension could no way justifie his Usurpation, as has been already shewn in the Time of *Hen.* II.

Q 4

Next, I come to the Time of *Hen* III. in whose Time the Tractate of *Bracton* was written, and thereby in *Lib* 2. *cap* 30, & 31. and *Lib* 5. *cap.* it appears, That there is so little Variance as to Point of Descents between the Law as it was taken when *Bracton* wrote, and the Law as afterwards taken in *Edw.* I.'s Time, when *Britton* and *Fleta* wrote, that there is very little Difference between them, as may easily appear by comparing *Bracton ubi supra*, & *Fleta, Lib* 5. *cap* 9. *Lib.* 6. *cap* 1, 2. that the latter seem to be only Transcripts or Abstracts of the former. Wherefore I shall set down the Substance of what both say, and thereby it will appear, that the Rules of Descents in *Hen.* III. and *Edw.* I.'s Time were very much one

First, At this Time the Law seems to be unquestionably settled, that the eldest Son was of Common Right Heir, not only in Cases of Knight Service Lands, but also of Socage Lands, (unless there were a special Custom to the contrary, as in *Kent* and some other Places) and so that Point of the Common Law was fully settled.

Secondly, That all the Descendants in infinitum, from any Person that had been Heir, if living, were inheritable, *Jure representationis*; as, the Descendants of the Son, of the Brother, of the Uncle, &c. And also,

Thirdly, That the eldest Son dying in the Life-time of the Father, his Son or Issue

was

was to have the Preference as Heir to the Father before the younger Brother, and so the Doubt in *Glanville's* Time was settled, *Glanvil Lib.* 7. *cap* 3. *Cum quis autem moriatur habens Filium postnatum, & ex primogenito Filio præmortuo Nepotem, Magna quidem Juris dubitatio solet esse uter illorum preferendus sit alii in illa Successione, scilicet, utrum Filius aut Nepos?*

Fourthly, The Father, or Grandfather, could not by Law inherit immediately to the Son.

Fifthly, Leprosy, Though it were an Exception to a Plaintiff, because he ought not to converse in the Courts of Law, as *Bracton, Lib.* 5 *cap.* 20 'yet we no where find it to be an Impediment of a Descent.

So that upon the whole Matter, for any Thing I can observe in them, the Rules of Descents then stood settled in all Points as they are at this Day, except some few Matters (which yet soon after settled as they now stand), *viz.*

First, That Impediment or Hindrance of a Descent from him that did Homage to him that received it, seems to have been yet in Use at least till 13 *E* 1. and in *Fleta's* Time, for he puts the Case and admits it.

Secondly, Whereas both *Bracton* and *Fleta* agree, that half Blood to him that is a Purchaser is an Impediment of a Descent, yet in the Case of a Descent from the Common Ancestor, half Blood is no Impediment.

ment. As for Inftance, *A* has Iffue *B.* a Son
and *C* a Daughter by one Venter, and *D* a
Son by another Venter : If *B.* purchafes in
Fee and dies without Iffue, it fhall defcend
to the Sifter, and not to the Brother of the
half Blood ; but if the Land had defcended
from *A* to *B* and he had entred and died
without Iffue, it was a Doubt in *Bracton*
and *Britton*'s Time, whether it fhould go to
the younger Son, or to the Daughter? But
the Law is fince fettled, that in both Cafes
it defcends to the Daughter, *Et feifina facit
Stipitem & primum Gradum. Et poffeffio Fratris
de Feodo fimplici facit Sororem effe hæredem.*

Thus upon the whole it feems, That
abating thofe fmall and inconfiderable Vari-
ances, the States and Rules of Defcents as
they ftood in the Time of *Hen.* III. or at
leaft in the Time of *Edw* I. were reduced
to their full Complement and Perfection,
and vary nothing confiderably from what
they are at this Day, and have continued
ever fince that Time.

I fhall therefore fet down the State and
Rule of Defcents in Fee-Simple as it ftands
at this Day, without meddling with particular Limitations of Entails of Eftates,
which vary the Courfe of Defcents in fome
Cafes from the Common Rules of Defcents
or hereditary Succeffions ; and herein we
fhall fee what the Law has been and continued touching the fame ever fince *Bracton*'s
Time, who wrote in the Time of *Hen.* III.
now above 400 Years fince, and by that we
fhall

shall see what Alterations the Succession of Time has made therein

And now to give a short Scheme of the Rules of Descents, or hereditary Successions, of the Lands of Subjects as the Law stands at this Day, and has stood for above four hundred Years past, *viz.*

All possible hereditary Successions may be distinguished into these 3 Kinds, *viz.* either,

1*st*, *In the Descending Line*, as from Father to Son or Daughter, Nephew or Niece, *i.e.* Grandson or Grand-daughter. Or,

2*dly*, *In the Collateral Line*, as from Brother to Brother or Sister, and so to Brother and Sisters Children Or,

3*dly*, *In an Ascending Line*, either direct, as from Son to Father or Grandfather, (which is not admitted by the Law of *England*) or in the transversal Line, as to the Uncle or Aunt, Great-Uncle or Great-Aunt, *&c.* And because this Line is again divided into the Line of the Father, or the Line of the Mother, this transverse ascending Succession is either in the Line of the Father, Grandfather, *&c.* on the Blood of the Father, or in the Line of the Mother, Grandmother, *&c.* on the Blood of the Mother: The former are called *Adgnati*, the latter *Cognati*: I shall therefore set down a Scheme of Pedigrees as high as Great-Grandfather and Great-Grandmothers Grandsires, and as low as Great-Gandchild; which nevertheless will be applicable to more remote Successions with a little Variation, and will explain the whole Nature of Descents or hereditary Successions.

The

The *PATERNAL* Line   The *MATERNAL* Line

Tritavus, or Great-Grandfather's Great Grandfather			*Tritavia*, or Great-Grandmothers Great Grandmother		
Atavus, or Great-Grandfather's Grandfather			*Atavia*, or Great-Grandmothers Grandmother		
Abavus, or Great-Grandfather's Father			*Abavia*, or Great-Grandmothers Mother		

Proamita Magna Great Great-Aunt	*Propatruus Magnus* Great-Great-Uncle	*Proavus* Gr Grandfather.	*Proavia*, or Gr Grandmother	*Proavunculus* Gr. Great-Uncle	*Promatertera Magna* Great-Great Aunt
Amita Magna Great-Aunt.	*Patruus Magnus* Great Uncle	*Avus*, or Grandfather	*Avia*, or Grandmother	*Avunculus Magnus* Great-Uncle	*Matertera Magna* Great-Aunt
Amita, or Aunt	*Patruus*, or Uncle	*Pater*, or FATHER	*Mater*, or MOTHER	*Avunculus* Mothers Brother	*Matertera* Mothers Sister

Soror, his Sister.	*Frater*, his Brother	*Filius Primus*, eldest Son	
Nepos. Nephew *Neptis.* Niece	*Nepos* Nephew *Neptis.* Niece.	*Nepos*, or Grandson	*Neptis*, or Grandaughter

Note, The Descendants from all these Six in the next Degree, if Male, is called *Pronepos*, if Female, *Proneptis* i e *Great-Grandson,* or *Great-Grand-daughter*

Consobrinus A Mothers Brother's Daughter.

Consobrinus A Mothers Brother's Son

Consobrina A Mothers Sisters Daughter

Consobrinus A Mothers Sisters Son.

This Pedigree, with its Application, will give a plain Account of all Hereditary Succeffions under their feveral Cafes and Limitations, as will appear by the following Rules, taking our Mark or *Epocha* from the FATHER and MOTHER.

But firft, I fhall premife certain general Rules, which will direct us much in the Courfe of Defcents as they ftand here in *England* (*Viz.*)

Firft, In Defcents, the Law prefers the worthieft of Blood : As, 1 Rule

1*ft*, In all Defcents immediate, the Male is preferred before the Female, whether in Succeffions Defcending, Afcending, or Collateral: Therefore in Defcents, the Son inherits and excludes the Daughter, the Brother is preferred before the Sifter, the Uncle before the Aunt

2*dly*, In all Defcents immediate, the Defcendants from Males are to be preferred before the Defcendants from Females: And hence it is, That the Daughter of the eldeft Son is preferred in Defcents from the Father before the Son of the younger Son; and the Daughter of the eldeft Brother, or Uncle, is preferred before the Son of the younger ; and the Uncle, nay, the Great-Uncle, *i e* the Grandfather's Brother, fhall inherit before the Uncle of the Mothers Side.

Secondly, In Defcents, the next of Blood is preferred before the more remote, tho' equally or more worthy. And hence it is, 2 Rule.

1*ft*, The

1*st*, The Sister of the whole Blood is preferred in Descents before the Brother of the half Blood, because she is more strictly joined to the Brother of the whole Blood (*viz.* by Father and by Mother) than the half Brother, though otherwise he is the more worthy.

2*dly*, Because the Son or Daughter being nearer than the Brother, and the Brother or Sister than the Uncle, the Son or Daughter shall inherit before the Brother or Sister, and they before the Uncle.

3*dly*, That yet the Father or Grandfather, or Mother or Grandmother, in a direct ascending Line, shall never succeed immediately the Son or Grandchild; but the Father's Brother (or Sisters) shall be preferred before the Father himself; and the Grandfather's Brother (or Sisters) before the Grandfather: And yet upon a strict Account, the Father is nearer of Blood to the Son than the Uncle, yea than the Brother; for the Brother is therefore of the Blood of the Brother, because both derive from the same Parent, the Common Fountain of both their Blood And therefore the Father at this Day is preferred in the Administration of the Goods before the Son's Brother of the whole Blood, and a Remainder limited *Proximo de Sanguine* of the Son shall vest in the Father before it shall vest in the Uncle. *Vide Littleton, Lib.* 1 *fo.* 8, 10.

3 Rule   *Thirdly*, That all the Descendants from such a Person as by the Laws of *England*

I   might

might have been Heir to another, hold the fame Right by Reprefentation as that Common Root from whence they are derived; and therefore,

1ʃ, They are in Law in the fame Right of Worthinefs and Proximity of Blood, as their Root that might have been Heir was, in cafe he had been living: And hence it is, that the Son or Grandchild, whether Son or Daughter of the eldeſt Son, ſucceeds before the younger Son; and the Son or Grandchild of the eldeſt Brother, before the youngeſt Brother, and ſo through all the Degrees of Succeſſion, by the Right of Reprefentation, the Right of Proximity is tranferred from the Root to the Branches, and gives them the fame Preference as the next and worthieſt of Blood.

2*dly*, This Right transferred by Reprefentation is infinite and unlimited in the Degrees of thofe that defcend from the Reprefented; for *Filius* the Son, the *Nepos* the Grandfon, the *Abnepos* the Great-Grandfon, and ſo *in infinitum* enjoy the fame Privilege of Reprefentation as thofe from whom they derive their Pedigree have, whether it be in Defcents Lineal, or Tranſverſal; and therefore the Great-Grandchild of the eldeſt Brother, whether it be Son or Daughter, ſhall be preferred before the younger Brother, becaufe tho' the Female be lefs worthy than the Male, yet ſhe ſtands in Right of Reprefentation of the eldeſt Brother, who was more worthy than the younger. And upon this Account it is,

3*dly*, That

3dly, That if a Man have two Daughters and the eldeſt dies in the Life of the Father, leaving ſix Daughters, and then the Father dies; the youngeſt Daughter ſhall have an equal Share with the other ſix Daughters, becauſe they ſtand in Repreſentation and Stead of their Mother, who could have had but a Moiety

4 Rule.   *Fourthly*, That by the Law of *England*, without a ſpecial Cuſtom to the contrary, the eldeſt Son, or Brother, or Uncle, excludes the younger, and the Males in an equal Degree do not all inherit· But all the Daughters, whether by the ſame or divers Venters, do inherit together to the Father, and all the Siſters by the ſame Venter do inherit to the Brother.

5 Rule   *Fifthly*, That the laſt actual Seiſin in any Anceſtor, makes him, as it were, the Root of the Deſcent equally to many Intents as if he had been a Purchaſer, and therefore he that cannot, according to the Rules of Deſcents, derive his Succeſſion from him that was laſt actually ſeized, tho' he might have derived it from ſome precedent Anceſtor, ſhall not inherit And hence it is, That where Lands deſcend to the eldeſt Son from the Father, and the Son enters and dies without Iſſue, his Siſter of the whole Blood ſhall inherit as Heir to the Brother, and not the younger Son of the half Blood, becauſe he cannot be Heir to the Brother of the half Blood, but if the eldeſt Son had ſur-

          vived

vived the Father and died before Entry, the youngeſt Son ſhould inherit as Heir to the Father, and not the Siſter, becauſe he is Heir to the Father that was laſt actually ſeized And hence it is, That tho' the Uncle is preferred before the Father in Deſcents to the Son, yet if the Uncle enter after the Death of the Son and die without Iſſue, the Father ſhall inherit to the Uncle, *quia Seiſina facit Stipitem.*

Sixthly, That whoſoever derives a Title to any Iand, muſt be of the Blood to him that firſt purchaſed it And this is the Reaſon why, if the Son purchaſe Lands and dies without Iſſue, it ſhall deſcend to the Heirs of the Part of the Father ; and if he has none, then to the Heirs on the Part of the Mother, becauſe tho' the Son has both the Blood of the Father and of the Mother in him, yet he is of the whole Blood of the Mother, and the Conſanguinity of the Mother are *Conſanguinei Cognati* of the Son

And of the other Side, if the Father had purchaſed Lands, and it had deſcended to the Son, and the Son had died without Iſſue, and without any Heir of the Part of the Father, it ſhould never have deſcended in the Iine of the Mother, but eſcheated For tho' the *Conſanguinei* of the Mother were the *Conſanguinei* of the Son, yet they were not of Conſanguinity to the Father, who was the Purchaſer, but if there had been none of the Blood of the Grandfather, yet it might

6 Rule.

R   have

have reſorted to the Line of the Grandmother, becauſe her *Conſanguinei* were as well
of the Blood of the Father, as the Mother's
Conſanguinity is of the Blood of the Son:
And conſequently alſo, if the Grandfather
had purchaſed Lands, and they had deſcended to the Father, and from him to the
Son; if the Son had entred and died without Iſſue, his Father's Brothers or Siſters,
or their Deſcendants, or, for want of them,
his Great Grandfather's Brothers or Siſters,
or their Deſcendants, or, for want of them,
any of the Conſanguinity of the Great
Grandfather, or Brothers or Siſters of the
Great Grandmother, or their Deſcendants,
might have inherited, for the Conſanguinity of the Great Grandmother was the
Conſanguinity of the Grandfather, but none
of the Line of the Mother, or Grandmother,
viz. the Grandfather's Wife, ſhould have inherited, for that they were not of the Blood
of the firſt Purchaſer And the ſame Rule
e converſo holds in Purchaſes in the Line
of the Mother or Grandmother, they ſhall
always keep in the ſame Line that the firſt
Purchaſer ſettled them in.

But it is not neceſſary, That he that inherits be always Heir to the Purchaſer; it is
ſufficient if he be of his Blood, and Heir
to him that was laſt ſeized The Father
purchaſes Lands which deſcended to the Son,
who dies without Iſſue, they ſhall never deſcend to the Heir of the Part of the Son's
Mother, but if the Son's Grandmother has a
Brother, and the Son's Great Grandmother
hath

hath a Brother, and there are no other Kindred, they fhall defcend to the Grandmother's Brother, and yet if the Father had
died without Iffue, his Grandmother's Brother fhould have been preferred before his
Mother's Brother, becaufe the former was
Heir of the Part of his Father tho' a Female, and the latter was only Heir of the
Part of his Mother; but where the Son is
once feized and dies without Iffue, his
Grandmother's Brother is to him Heir of
the Part of his Father, and being nearer
than his Great Grandmothers Brother, is
preferred in the Defcent

But *Note*, This is always intended fo long
as the Line of Defcent is not broken; for if
the Son alien thofe Lands, and then re-
purchafe them again in Fee, now the Rules
of Defcents are to be obferved as if he were
the original Purchafer, and as if it had been
in the Line of the Father or Mother.

Seventhly, In all Succeffions, as well in
the *Line Defcending, Tranfverfal,* or *Afcending*,
the Line that is firft derived from a Male
Root has always the Preference. 7. Rule

Inftances whereof in the *Line Defcending*,
&c *viz.*

A. has Iffue two Sons *B* and *C* *B.* has
Iffue a Son and a Daughter *D.* and *E.*
D the Son has Iffue a Daughter *F.* and *E.*
the Daughter has Iffue a Son *G.* Neither *C.* nor any of his Defcendants, fhall
inherit fo long as there are any Defcendants
from

from *D* and *E* and neither *E* the Daughter, nor any of her Defcendants, fhall inherit fo long as there are any Defcendants from *D* the Son, whether they be Male or Female

So in Defcents Collateral, as Brothers and Sifters, the fame Inftances applied thereto, evidence the fame Conclufions

But in Succeffions in the Line Afcending, there muft be a fuller Explication, becaufe it is darker and more obfcure, I fhall therefore fet forth the whole Method of *Tranfverfal Afcending Defcents* under the Eight enfuing Rules, *viz*

Rules in the Line Afcending

1. Rule *Firft*, If the Son purchafes Lands in Fee-Simple and dies without Iffue, thofe of the Male Line afcending, *ufque infinitum* fhall be preferred in the Defcent, according to their Proximity of Degree to the Son, and therefore the Father's Brothers and Sifters and their Defcendants fhall be preferred before the Brothers of the Grandfather and their Defcendants, and if the Father had no Brothers nor Sifters, the Grandfather's Brothers and their Defcendants, and for want of Brothers, his Sifters and their Defcendants, fhall be preferred before the Brothers of the Great Grandfather. For altho' by the Law of *England* the Father or Grandfather cannot immediately inherit to the Son, yet the Direction of the Defcent to the *Collateral Afcending Line*, is as much as if the Father or Grandfather had been by Law inheritable, and therefore as in cafe

the

the Father had been inheritable, and should
have inherited to the Son before the Grandfather, and the Grandfather before the
Great Grandfather, and consequently if
the Father had inherited and died without
Issue, his eldest Brother and his Descendants should have inherited before the
younger Brother and his Descendants; and
if he had no Brothers but Sisters, the Sisters
and their Descendants should have inherited
before his Uncles or the Grandfather's Brothers and their Descendants So though the
Law of *England* excludes the Father from
inheriting, yet it substitutes and directs the
Descent as it should have been, had the
Father inherited, viz It lets in those first
that are in the next Degree to him

Secondly, The second Rule is this That 2 Rule
the Line of the Part of the Mother shall
never inherit as long as there are any, tho'
never so remote, of the Line of the Part of
the Father , and therefore, tho' the Mother
has a Brother, yet if the *Atavus* or *Atavia
Patris* (i e the Great-Great Great-Grandfather, or Great Great-Great-Grandmother
of the Father) has a Brother or a Sister,
he or she shall be preferred, and exclude
the Mothers Brother though he is much
nearer.

Thirdly, But yet further, The Male Line 3. Rule
of the Part of the Father ascending, shall
in *Æternum* exclude the Female Line of the
Part of the Father ascending; and therefore

fore in the Cafe propofed of the Son's purchafing Lands and dying without Iffue,
the Sifter of the Father's Grandfather, or
of his Great Grandfather, and fo *in infinitum*
fhall be preferred before the Father's Mothers Brother, tho' the Father's Mothers
Brother be a Male, and the Father's Grandfather or Great Grandfather's Sifter be a
Female, and more remote, becaufe fhe is
of the Male Line, which is more worthy
than the Female Line, though the Female
Line be alfo of the Blood of the Father.

4 Rule   *Fourthly*, But as in the Male Line afcending, the more near is preferred before the
more remote; fo in the Female Line defcending, fo it be of the Blood of the Father, it is preferred before the more remote.
The Son therefore purchafing Lands, and
dying without Iffue, and the Father, Grandfather, and Great Grandfather, and fo up-
ward, all the Male Line being dead without any Brother or Sifter, or any defcending from them; but the Father's Mother
has a Sifter or Brother, and alfo the Father's
Grandmother has a Brother, and likewife
the Father's Great Grandmother has a Brother: Tho' it is true, that all thefe are of
the Blood of the Father; and tho' the very
remoteft of them, fhall exclude the Son's
Mothers Brother; and tho' it be alfo true,
that the Great Grandmother's Blood has
paffed through more Males of the Father's
Blood than the Blood of the Grandmother
or Mother of the Father, yet in this Cafe,
the

the Father's Mothers Sister shall be preferred before the Father's Grandmothers Brother, or the Great Grandmothers Brother,
because they are all in the Female Line,
viz. *Cognati* (and not *Adgnati*), and the Father's Mothers Sister is the nearest, and
therefore shall have the Preference as well
as in the Male Line ascending, the Father's Brother or his Sister shall be preferred before the Grandfather's Brother.

Fifthly, But yet in the last Case, where
the Son purchases Lands and dies without
Issue, and without any Heir on the Part of
the Grandfather, the Lands should descend
to the Grandmothers Brother or Sister, as
Heir on the Part of his Father; yet if the
Father had purchased this Land and died,
and it descended to his Son, who died
without Issue, the Lands should not have
descended to the Father's Mothers Brother
or Sister, for the Reasons before given in
the *Third Rule* But for want of Brothers
or Sisters of the Grandfather, Great Grandfather, and so upwards in the Male ascending Line, it should descend to the Father's
Grandmothers Brother or Sister which is
his Heir of the Part of his Father, who
should be preferred before the Father's
Mothers Brother, who is in Truth the Heir
of the Part of the Mother of the Purchaser,
tho' the next Heir of the Part of the Father of him that last died seized; and
therefore, as if the Father that was the Purchaser had died without Issue, the Heirs

5. Rule.

R 4   of

of the Part of the Father, whether of the
Male or Female Line, should have been
preferred before the Heirs of the Part of
the Mother, so the Son, who stands now
in the Place of the Father, and inherits
to him primarily, in his Father's Line dying without Issue, the same Devolution and
hereditary Succession should have been as
if his Father had immediately died without Issue, which should have been to his
Grandmothers Brother, as Heir of the
Part of the Father, tho' by the Female
Line, and not to his Mothers Brother,
who was only Heir of the Part of his
Mother, and who is not to take till the
Father's Line both Male and Female be
spent

6 Ru..   Sixth, If the Son purchases Lands and
dies without Issue, and it descends to any
Heir of the Part of the Father, and then
if the Line of the Father (after Entry and
Possession) fail, it shall never return to
the Line of the Mother; tho' in the first
Instance, or first Descent from the Son, it
might have descended to the Heir of the Part
of the Mother, for now by this Descent
and Seisin it is lodged in the Father's Line,
to whom the Heir of the Part of the Mother can never derive a Title as Heir,
but it shall rather escheat. But if the
Heir of the Part of the Father had not
entred, and then that Line had failed, it
might have descended to the Heir of the
Part of the Mother as Heir to the Son,

to

to whom immediately, for want of Heirs of the Part of the Father, it might have defcended

Seventhly, And upon the fame Reafon, 7. Rule. if it had once defcended to the Heir of the Part of the Father of the Grandfather's Line, and that Heir had entred, it fhould never defcend to the Heir of the Part of the Father of the Grandmothers Line, becaufe the Line of the Grandmother was not of the Blood or Confanguinity of the Line of the Grandmothers Side.

Eighthly, If for Default of Heirs of the 8 Rule. Purchafer of the Part of the Father, the Lands defcend to the Line of the Mother, the Heirs of the Mother of the Part of her Father's Side, fhall be preferred in the Succeffion before her Heirs of the Part of her Mothers Side, becaufe they are the more worthy.

And thus the Law ftands in Point of Defcents or Hereditary Succeffions in *England* at this Day, and has fo ftood and continued for above four Hundred Years paft, as by what has before been faid, may eafily appear. And *Note,* The moft Part of the Eight Rules and Differences above fpecified and explained, may be collected out of the Refolutions in the Cafe of *Clare verfus Brook, &c.* in *Plowden's Commentaries, Folio* 444.

But

But for the better illuftrating and clearing of the Rules and Methods of Defcents, and of the different Directions of the Civil Law, the Canon Law, and the Common Law therein; I fhall here fubjoin the fo much famed *Arbor Civilis* of the *Civilians* and *Canonifts*, which being compared with the *Gradus Parentelæ* in the *Firft Inftitutes*, will fully illuftrate what has been already faid.

CHAP.

Arbor   Tritavu Tritavia   Civilis

| Adanati | | | | Cognati |

Tritavu Tritavia

Abpatruus Itramita | Atavus Atavia | Atavunculus Itmatertera

horu filius & filia | Abpatruus Abamita | Abavus Abavia | Abavunculus Itmatertera | horu filius & filia

horu filius & filia | Propatruus Proamita | Proavus Proavia | Proavunculus Promatertera | horu filius & filia

horu filius & filia | Patruus magnus Amita magna | Avus Avia | Avunculus magnus Matertera magna | horu filius & filia

Propior Sobrinus & Sobrina | Patruus Amita | Pater Mater | Avunculus Matertera | Propior Sobrinus & Sobrina

Patrui filius vel filia | Frater | Persona proposita | Soror | Consobrinus Consobrina

Fratris filius vel filia | Filius Filia | Consobrini filius vel filia

Nepos Neptis

Pronepos Proneptis

Abnepos Abneptis

Atnepos Atneptis

Trinepos Trineptis

CHAP. XII.

Touching Trials by Jury.

HAving in the former Chapter somewhat largly treated of the Course of Descents, I shall now with more Brevity consider that other Title of our Law which I before propounded (in order to evidence the Excellency of the Laws of *England* above those of other Nations), *viz. The Trial by a Jury of Twelve Men*, which upon all Accounts, as it is settled here in this Kingdom, seems to be the best Trial in the World: I shall therefore give a short Account of the Method and Manner of that Trial, *viz*

First, The Writ to return a Jury, issues to the Sheriff of the County. And,

1*st*, He is to be a Person of Worth and Value, that so he may be responsible for any Defaults, either of himself or his Officers And, 2*dly*, Is *Sworn*, faithfully and honestly, to execute his Office This Officer is entrusted to elect and return the Jury, which he is obliged to do in this Manner : 1. Without the Nomination of either Party 2. They are to be such Persons as for Estate and Quality are fit to serve upon that Employment 3 They are to be of the Neighbourhood of the Fact to be be inquired, or at least of the County or Bailywick. And, 4 Anciently Four, and now Two of them at least are to be of the Hundred. *But* Note, *This is now in great Measure altered by Statute*

Secondly, Touching the Number and Qualifications of the Jury   2.

1*st*, As to their Number, though only Twelve are sworn, yet Twenty four are to be returned to supply the Defects or Want of Appearance of those that are Challenged off, or make Default 2*dly*, Their Qualifications are many, and are generally set down in the Writ that summons them, *viz* 1. They are to be *Probi & legales Homines* 2. Of sufficient Freeholds, according to several Provisions of Acts of Parliament 3. Not Convict of any Notorious Crime that may render them unfit for that Employment. 4. They are not to be of the Kindred or Alliance of any of the Parties And, 5. Not to be such as are prepossessed or prejudiced before they hear their Evidence

Thirdly, The Time of their Return   3

Indeed, in Affizes, the Jury is to be ready at the Bar the first Day of the Return of the Writ. But in other Cases the Pannel is first returned upon the *Venire F cias*, or ought to be so, and the Proofs or Witnesses are to be brought or summoned by *Distringas* or *Habeas Corpora* for their Appearance at the Trial, whereby the Parties may have Notice of the Jurors, and of their Sufficiency and Indifferency, that so they may make
their

their Challenges upon the Appearance of
the Jurors if there be juft Caufe

4

Fourthly, The Place of their Appearance.

If it be in Cafes of fuch Weight and Confequence as by the Judgment of the Court
is fit to be tried at the Bar, then their Appearance is directed to be there; but in ordinary Cafes, the Place of Appearance is in
the Country at the Affifes, or *Nifi Prius*, in
the County where the Iffue to be tried arifes:
And certainly this is an excellent Conftitution The great Charge of Suits is the attendance of the Parties, the Jury-Men and
Witneffes: And therefore tho' the Prepara-
tion of the Caufes in Point of pleading to
Iffue, and the Judgment, is for the moft part
in the Courts at *Weftminfter*, whereby there
is kept a great Order and Uniformity of
Proceedings in the whole Kingdom, to prevent Multiplicity of Laws and Forms; yet
thofe are but of fmall Charge, or Trouble,
or Attendance, one Attorney being able
to difpatch Forty Men's Bufinefs with the
fame Eafe, and no greater Attendance than
one Man would difpatch his own Bufinefs:
But the great Charge and Attendance is at
the Trial, which is therefore brought Home
to the Parties in the Counties, and for the
moft part near where they live.

5.

Fifthly, The Perfons before whom they
are to appear

If the Trial be at the Bar, it is to be
before that Court where the Trial is; if in
the Country, then before the Juftices of
Affizes, or *Nifi Prius*, who are Perfons well

I   acquainted

acquainted with the Common Law, and for the moſt part are Two of thoſe Twelve ordinary Juſtices who are appointed for the Common Diſpenſation of Juſtice in the Three great Courts at *Weſtminſter*. And this certainly was a moſt wiſe Conſtitution: For,

1ſt, It prevents Factions and Parties in the Carriage of Buſineſs, which would ſoon appear in every Cauſe of Moment, were the Trial only before Men reſiding in the Counties, as Juſtices of the Peace, or the like, or before Men of little or no Place, Countenance or Preheminence above others; and the more to prevent Partiality in this Kind, thoſe Judges are by Law prohibited to hold their Seſſions in Counties where they were born or dwell.

2*dly*, As it prevents Factions and Part-takings, ſo it keeps both the Rule and the Adminiſtration of the Laws of the Kingdom uniform; for thoſe Men are employed as Juſtices, who as they have had a Common Education in the Study of the Law, ſo they daily in Term-time Converſe and Conſult with one another; acquaint one another with their Judgments, ſit near one another in *Weſtminſter-Hall*, whereby their Judgments and Deciſions are neceſſarily communicated to one another, either immediately or by Relations of others, and by this Means their Judgments and their Adminiſtrations of Common Juſtice carry a Conſonancy, Congruity, and Uniformity one to another, whereby both the Laws and the Adminiſtrations thereof are preſerved from that Con-

Confuſion and Diſparity that would una-
voidably enſue, if the Adminiſtration was
by ſeveral incommunicating Hands, or by
provincial Eſtabliſhments And beſides all
this, all thoſe Judges are ſolemnly ſworn
to obſerve and judge according to the Laws
of the Kingdom, according to the beſt of
their Knowledge and Underſtanding.

6.   *Sixthly*, When the Jurors appear, and are
called, each Party has Liberty to take his
Challenge to the Array it ſelf, if unduly
or partially made by the Sheriff; or if the
Sheriff be of Kin to either Party, or to the
Polls, either for Inſufficiency of Freehold,
or Kindred or Alliance to the other Party,
or ſuch other Challenges, either Principal,
or to the Favour, as renders the Juror
unfit and incompetent to try the Cauſe, and
the Challenge being confeſs'd or found true
by ſome of the reſt of the Jury, that particular incompetent Perſon is withdrawn

7.   *Seventhly*, Then Twelve, and no leſs, of
ſuch as are indifferent and are return'd
upon the Principal Pannel, or the Tales, are
ſworn to try the ſame according to their
Evidence.

8.   *Eightly*, Being thus ſworn, the Evidence
on either Part is given in upon the Oath of
Witneſſes, or other Evidence by Law allowed, (as Records and ancient Deeds, but
later Deeds and Copies of Records muſt be
atteſted by the Oaths of Witneſſes) and
other Evidence in the open Court, and in
the Preſence of the Parties, their Attornies,
Council, and all By-ſtanders, and before

the Judge and Jury, where each Party has
Liberty of excepting, either to the Competency
of the Evidence, or the Competency
or Credit of the Witnesses, which Exceptions
are publickly stated, and by the Judges
openly and publickly allowed or disallowed,
wherein if the Judge be partial, his Partiality and Injustice will be evident
to all By-standers; and if in his Direction
or Decision he mistake the Law, either
through Partiality, Ignorance, or Inadvertency,
either Party may require him to
seal a Bill of Exception, thereby to deduce
the Error of the Judge (if any were) to a
due Ratification or Reversal by Writ of
Error

Bills of Exception

Ninthly, The Excellency of this open
Course of Evidence to the Jury in Presence
of the Judge, Jury, Parties and Council,
and even of the adverse Witnesses, appears
in these Particulars:

9. Excellency of his Trial.

1st, That it is openly, and not in private
before a Commissioner or Two, and a
couple of Clerks, where oftentimes Witnesses
will deliver that which they will be
ashamed to testifie publickly.

2dly, That it is *Ore Tenus* personally; and
not in Writing, wherein oftentimes, yea
too often, a crafty Clerk, Commissioner, or
Examiner, will make a Witness speak what
he truly never meant, by his dressing of it up
in his own Terms, Phrases, and Expressions;
whereas on the other Hand, many times
the very Manner of a Witness's delivering
his Testimony will give a probable
Indi-

Indication whether he speaks truly or falsly;
and by this Means also he has Opportunity
to correct, amend, or explain his Testimony upon further Questioning with him,
which he can never have after a Deposition
is set down in Writing

3dly, That by this Course of personal and
open Examination, there is Opportunity
for all Persons concern'd, *viz.* The Judge,
or any of the Jury, or Parties, or their
Council or Attornies, to propound occasional Questions, which beats and bolts out
the Truth much better than when the Witness only delivers a formal Series of his
Knowledge without being interrogated;
and on the other Side, preparatory limited,
and formal Interrogatories in Writing, pre-
clude this Way of occasional Interrogations,
and the best Method of searching and sifting
out the Truth is choak'd and suppress'd.

4thly, Also by this personal Appearance
and Testimony of Witnesses, there is Opportunity of confronting the adverse Witnesses, of observing the Contradiction of
Witnesses sometimes of the same Side, and
by this Means great Opportunities are gained for the true and clear Discovery of the
Truth

5thly, And further, The very Quality,
Carriage, Age, Condition, Education, and
Place of Commorance of Witnesses, is by
this Means plainly and evidently set forth to
the Court and the Jury, whereby the Judge
and Jurors may have a full Information of
them, and the Jurors as they see Cause may
give

give the more or lefs Credit to their Teftimony, for the Jurors are not only Judges of
the Fact, but many times of the Truth of
Evidence ; and if there be juft Caufe to
disbelieve what a Witnefs fwears, they are
not bound to give their Verdict according
to the Evidence or Teftimony of that Wit
nefs, and they may fometimes give Credit
to one Witnefs, tho' oppos'd by more than
one. And indeed, it is one of the Excellencies of this Trial above the Trial by
Witneffes, that altho' the Jury ought to
give a great Regard to Witneffes and their
Teftimony, yet they are not always bound *Fac pr.*
by it, but may either upon reafonable Cir- *Pag*
cumftances, inducing a Blemifh upon their
Credibility, tho' otherwife in themfelves in
Strictnefs of Law they are to be heard, pronounce a Verdict contrary to fuch Teftimonies, the Truth whereof they have juft
Caufe to fufpect, and may and do often
pronounce their Verdict upon one fingle
Teftimony, which Thing the Civil Law
admits not of

 Tenthly, Another Excellency of this Trial   10
is this, That the Judge is always prefent
at the Time of the Evidence given in it :
Herein he is able in Matters of Law emerg-
ing upon the Evidence to direct them, and
alfo, in Matters of Fact, to give them a
great Light and Affiftance by his weighing
the Evidence before them, and obferving
where the Queftion and Knot of the Bufinefs lies, and by fhewing them his Opinion
even in Matter of Fact, which is a great

Advantage and Light to Lay-Men: And
thus, as the Jury affifts the Judge in determining the Matter of Fact, fo the Judge
affifts the Jury in determining Points of
Law, and alfo very much in inveftigating
and enlightening the Matter of Fact, whereof the Jury are Judges

11   *Eleventhly,* When the Evidence is fully
given, the Jurors withdraw to a private
Place, and are kept from all Speech with
either of the Parties till their Verdict is delivered up, and from receiving any Evidence other than in open Court, where it
may be fearch'd into, difcufs'd and exa-
min'd   In this Recefs of the Jury they are
to confider their Evidence, and if any Writings under Seal were given in Evidence,
they are to have them with them; they are
to weigh the Credibility of Witneffes, and
the Force and Efficacy of their Teftimonies,
wherein (as I before faid) they are not precifely bound to the Rules of the Civil Law,
viz. To have Two Witneffes to prove every
In Trea-   Fact, unlefs it be in Cafes of Treafon, nor
fon, Two   to reject one Witnefs becaufe he is fingle,
Witnef-   or always to believe Two Witneffes if the
fes   Probability of the Fact does upon other
Circumftances reafonably encounter them;
for the Trial is not here fimply by Witneffes,
but by Jury, nay, it may fo fall out, that
the Jury upon their own Knowledge may
know a Thing to be falfe that a Witnefs
fwore to be true, or may know a Witnefs
to be incompetent or incredible, tho' nothing

thing be objected againſt him, and may give their Verdict accordingly

Twelfthly, When the whole Twelve Men are agreed, then, and not till then, is their Verdict to be received, and therefore the Majority of Aſſentors does not conclude the Minority, as is done in ſome Countries where Trials by Jury are admitted : But if any One of the Twelve diſſent, it is no Verdict, nor ought to be received. It is true, That in ancient Times, as *Hen* II. and *Hen* III's Time, yea, and by *Fleta* in the Beginning of *Edw* I.'s Time, if the Jurors diſſented, ſometimes there was added a Number equal to the greater Party, and they were then to give up their Verdict by Twelve of the old Jurors, and the Jurors ſo added; but this Method has been long Time antiquated, notwithſtanding the Practice in *Bracton*'s Time, *Lib.* 4 *cap.* 9. and *Fleta*, *lib.* 4. *cap* 9. for at this Day the entire Number firſt empannell'd and ſworn are to give up an unanimous Verdict, otherwiſe it is none. And indeed this gives a great Weight, Value and Credit to ſuch a Verdict, wherein Twelve Men muſt unanimouſly agree in a Matter of Fact, and none diſſent; though it muſt be agreed, that an ignorant Parcel of Men are ſometimes governed by a few that are more Knowing, or of greater Intereſt or Reputation than the reſt.

Thirteenthly, But if there be Matter of Law that carries in it any Difficulty, the Jury may, to deliver themſelves from the Danger of an Attaint, find it ſpecially, that ſo it may be

12

Verdict unanimous.

13.

Special Verdict.

S 3

be decided in that Court where the Verdict
is returnable, and if the Judge over-rule the
Point of Law contrary to Law, whereby
the Jury are perfwaded to find a general
Verdict (which yet they are not bound to
do if they doubt it), then the Judge, upon
the Requeft of the Party defiring it, is bound
by Law in convenient Time to feal a Bill
**Bill of
Excep-
tions** of Exceptions, containing the whole Matter excepted to, that fo the Party grieved,
by fuch Indifcretion or Error of the Judge,
may have Relief by Writ of Error on the
Statute of *Weftminfter* 2

14 *Fourteenthly.* Altho' upon general Verdicts
given at the Bar in the Courts at *Weftminfter*,
**Judg-
ment** the Judgment is given within Four Days, in
Prefumption that there cannot be any confiderable Surprize in fo folemn a Trial, or at
leaft it may be foon efpied; yet upon Trials
by *Nifi prius* in the Country, the Judgment
is not given prefently by the Judge of *Nifi
prius*, unlefs in Cafes of *Quare Impedits* But
the Verdict is returned after Trial into that
Court from whence the Caufe iffued, that
thereby, if any Surprize happened either
through much Bufinefs of the Court, or
through Inadvertency of the Attorney or
Council or through any Mifcarriage of the
Jury, or through any other Cafualty, the
Party may have his Redrefs in that Court
from whence the Record iffued

And thus ftands this excellent Order of
Trial by Jury, which is far beyond the
Trial by Witneffes according to the Pro-
ceedings

ceedings of the Civil Law, and of the
Courts of Equity, both for the Certainty,
the Difpatch, and the Cheapnefs thereof ·
It has all the Helps to inveftigate the
Truth that the Civil Law has, and many
more. For, as to Certainty,

1*ft*, It has the Teftimony of Witneffes,
as well as the Civil Law and Equity Courts

2*dly*, It has this Teftimony in a much
more advantageous Way than thofe Courts
for difcovery of Truth

3*dly*, It has the Advantage of the Judge's
Obfervation, Attention, and Affiftance, in
Point of Law by way of Decifion, and in
Point of Fact by way of Direction to the
Jury.

4*thly*, It has the Advantage of the Jury,
and of their being *de Viceneto*, who oftentimes know the Witneffes and the Parties :
And,

5*thly*, It has the unanimous Suffrage and
Opinion of Twelve Men, which carries in it
felf a much greater Weight and Prepondera-
tion to difcover the Truth of a Fact than
any other Trial whatfoever

And as this Method is more certain, fo it
is much more expeditious and cheap; for
oftentimes the Seffion of one Commiffion for
the Examination of Witneffes for one Caufe
in the Ecclefiaftical Courts, or Courts of
Equity, lafts as long as a whole Seffion of
Nifi prius, where a Hundred Caufes are
examined and tried.

S 4   And

And thus much concerning Trials in Civil Causes As for Trials in Causes Criminal, they have this further Advantage, That regularly the Accusation as Preparatory to the Trial is by a Grand Jury: So that as no Man's Interest, according to the Course of the Common Law, is to be tried or determined without the Oaths of a Jury of Twelve Men; so no Man's Life is to be tried but by the Oaths of Twelve Men, and by the Preparatory Accusation or Indictment by Twelve Men or more precedent to his Trial, unless it be in the Case of an Appeal at the Suit of the Party.

I might here shew the Antiquity of this Method of Trial, both from the *Saxon* and the *British* Laws, and demonstrate it to have been in Use long before the Time of *William* I. and indeed it seems to have been one of the first Principles upon which our Constitution was erected and established.

Sed de his Satis.

THE
TABLE.

A.

The TABLE.

B.

C.

The TABLE.

Exche-

The T A B L E.

King

The TABLE.

4   ——Not

The *TABLE*.

The TABLE.

3   Petitions

The TABLE.

T   S. Saxon

The TABLE.

S.

T.

The TABLE.

The TABLE.

Y.

FINIS.

Lightning Source UK Ltd.
Milton Keynes UK
UKHW021920140521
383755UK00003B/133

9 781379 662600